ABILENE DAILY

SNAPSHOTS OF HOME

Cover design by London Moore

Cover photo: Amelia Earhart's Auto-Giro crash, 1931

Layout by Tinyah M. Hawkins/Goofidity Designs

ISBN: 978-0-9973706-8-3

Printed in the U.S.A.

Published by TexasStarTrading.com
174 Cypress St., Abilene, Texas 79601
info@TexasStarTrading.com
(325) 672-9696

ABILENE DAILY

SNAPSHOTS OF HOME

JAY MOORE

INTRODUCTION

Dear Reader,

In 2021, Abilene celebrated its 140th birthday (see March 15). Figuring in the 34 Leap Years (Feb. 29), by the end of 2021 this old West Texas city will have passed through 51,061 days. Some of those days were chock-full of drama and historic hubbub (April 28), while others weigh in—save for the blowing wind (June 10)—as run-of-the-mill humdrum.

However, toss a dart at the calendar and, with a bit of digging, you are bound to find that on that particular day along the 140-year span there was some notable incident or striking mishap (Jan. 2) offering interest for the reader. Abilene Daily is a full calendar year recounting both the momentous and the mundane, the makings of the Key City (June 16).

Jay Moore

JANUARY

A Sun Bowl Triumph
for Hardin-Simmons

The third annual Sun Bowl pitted the Cowboys of Hardin-Simmons against the Miners of the Texas College of Mines [now UT El Paso], playing at Jones Stadium in El Paso with some 9,000 fans turning out to witness the hard fought affair. The Abilene squad came out on top 34-6, but the contest was not one to make a mama proud. A fistfight sent Cowboy end Ed Harris to the showers early, while HSU halfback Burns McKinney received a Miner kick to the head. Red Andrews suffered a laceration requiring five stitches when Cowboy back Ed Cherry slugged him. By the end of the contest, five other Miners headed for medical treatment to touch up cut noses, torn mouths and split lips.

The game was HSU's second straight Sun Bowl appearance, following its disappointing 1936 tilt against New Mexico State ending in a 14-14 tie. (The first Sun Bowl featured two high school squads.) In the 1937 contest, future Abilene businessman Si Addington drew first blood (figuratively speaking) scoring on a 13-yard run as the Cowboys ran up

Future football coach
Gordon Wood, 1938

511 yards to the Miners' 146. The victory earned each HSU squad member a gold watch to commemorate the smash-mouth occasion.

The Cowboys finished the season with 9 wins and 2 losses—one to Baylor and a slim 3-0 loss at home to top-ranked Texas A&M, decided by a last-second field goal. For the season, the Cowboys outscored their opponents 302-41. Sporting number 85 on the 1937 roster was a junior end from nearby Wylie who, before coming to Hardin-Simmons, had never played football. However, he would go on to coach football to Texas schoolboys for 43 seasons and turn in one of the winningest records of all time—396 wins and 11 state titles—Gordon Wood.

ALSO ON THIS DAY IN 1938...
Daddy Dearest

Thomas LeSueur, a 30-year Abilene resident and the father of actress Joan Crawford, died from a cerebral hemorrhage in his two-story home along South First Street. He was just one day shy of turning 71. As a young father, LaSueur walked away from his wife and his 10-month old daughter, Lucille Fay (later known as Joan Crawford), leaving them in San Antonio while he moved to Abilene. Despite a strained relationship, LeSueur was justifiably proud of his famous daughter and her Hollywood success; however, he was not much of a movie buff, never attending showings of her films. Due to a prior commitment, Joan could not attend the Abilene funeral of her father, but she did send a wreath. Mr. LeSueur is buried in the Masonic section of the City Cemetery.

JANUARY 2, 1952

"Hello Girl" Postpones Good-bye

In the early days of telephoning, "Hello Girl" was a common name applied to female operators who would greet callers with a cheery "hello" when answering the switchboard. After 36 years as one of Abilene's "Hello Girls," 58-year-old Evelyn Robert Reese (dad hoping for a son, perhaps?), was set to finally hang it up as a telephone operator for Southwestern Bell. On January 2, the night before her last day at the switchboard, an ice storm side-swiped Abilene, creating slickened streets and glassy sidewalks. As Evelyn left the phone company building on Cypress Street, following her late shift, she fell victim to the slippery conditions, suffering a broken ankle. Still a phone company employee for a few more hours, she remained eligible for one year of disability pay, enabling Evelyn to spend a recuperative 12 months at home while collecting one more year of service and falling into $2,500 she had not counted on.

ALSO ON THIS DAY IN 1883

Abilene, Inc.

Voters opted to incorporate Abilene as a city, electing attorney Daniel Burford Corley as the first mayor a few weeks later.

Cruel Conditions in the County Clink

Newly elected Taylor County Sheriff George Maxwell ordered a clean sweep of the county jail but first granted prisoners a chance to register any complaints. The most common gripe was the meager daily dose of weak coffee. One felon asked why inmates could not have copies of the local newspaper. Maxwell replied that he had to approve all reading materials and since the prisoners only wanted to read about their own criminal activity, he would not give them the pleasure. The sheriff then directed the men on the third floor to clean up their ongoing mess or risk losing their cigarette, Jell-O and dried fruit rations. He also directed the cook to quit serving costly cans of salmon as they were denting the budget at 65 cents each.

The Opera House Burns

An unseasonably warm 70 degrees helped draw an immense noontime crowd of gawkers along South First and Chestnut. The rubberneckers assembled to watch Abilene firefighters struggle to contain a raging fire consuming the second-story opera house. First floor tenants scrambled to save their inventory and records with some helpful onlookers pitching in to save Mr. Fuller's furniture store, Adams Confectionery, Courtney's Shoe Shop and the Lion Harness Company. Attorney Harry Tom King, a recent returnee to Abilene from Galveston, was ready to occupy his upstairs office space but suffered a serious setback when his law library and other papers went up in smoke.

The opera house was located upstairs in the building at the corner of Chestnut and South First

In appreciation for the brave work by the fire brigade keeping the fire from spreading to their neighboring building, Farmers and Merchants Bank donated $50 to the department. Building owner Morgan Jones, who was out of town during the fire, learned of the heroic efforts and wrote an appreciation check for $100.

The buildings fronting South First and Chestnut would ultimately give way to the Pine Street underpass.

JANUARY 5, 1938

Harsh Words for the Mayor

Judged by the Aviation Committee of the Chamber of Commerce as the one responsible for delaying improvements to the city airport, Mayor Will Hair was denounced by the committee chairman as *"the most high-handed, arbitrary, dilatory, misfit one-man rule ever to afflict this city—a mayor who knows only one answer, 'no money.'"*

The aim of the chamber committee was to insure upgrades to the airport so the facility would meet new post office standards and earn Abilene the designation as an approved westbound stop for airmail. (With eastbound air service already in place for Abilene, one wonders what upgrades only affected planes heading west.) At any rate, committee chair

George Paxton Jr. noted that there was only one obstacle in procuring the improvements, to wit, the mayor himself. Paxton ended his diatribe with, "*This committee is thoroughly disheartened, disappointed and disgusted with our fine old gentleman, the mayor.*"

The following day, three committee members—W. G. Swenson, Max Bentley and Dr. M.T. Ramsey—issued their own statement, disavowing Paxton's statement, of which they had no prior knowledge, adding that he did not speak for them. Four months later, westbound airmail service began landing in Abilene.

JANUARY 6, 1947
Coldest Ever

A ten-day blizzard brought the coldest temperatures yet recorded in Abilene. Things improved slightly on January 6 as thermometers registered in the low 20s. Two days before, the weather bureau recorded an all-time low of -7.6 degrees. The prolonged cold brought some unusual sights: ice skaters gliding across a frozen Lytle Lake, a 28-foot icicle suspended from the Tuscola water tower, and an improvised snow plow clearing school sidewalks. Lake Abilene and Lake Kirby froze solid, as did water pipes and car radiators all across town.

The bone-chilling cold caused a 10-inch water main near Abilene Christian to freeze. Trash piled up as the city trucks were unable to make their runs. Hotel rooms were fully booked. The *Reporter-News* equipped news carriers with whistles, instructing them to blow a tweet in order to alert subscribers that the newspaper was in the yard, as it was not feasible nor fair for newsboys to put it in the usual spot between the front door and screen. Ruth Rollins phoned the newspaper circulation manager insisting that he instruct her paperboy to knock on her door and come inside to warm up. Newsboy Clarence Hastings complied, coming in from the frigid cold to enjoy a warm drink (and saving Ruth a trip outside to get the paper).

A Dust-up in the East

The 1954 development of property around Lytle Lake set off a testy dispute, with the dust settling in 1956 only to whip up once again two days before Christmas in 1957, before finally being tamped down on this day in 1960. The Sayles Company developed the acreage, adjacent to the Abilene city limits, in late 1954 touting "where you can swim, fish and sail in your own backyard." Rumblings soon began at City Hall about annexing the property, with lake homeowners in firm opposition. The civic clash caused lake residents to counter annexation by taking steps to turn the new neighborhood into its own town, setting an incorporation election for December 27, 1956. The new town would be named "East Abilene."

The startled Abilene mayor and city commissioners held pre-election talks with the breakaway neighbors, agreeing that if the residents would cancel the vote to become a new city then Abilene city officials would not bring up the annexation issue again until, at the earliest, 1960. However, in 1957, Abilene voters elected Jesse Winters as the new mayor and opted to replace three of the four commissioners.

With the new civic officials not feeling bound to the gentleman's agreement put in place by the last administration, they voted to go ahead and annex the Lytle Lake area into Abilene. Lake residents and former commissioners marched into City Hall protesting the move. Mayor Winters told the complainants that people don't expect Coach Royal at the University of Texas to use the plays of former coach Ed Price, prompting former Commissioner Crutcher Scott to retort, "That may be true Mr. Mayor, but Coach Royal did honor the scholarships Price had given the players."

Following the early annexation, Lytle residents filed suit in the 42nd District Court which upheld the city's right to ignore the prior agreement and expand the city limits. The Lytle group appealed and in 1959 the superior court voided the annexation, ruling that the agreement to postpone annexation talks until 1960 was valid and further decreed that property taxes collected for 1958 must be refunded to the East Abilenians. A few months later, 1959 gave way to 1960, and seven days into the new year, Abilene annexed Lytle Shores. Ever so slowly, the dust settled in the East.

JANUARY 8, 1884
Crooked Bartender

Abilene City Alderman Frank Collins and his brother Walter— a Taylor County Deputy Sheriff—entered the Cattle Exchange Saloon at North First and Pine Street just after 4 p.m. to have a word with the proprietor, Zeno Hemphill. An 1883 Abilene ordinance outlawed gambling in the city and the Collins brothers intended to confront Hemphill concerning non-compliance within his establishment. It did not go well.

Angry words turned into clenched fists, which led to the drawing of guns. After Zeno clocked Frank in the jaw, Frank unholstered his gun. Brother Walter jumped in between ordering them to stop fighting. That advice went unheeded with Zeno drawing his own gun and firing, striking Deputy Walter and resulting in Frank and Zeno simultaneously emptying their revolvers in the general direction of the other. When the smoke cleared, all three men lay bleeding on the floor. Deputy Walter and barkeep Zeno died before sunset while Alderman Frank lingered for two months before succumbing to his wounds.

The day after the shootout, Walter Collins, 28, and Zeno Hemphill, 31, were buried in the City Cemetery only yards from one another. Per a family request, Zeno was buried with his coffin angled to the northwest because his brother indicated that Zeno did not like the sun in his face. In March, Frank Collins was laid to rest beside his brother.

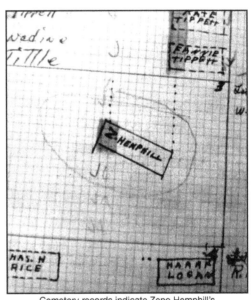

Cemetery records indicate Zeno Hemphill's unconventional, aslant burial

JANUARY 9, 1882
Ambitious Arsonist

The *New York Times* carried a short dispatch on page 2 reporting, "An attempt was made at an early hour on January 9 to burn the south side of Abilene, Texas. The flames were quickly extinguished and only slight damage was done. An inquiry is now being held and suspected persons are under surveillance." A few days later an arrest was made and Willie Featherstone was charged with "incendiarism in order to burn down the whole village." His bail was set at $20,000. At the inquest, 38 witnesses presented their testimony, with many stating they saw Featherstone standing by watching the flames. It appears that Mr. Featherstone was allowed to slip the arson charge since no one saw him set the fire—and watching the flames is exactly what everyone else in the vicinity was doing.

JANUARY 10, 1964
Tough Call

Hardin-Simmons University President Dr. James Landes assured students, faculty and alumni that the decision by the school's board to discontinue the football program was necessary and based on the urgent need to save money. Cowboy football cost the school nearly $1 million over the previous nine years and was producing annual loss of yardage to the tune of $60,000. The disappointing news produced a glum spirit on campus, but the majority expressed an understanding. "You see the financial necessity, but it just hurts to see football go," replied cheerleader Myrtle Lewis. The school honored all existing football scholarships and timed the announcement so that football players with remaining eligibility had plenty of time to decide where to transfer in order to punt, pass and kick for a bit longer.

At a student meeting, one disappointed Cowboy asked about the chances of reviving football in the future. Dr. Landes replied, "The financial situation will be reviewed regularly and there is every opportunity left for football to return in the future." HSU President Dr. Jesse Fletcher and the school's board revived football in 1989.

JANUARY 11, 1949
Icy Issues, Warm Welcome

An ice storm brought about a variety of problems due to slick roads and downed power lines. Travelers exited the Bankhead Highway to escape the treacherous conditions, uniting one band of 11 strangers over their common plight at the Abilene Courts. The group huddled at the Courts Café on South 11th where they swapped stories, held a sing-along, and the next day were taken downtown to shop and later escorted by locals to a barn dance.

Flights were cancelled along with sporting events. Electricity was out at the jail, prompting 21 prisoners to cool their heels more literally than they had anticipated. The icy storm brought down more than one postman, completely shut down long-distance phone service and caved in the roof of a car belonging to an HSU student when a hefty, ice-laden mesquite limb at a Beech Street home succumbed to gravity. Hendrick Memorial Hospital lost power for nearly two hours, making it necessary for nurses to hand-pump the iron lung serving as the lifeline for 14-year-old polio patient Katherine Stanfield.

Motels quickly filled and the Chamber of Commerce sprang into action asking locals to offer spare bedrooms to the stranded motorists. Stella Davis offered a room in her Swenson Avenue home but, while awaiting a claim to her hospitality, her son brought in a baby calf born on their ranch, setting up the shivering newborn in the living room to warm by the fireplace. Shortly after, the chamber sent over a traveler from Chicago to lodge at the Davis home. Asked if he was okay to put up with livestock, the guest noted that city folk seldom got to see a newborn calf, and that he was pleased to be under the same roof.

JANUARY 12, 1931
Mystery Donor

Dr. J.D. Sandefer, president of Simmons University, publicly announced that for the 36th month in a row, the school had received a check in the amount of $1,000 from an anonymous Philadelphia donor. (In 2021 dollars, the $1,000 gift would be worth $17,000.) With the school suffering the effects of the Great Depression, the monthly checks went a long way in filling the financial void. Dr. Sandefer recounted that three years before, in 1928, the multi-millionaire visitor passed through Abilene en route to California. After staying the night, two local bankers took the man on a driving tour so he might examine possible real estate investments. The tour included a stop at Simmons where he met Dr. Sandefer, who told how Simmons began and of the ongoing operation and financial challenges. Ten days later, Dr. Sandefer opened an envelope in his office and fluttering to the ground was the first $1,000 check. Checks continued to arrive in Sandefer's office from 1928 until the death of the anonymous donor at age 73 in 1936.

The generous mystery donor to the Baptist college turned out not to be Baptist at all; rather, a Presbyterian named Horace Coates Coleman, an industrialist and insurance broker living in the Philadelphia suburb of Norristown.

JANUARY 13, 1895
Mind Reader

The nation's best known mind reader was in town showing off his paranormal powers. Charles F. Haynes traveled far and wide demonstrating his ability to astonish, often right on the street. Surrounded by a large crowd on Pine Street, Haynes performed a rather convoluted bit of psychic trickery. He first asked three citizens to jointly write a letter to a friend, put it into a blank envelope and seal it. Haynes was then blindfolded and sent the men off with the letter. The three-man committee took the letter to the post office, placed it in the mailbox for J.A. Boyce, then hid the mailbox key several blocks away in a culvert.

The trio returned to Haynes' position where several hundred were patiently waiting. Still blindfolded, Haynes was led to a carriage where he took up the reins and whipped the team into a full gallop headed up Pine Street. Approaching the culvert, he announced the key was nearby and brought the horses to a stop. After a few minutes of digging in the dirt, he turned up the key then headed to the post office where he walked straight to Boyce's box and produced the sealed letter.

With the crowd traipsing along, the unmarked envelope was taken to Harris Brothers Drugstore, the spot Haynes' otherworldly powers revealed to him as the location of the intended recipient, Sam Stevenson. Sam happened to be out for lunch, so the nation's preeminent mind reader asked the crowd to follow him, à la the Pied Piper, to a nearby boarding house where Haynes handed the envelope and letter to a rather startled Sam Stevenson, who, no doubt, was surprised to find a couple hundred people intruding on his lunch break.

JANUARY 14, 1963
Integration, Finally

Despite the Supreme Court's 1954 decision in Brown v. The Topeka Board of Education, Abilene schools remained segregated in 1962. A vote by the school board on January 14, 1963 changed that and, seven days later, 38 black students, all children of families stationed at Dyess AFB, entered the classrooms of Dyess Elementary. The change in local policy was prompted by two letters. The first was written by a group of mothers who asked the school board to allow their children to attend Dyess rather than be bused from the base several miles away to Woodson Elementary. A second letter, written by Captain John Price, strengthened the case. He wrote to the Abilene school superintendent in March of 1962:

Dear Sir:

After a great deal of soul searching and contemplation, I have decided to write to you to get some firm, definitive answers to a question that has to be answered sooner or later. To come at once to the heart of the matter: I am a Negro officer stationed at Dyess Air Force Base with onbase quarters. I have two children, the eldest of whom will soon be eligible to attend grade school. I am informed that solely because of color and because of the existing segregation policy, my son will not be able to attend the William E. Dyess school which is only a few hundred yards from our home. He can look across the yard at this school and see the white, Latin-American, part-Japanese, and so on, children attending this school but he must or will have to ride a bus to attend the "colored" school which is about five or six miles away.

The board responded by approving the integration of Dyess beginning at the start of the January semester and mandated that all elementary schools, plus the seventh grade in all junior high schools, be integrated by the fall of 1963. The remaining grades integrated one year at a time until complete desegregation had been achieved beginning with the 1968-1969 school year.

JANUARY 15, 1928
Episcopalians Mark the Spot

Following a noontime meal at the Hilton Hotel, a group of Episcopalians left in a line of cars heading south to a spot just over the Callahan County line near Dudley. Fifty years prior, Bishop Alexander Garrett traveled to the same spot on horseback and held the first Episcopal service on the western frontier. In 1878 Garrett arrived from Dallas to the home of Captain John Trent, where neighbors gathered for the rare religious service. Garrett later recalled, "At the appointed hour Captain Trent's house was filled to its utmost capacity, and for the first time in these wild mountains the service of the church so dear to all its children was celebrated."

Parson Willis Gerhart at the Garrett marker near Dudley

The Trent homestead was later purchased by a local parishioner, and on this day the Episcopalian entourage held a memorial service at the spot and received the deed to the one-acre site. Plans to erect a monument on the exact spot of the Trent's old fireplace were underway with money being raised to erect a 20-foot-high monolithic shaft with a cross on each side and designed by artist and designer Louis Tiffany. The monument was to be cut from Leuders limestone and planned as a near duplicate to one in the Hillside Cemetery in Scotch Plains, New Jersey.

Fundraising for the project slowed with the onset of the Great Depression, delaying the erection of the monument until 1932 and reducing its size to 16 feet. Rather than cutting the marker from limestone, it was instead formed from polished concrete. The actual marker differed from Tiffany's design as well. The final plan of the art-deco inspired monolith was redesigned by Abilene draftsman Henry Fowler.

To see the marker noting Bishop Garrett's 1878 visit, head south on Highway 36, turn south onto FM 1178 and go three miles. Look to the east, can't miss it.

JANUARY 16, 1881
The Tracks Arrive

The Dallas *Daily Herald* announced that the Texas & Pacific Railway had successfully reached the site of Abilene, having laid their rails and ties to a point 192 miles west of Dallas. An intrepid reporter ventured to the end of the line a week later and reported that people were living in tents and wagons at the future site of Abilene, noting that there is no lumber or building materials. But he predicted that in a few months "where now you see only a tented field there will be a thriving town. Abilene is generally looked at as the future great, but this writer predicts that Baird will, in time, be the better point for business." (A swing and a miss.)

Sunday Cinema Skirmish

Following sixty minutes listening to Abilene preachers, laymen and college presidents who pointedly protested a proposed ordinance to allow for Sunday night movies—punctuated by frequent "amens" from the overflow crowd—commissioners prepared to vote on the motion.

The opposition speakers pointed out that such a move would desecrate the Sabbath, compete with evening church services, and lay a foundation "for more vicious things to come" (nothing specific was mentioned). One Methodist preacher proclaimed that "some folk would vote to repeal the Ten Commandments if they could." On the other hand, the pro-movie crowd pointed out that Sunday night movies would offer wholesome entertainment for the soldiers stationed at Camp Barkeley as well as for Abilenians compelled to leave town each Sabbath heading for Sweetwater or Baird to buy beer and take in a flick.

Following the tense public debate, it came time to vote. Commissioners decided 3-1 to dim the lights and let the reels roll on Sunday night. Following the vote, one anti-movie protestor rebuked the commissioners, "We lost, but we'll remember it on election day!"

JANUARY 18, 1946
Leo on the Loose?

The Assistant District Agent for the U.S. Fish and Wildlife Service came to Cedar Gap to investigate the rumored sighting and screeching of a mountain lion. J.A. Gibson spent two days trouncing around the hills and working with nearby ranchers to locate lion tracks. Following his thorough scrutiny, Gibson reported that there was no lion, rather the screeching was produced by either "lyin' pranksters or a monkey-faced owl, which can make the most terrible noise one can imagine."

JANUARY 19, 1981
LaJet Swings a Tourney

The Professional Golf Association officially sanctioned the LaJet Classic golf tournament to be held at the Fairway Oaks Golf Club in Abilene. LaJet, an Abilene based crude oil gathering and refining company, put up the prize money and hosted the event. The tournament would be one of five PGA competitions held in Texas and offered a purse of $350,000, the eighth largest prize on the entire tour.

The LaJet Classic was staged in September of 1981 with Tom Weiskopf besting Gil Morgan by

Fairway Oaks clubhouse under construction, 1980

two strokes to take home the top check of $63,000. In 1983, the LaJet Classic added a sponsor and became the LaJet Coors Classic. The tourney was renamed again in 1985, this time becoming the Southwest Golf Classic. In 1988, it took on its fourth name, the Gatlin Brothers-Southwest Golf Classic, and the following year it became a tour stop on the Senior PGA circuit. The last professional tournament at Fairway Oaks was in 1990. Bruce Crampton won $45,000, beating Lee Trevino by four strokes.

JANUARY 20, 1920
Dammit, He's Dead

A crowd of over 600 gathered at 4 p.m. to say good-bye to the faithful white bulldog who had served for four years as the unofficial mascot of Simmons College. The freshman pup arrived on campus in 1916 as the tag-a-long companion to Gib Sandefer, son of the school president. With a proclivity for getting underfoot, the pup was aptly named "Dammit" by the Bible-toting students. During his four years on campus Dammit was known to be a solid stick-chaser and habitual rock-chewer who regularly attended chapel and classes, although not always remaining awake for the full lecture.

Just one semester shy of graduation, the beloved Dammit succumbed and was laid to rest on campus. Ira Harrison delivered the sermon titled "Every Dog Has His Day," followed by a wreath-laying next to the marble marker etched with the eternal statement and temporary sentiment, "Dammit, He's Dead."

Laying a wreath at the grave of Dammit the dog, 1920

JANUARY 21, 1953
Abilene and the Mob

Mafia crime boss Francesco Castiglia, better known as Frank Costello and head of New York's Luciano crime family, was the subject of an income tax lien filed in Abilene's federal court by the IRS. Dubbed as the "King of the slot machines," Costello was a powerful mobster who claimed to be a retired investor. However, the document filed in Abilene claimed he skirted paying his fair share of income taxes from 1941 to 1945, and a $388,000 lien was placed against oil leases alleged to be owned by Costello in Jack and Wise counties. Costello did not appear in the Abilene court, and would have had a hard time doing so, as he was serving an 18-month sentence for contempt of Congress, having walked out while testifying before a Senate crime committee in 1952. Costello retired for real after surviving an attempted assassination in 1957, turning his turf over to the Genovese family.

JANUARY 22, 1932
Football Profits Handed Off to Payroll

The Great Depression put a real pinch on local school finances with the school board unable to round up enough cash to pay Abilene teachers for January of 1932. In order to tide the bank account over, the Abilene High athletic council agreed to loan the school board $9,000 to meet the district payroll needs. Eagle football proceeds for the 1931 season were plump due to Coach Mayhew's state-championship winning season which produced a strong ticket-buying public. The balance of extra athletic funds covered the cost of constructing Eagle Field at Fair Park [now Rose Park].

Big Country is Born

Referring to our corner of the world as "West Central Texas" is a bit of a mouthful, failing a gentle roll off the tongue. Dr. Virgil Pate of Abilene proposed that a more suitable nickname should be found, an idea fostered by assistant newspaper editor Katharyn Duff and resulting in the *Abilene Reporter-News* launching a "name-the-area" contest in early January 1966.

Nominations were accepted over a two week period, with a committee set to review submissions and select the winner. An award of $100 awaited the person whose suggestion best described the multi-county area. Local businessmen Elbert Hall, Raymond Thomason and Sonny Bentley represented Abilene on the selection committee. Also on the panel: the owner of Sweetwater radio station KXOX, mayor of Winters, publisher of the Cross Plains newspaper, and representatives from Knox City and Breckenridge, with the managing editor of the *Reporter-News*, Ed Wishcamper, rounding out the group. The committee met over lunch on January 19 to make its choice from over 6,000 submissions. The winner was announced in the Sunday editions of area papers.

An employee of the Texas Railroad Commission, James Brooke of 309 Fannin Street, took home the cash for submitting the winning selection. The same name had also been suggested by Steve Arthur, Sam Crume and a man living in Benjamin, but Mr. Brooke's was the first received. His suggestion? "Big Country." Two other entries proffered "The Big Country," but the two-word phrase won out. In accepting his prize money, Mr. Brooke quipped, "It will help the poverty program out at 309 Fannin Street."

JANUARY 24, 1973
Fire Sale

The crowd gathered outside of Waldrop's Furniture Store was so thick that one woman remarked, "I just got up on my tiptoes to get a breath of fresh air and now I can't get down again." An older gentleman hoping to get inside said, "You'd think we were waiting for the last lifeboat on the Titanic!" The huge crowd lining the sidewalk in front of the Walnut Street store came to snag bargains marked down by as much as 75 percent due to smoke damage.

An early morning fire on December 22 destroyed the southeast corner of the store's service area, causing smoke to roll throughout the showroom. In order to remodel the store, the damaged inventory needed to head out the door. But first, shoppers had to get past the door. Every few minutes, the store manager allowed another 15 shoppers inside.

JANUARY 25, 1930
Driverless Car

Movie stunt flier Gloria Hall, also known as "Radio Girl," maneuvered an empty Dodge through the downtown Abilene streets, steering the car as she rode in a separate, trailing auto more than 20 feet behind the driverless Dodge. The car, supplied by Allison-Stevens Motor company, was manipulated by a radio transmitting to a device attached to the steering wheel. The stunt was intended to stir up interest in a larger demonstration scheduled for the following day when Radio Girl would pilot the empty car while she flew overhead. From her seat in a Travelair plane, piloted by airport manager L.E. Derryberry, Gloria managed to move the car around the field during two afternoon exhibitions.

Marketing Murder in Abilene

The following notice appeared this day in the Abilene paper: *The citizens of Abilene were thrown into a state of wild excitement due to a murder at Abilene. Such a crime as was committed here is unprecedented and horrible to relate. All the residents for miles around have been flocking to town to learn the details, and have returned surprised and dumbfounded that such an act could be perpetrated in this civilized land of ours. Mr. A.M. Robertson shot off his gun loaded with reduction and murdered high prices. Go by and see the remains at Robertson Grocery.* Now that is marketing!

A Rowdy Crowd Awaits Their Hometown

The former Tennessee Governor-turned-Texas & Pacific Railway Vice-President John Calvin Brown accepted the 30-mile stretch of track completed between Baird and Tebo Station [Tye] while speculators, wanna-be-merchants, -ranchers, -farmers and dreamers already began gathering at the site designated for infant Abilene. Estimates were that around 1,000 hearty souls pitched tents, slept in boarding cars or simply bedded down near a fire in anticipation of the opening of the "Future Great City of West Texas."

At least one slap-dash saloon operated under a canvas cover where soon-to-be-Abilenians imbibed and traded rumors about the depot location and the future site of the T&P stock pens. The auction of lots took place six weeks later on March 15-16. By sunset on the 16th, a drunken row between a Buffalo Gap cowboy and a newly-arrived barber resulted in the barber becoming the first murder victim in the newly-launched, and quite rowdy, town of Abilene. Speculation then turned to just where the cemetery might be located.

JANUARY 28, 1885
Put Your Weapon Down

Abilene Mayor Dan Corley signed into effect an ordinance setting a fine ranging from $25 to $100 if you were found to be carrying a weapon on your person, your saddle, or in your saddle bags, buggy, hack or carriage. The list of prohibited weapons included: pistols, dirks, daggers, razors, slingshots, a sword cane, a Bowie knife, or any other kind of knife used for offense or defense, brass knuckles, steel knuckles or knuckles made out of any other material. In case you forgot, a dirk is a long thrusting dagger and, as a local resident, you need to put yours away.

JANUARY 29, 1958
School's Out for Mike

Eight-year-old Mike Johnson lived on Cherry Street with his mother. It seems Mike got itchy feet and sauntered away from Locust Elementary soon after the bell rang at 8 a.m., taking his dog with him on his walkabout. Abilene police received a rash of reports from all over town as concerned citizens spotted Mike and his dog at the bus station, at the hospital, near South First and Sayles, and out along College Street.

Mike Johnson was well known to local law enforcement, for he was a regular roamer. A few years before, he managed to pedal his tricycle to the feed mill off of Treadaway and somehow managed to climb on top. Another time, he took his trike and headed for the airport. An officer picked him up along the way and told him that if he ever caught him gallivanting around again, he would give him a spanking. Mike replied, "You don't have to. My mom will do that when I get home."

Mike's tuckered-out dog gave up early, showing back up at Cherry Street around 8 p.m., with Mike walking in closer to 9:30, ready to pay the price.

What Abilene Needs

When Abilene Booster Club members decided to find out just what city residents wanted in their town, they held community meetings and also asked newspaper readers to submit their suggestions to the editorial page. "What Does Abilene Need?" became a regular column; turns out we needed a lot of things.

Marian Burks of Chestnut Street pointed out the age-old complaint, that there were no amusements for Abilene youth. Sure, there were a couple of nice parks and night clubs for the older crowd, but Marian suggested the city "find a vacant lot and put a skating rink, swimming pool or carnival void of gambling stands on it." She even proposed that it could close at 10 or 10:30 p.m. and police could patrol in order to snuff out cigarette smoking, drinking and rough talk.

One reader suggested the city should hire a dog catcher, while a second wrote that the city needed to clear out excess bootlegging joints and drunks splayed about on the post office lawn. Others recommended a Dad's Club, a Junior Patrol posting boys on every corner, a city manager, boys clubs, girls clubs, a tax-supported Chamber of Commerce, wrestling venues, a place to do chin-ups, and a host of other ideas. The Booster Club learned its lesson, never asking again.

JANUARY 31, 1913

Did You Just Call Us That!?

With more than 3,800 poll taxes assessed in Taylor County, it seems not everyone was rushing to pay up, causing the newspaper to employ the shame factor.

Bohunk — *noun*: a rough or stupid person.

FEBRUARY

Slingin' Sammy Baugh Tackles HSU Job

Heavy pressure from the Hardin-Simmons athletic committee produced results as former Washington Redskins star Sammy Baugh agreed to coach the Cowboys. Rev. Sterling Price told Baugh that the committee considered him the only man for the job, offering the Rotan native a five-year contract. The former NFL star shunned more lucrative coaching offers, agreeing to take the position for $7,000 a year. As one of the greatest football players of all time, Baugh found that the sideline held less success. During his tenure as head coach, the Cowboys posted a mediocre record of 23 wins and 28 losses. At the end of his contract in 1960, Baugh resigned to accept the head-coaching job of the new American Football League's New York Titans. Hardin-Simmons axed the school's football program four years after Baugh's departure, not playing again until 1989.

Coach Sammy Baugh

FEBRUARY 2, 1971
On the Level

A contentious meeting of the five-member County Commissioners Court resulted in the first split vote for the group in over two years. At issue was the leveling of the cornerstone for the new Taylor County Courthouse that was under construction. Following a heated discussion, County Judge Roy Skaggs and Commissioner Joe McDuff voted to give Abilene Masons permission to level the cornerstone, a tradition dating back to Solomon's Temple. Skaggs pointed out the Abilene Lodge of Ancient Free and Accepted Masons laid the cornerstone for the existing courthouse back in 1914 and later did the same for the Civic Center. The other three commissioners abstained from voting, effectively stopping the Masons' chance to administer their sacred ritual. Commissioners Grover Nelson, Felton Saverance and Jake McMillon felt they needed to visit with constituents before voting. Additionally, they wondered if perhaps some other group would like the honor of leveling the stone. Judge Skaggs called their arguments "ridiculous and ludicrous," characterizing it as "a slap in the face to all Masons."

A week later, cooperative bliss returned to the Commissioners Court with a unanimous vote to approve the Masons' request, granting them the opportunity to level the courthouse cornerstone. The Masons symbolically applied "the corn of nourishment, the wine of refreshment and the oil of joy" as they set the stone true and level.

FEBRUARY 3, 1929
Fire Came Too Soon

Just one month into the last semester for Abilene Christian College to inhabit the school's original North First Street campus (ACC planned to move the upcoming fall to the spacious new facility under construction in northeast Abilene), an early morning fire destroyed the administration building, which held most of the classrooms. The 22-year-old brick structure was a complete loss; however, school records were saved along with about half of the library books. With the new campus not yet ready, the school board faced the quandary of where to hold classes and the possibility of spending money on a campus soon to be vacated. They decided to quickly erect a provisional frame structure containing six classrooms and space for offices but with the idea that this temporary building would be dismantled, once the semester ended, and the lumber hauled to the new campus and put to use in constructing new buildings. Despite a sleet storm on this day, work continued in the bitter cold with the new building completed in less than ten days.

FEBRUARY 4, 1927
February Graduation

For the first time, Abilene High school students completing their credits by Christmas were given their own graduation exercise, not having to wait until the end of the Spring semester when everyone else knocked out their classwork. Considered as graduates from the class of '27, the 26 December grads filled the city hall auditorium donning gray caps and gowns rather than the traditional black ones. The crowd was serenaded

by the girls' and boys' glee clubs before Professor Rupert Richardson
of Simmons University addressed the group on "The Spirit of Youth,"
reminding class members they will grow to be like those things they
love. Class valedictorian and future artist Juanita Tittle chose to speak
on "Civilization and Courage," with Mary Pence following up with her
salutatorian speech. In a well-thought out marketing maneuver, Abilene
Baptists hosted a post-graduation banquet, hoping to lure the graduates
to Simmons.

FEBRUARY 5, 1973

Harte-Hanks, Inc. Goes Public, Then Private, Then Public

Newspapermen Bernard Hanks of Abilene and Houston Harte
of San Angelo combined their holdings in 1923 to create Harte-
Hanks Newspapers, with the privately-held company publishing Texas
newspapers for 50 years. On the anniversary of their merger, Harte-
Hanks, Inc. went public in 1973, selling stock under the ticker symbol of
HHN. The company offered 4.5 million shares when the market opened
on February 5, 1973, and Harte-Hanks CEO Robert Marbut purchased
the first 100 shares at $26 a share. Eleven years later, the company
backpedaled, delisting from the New York Stock Exchange, once again
becoming privately traded. A second about-face in 1993 returned Harte-
Hanks to the Big Board, once more trading their stock to all comers.
Harte-Hanks sold the Abilene, San Angelo, and other newspapers to
Scripps in 1997.

The Rehab is Born

Immediately following the noontime meeting of the Kiwanis Club at the Hotel Wooten, the Taylor County Chapter of the Texas Society for Crippled Children organized. The new chapter aimed to provide therapy services for area children suffering from cerebral palsy. Julia Benson, wife of Citizens National Bank executive vice president Joe Benson, was elected president, with insurance man Elbert Hall chosen as vice president. Mrs. Benson announced that the school district offered a special education classroom at Fannin Elementary to serve as the treatment center until a building could be secured. With the construction of Bonham Elementary in 1953, the therapy center relocated to two rooms in a special wing of that school.

Local physicians volunteered their services while the search for a full-time physical therapist immediately got underway. In July of 1953, the director of the Handicapped Children's Treatment Center in San Angelo accepted the position as physical therapist. Twenty-four year-old Georgetown native Shelley Smith would lead the effort to construct a new building for the therapy program and to operate under a new name—West Texas Rehabilitation Center for Crippled Children. Groundbreaking for the center on Harford Street took place in 1954 and stood ready to receive patients by September of 1955.

Shelley Smith with a young patient

FEBRUARY 7, 1940

Gone With the Wind
to See the Matinee Showing

Board members of the Carnegie Library Association met to review matters and to approve a personal request from City Librarian Maude Cole, who asked for an afternoon off so she could take in a matinee showing of "Gone With the Wind." The highly anticipated movie was set for an early West Texas premiere in Abilene on the 16th and reserved tickets for seats in the Paramount Theatre were going fast. Advance tickets had gone on sale three days before the library meeting, with 775 snapped up on the first day. Movie fans from surrounding towns joined Abilenians braving a cold wind to queue up in a line stretching around the block from the box office. Groups from Lubbock, Sweetwater, Big Spring and Stamford bought blocks of tickets to catch the highly anticipated movie set for a one-week Abilene run, and well in advance of release in their local hometown theaters. Despite a blizzard, opening night drew a packed house who remained warmly rapt right up until 12:10 a.m. when Scarlett noted that "Tomorrow is another day."

Librarian Cole hoped for permission to attend the lower-priced matinee—which may have been her way of pointing out that her meager salary did not afford the luxury of the evening show price. The board unanimously approved Mrs. Cole's request.

FEBRUARY 8, 1928
Whoa Nash!

The new advertising manager for the Mutual Motor Company held out hopes his poor driving would stay out of the paper. Alas, on this day, ad man Landry Johns opened up the *Abilene Daily Reporter* to read all about the embarrassing accident he had at work. It seems Mr. Johns was sent to bring a new Nash around from the back and park it in front of the sales room so a prospective buyer could have a look-see. Driving up in front of the plate glass, Johns momentarily forgot just exactly which pedal did what and proceeded to press harder on the accelerator, all the while wondering what was the matter with the brake. Three gentlemen seated on the other side of the glass found they were soon joined by the big Nash and thousands of glass shards. Mr. Johns managed to locate the brake and halt the action with no one receiving a scratch. However, the car suffered several while Mr. Johns suffered a good ribbing for days to come.

FEBRUARY 9, 1960
The Guitar Mansion is Saved (for a bit)

Workers began dismantling the carriage house situated at the rear of the former home of John and Laura Guitar along North First Street. The rest of the home was set to come down next. The Guitar mansion, built in 1902 at a cost of $75,000, was a landmark Abilene home. A native of Missouri, John Guitar had imported cut stone and lumber from Clinton, Missouri, so he might have a bit of his boyhood home in his new Abilene mansion. Forty-five years later the home stood vacant and by

1950 time and vandals began to take a toll on the grand manor. In 1960, heirs of the home sold the property to Franks and Hobbs Demolition of Austin, who planned to salvage the finer details then raze the magnificent home and clear the lot.

Before tearing into the main house, they opened the home up for Abilenians to take a final peek inside. In three days, over 7,000 came to see the 14-room mansion and to gawk at the five bathrooms, private bowling alley, hand-painted ceilings, secret floor vault, the solarium with a sprinkler system set to water the plants, and have a last look at the elaborate stone lions holding guitars that graced the exterior. The front door sold for $750 while other nostalgic Abilenians claimed a variety of fittings and woodwork decorating the venerable home. The extent of public sentiment expressed over the three-day open house prompted Earl Guitar and his siblings to buy out the demolition contract and save the grand old home from the wrecking ball…for a bit. In 1964, the Guitar Mansion was bulldozed to the ground.

The Guitar home along North First Street

FEBRUARY 10, 1944

Lt. "Tex" Farquhar is Killed

Wading ashore under fire at the Battle of Anzio, Italy, "Tex" Farquhar of Abilene, survived and soon grew accustomed to near daily attacks at a field hospital set up four miles from the enemy lines and forward of Allied heavy artillery. German bombs frequently dropped nearby. On one occasion, a piece of shrapnel hit an oxygen bottle at the end of the operating table, but it did not explode. And, more than once, Tex worked around the clock trying to aid wounded soldiers and helped out with over 100 surgeries. Twenty-eight-year-old Tex told a friend, "You don't have to be here long to know that a field hospital is where you can do the most good."

The Taylor County memorial wall showing Laverne Farquhar listed among the WWII casualties

On February 10, shells began to fall on the hospital once more, with one making a direct hit, instantly killing five U.S. Army nurses, including Second Lieutenant Laverne "Tex" Farquhar of Abilene. She and the other four nurses were the first Army women to die in WWII as the result of direct enemy action.

Prior to the war, Tex worked in Abilene for Dr. Snow, before entering the service on January 17, 1942, and training at Camp Barkeley. On the south side of the Taylor County courthouse is a granite memorial wall listing the names of Taylor County veterans who made the ultimate sacrifice. Laverne Farquhar's name is listed, although few know that she is the only female soldier from Abilene to die in battle.

FEBRUARY 11, 1966
Empty Cornerstone

With a new City Hall ready to open on Walnut Street, the old one at Cedar and North Second was set to come down. At the new civic headquarters, a time capsule was sealed behind a cornerstone, prompting many to wonder if a capsule might have been placed behind the stone at the old building when it was constructed in 1927. Public Works Director Jack McDaniel and a handful of city employees got busy with hammers and chisels to dislodge the old stone. After several hours of chipping and prying, the cornerstone was finally inched away from the building. A small crowd peered into the vacant space, disappointed to find only more brick and mortar, not a box to be seen.

FEBRUARY 12, 1941
Chinese Food!

Mr. H.G. Lee and partner Johnny Hop Long introduced Abilene to Chinese cuisine when the pair opened the Canton Café at 249 Pine Street. The restaurant, later operated by Johnny Ng, closed in 1946. For the next 15 years it was not possible to find Chinese food in an Abilene eatery. Finally, things turned around in 1961 when longtime restaurateur Christine Doyle, owner of Doyle's Café on North First Street, sold the location to Walter Gee, who changed the name to Ding How (meaning "very good" in Chinese) and began offering Chinese dishes to the dining public once more. (American and Mexican dishes were also on the menu.)

FEBRUARY 13, 1960

The Impact of Impact

The Saturday election to decide on the incorporation of Impact proceeded as scheduled despite Taylor County Judge Reed Ingalsbe revoking his election order two days earlier. Ingalsbe ruled that the area was part of a larger community and it was an area with no visible means to support itself and was ineligible to separately incorporate. (He later admitted that a rumor the new town might vote to sell liquor influenced his election revocation.) Complicating matters, on that same day Abilene city commissioners mounted a last-ditch effort to stop the action by proposing to annex the 47 acre site north of the city. However, the electorate —around 90 voters— living within the bounds of the proposed city of Impact turned out at the polling place (which doubled as the living room of Mr. and Mrs. Dallas Perkins) with 27 voters opting to incorporate the tiny town known as Impact. There were no opposing votes cast. Impact took its name from Mr. Perkins' public relations firm, Impact, Inc.

On Monday morning, the ballot box was submitted to Judge Ingalsbe, who refused to canvass the votes or accept the election as legitimate. (He also refused to approve the election expense of $48.) The lone ballot box was placed in a vault at the Taylor County clerk's office while Impact attorney Dan Sorrels filed a writ of mandamus in District Court seeking to force acceptance of the election.

Early 1960s billboard directing traffic to the new town of Impact

Court action sent the question on to the Court of Civil Appeals and finally to the Supreme Court of Texas. The uproar over the proposed new town was rooted in a fear that, once incorporated, Impact voters would return to the polls/living room for a local option liquor election. Nearly 18 months after the election, the Supreme Court of Texas ruled in July that the vote was legal and that Impact was lawfully incorporated. Two months later, Impact voters elected Dallas Perkins as mayor, and the following month Impactians returned to the ballot booth once more, this time voting 18 – 2 for their little town to go wet, prompting high blood pressure among Abilene clergy and voluminous legal proceedings over the next 14 months. Climax for the drawn-out Taylor County drama arrived at 9 a.m. on December 22, 1962—nearly three years since the initial election—with Impact mayor Dallas Perkins standing first in line to purchase a bottle of legal liquor at the Impact store. One amazed woman shopper remarked, "My goodness! I've never seen so much whiskey so close to Abilene in all my life."

FEBRUARY 14, 1962
What a Steal!

While the lone employee stepped out for 15 minutes, someone snuck in the back door of Toby's Bar-B-Q on Walnut Street. When the worker returned, he noticed a pan containing five pounds of freshly barbecued Polish sausage, a chicken and a dozen spare ribs was missing. If you ever had the palatable pleasure of food prepared by Toby Christian, and later by his son, Harold—"*What y'all gonna have to eat?*"—then you know that thief walked off with a tasty treasure indeed. Hope he swiped some sweet tea to soothe that "Damn Hot Sauce" burn.

Another Steal

Old Jack turned up stolen. Charles Fulwiler's livery stable rented Old Jack, his most valued and beloved horse, to a couple of young men who said they only needed Jack's service until noon. Well after lunch, the two thieves had failed to return with Jack, prompting Fulwiler to advertise a description of his prized animal in newspapers statewide. A few days later, the sheriff of Hunt County phoned Fulwiler to report he had the culprits in custody and had "sweated a confession" from them. An Abilene lawman was dispatched to Greenville to bring the horse thieves back to Abilene. Old Jack came home on a separate train.

FEBRUARY 15, 1938
Pupil Paddling

An unidentified mother phoned the *Reporter-News* asking with a note of distress, "Does a teacher have any right under the law to spank my child?" Feeling duty-bound to find out the answer, a reporter began digging into the legalities of student swatting. Local State Rep. Bryan Bradbury was consulted. He replied that it was legal but he understood that there was a maximum number of permissible swats on any one occasion of 39, admitting that as a schoolboy, he and his pals consoled one another with the knowledge that there was a limit. County Judge Lee York consulted his law books, finding a reference under "Injuries to the Person" which stated that "a teacher, schoolmaster or parent might whip a student but not with an instrument that might cause death." In that case, the whipper might be liable for manslaughter upon the whippee. The county school superintendent, Tom McGhee, produced a whole chapter from Texas Public School Laws showing that a student could legally be on the receiving end of the rod so long as it served up as punishment. (As of 2021, corporal punishment remains legal in Texas.)

FEBRUARY 16, 1931
Paderewski Plays

More than 2,000 locals packed the auditorium at Simmons University, scrounging up $3 during the Great Depression for a ticket to hear the "World's Greatest Pianist." Ignace Jan Paderewski arrived in Abilene before sunrise aboard his private Pullman car along with his wife, her secretary, his business manager, transportation manager, valet, masseur, two porters and chef. As was his schedule, he rose late and took a light lunch before practicing for the concert. The 75-year-old Polish Piano Punisher took the stage at 8:15 p.m. and for nearly three hours flawlessly tickled the ivories, bringing Beethoven, Chopin, Debussy, Brahms and Rachmaninoff to Abilene ears. The enthused crowd prompted six encores before the virtuoso returned to his train car and a gourmet dinner.

FEBRUARY 17, 1976
The Drys Have It

The weather seemed to foretell what the day held; a dust storm blew through town, highlighting the dry conditions just as voters headed to the polls to decide if Abilene would be wet or dry, alcoholically speaking. The bitterly fought debate allied religious and college leaders in a group dubbed Citizens for a Better Community against a pro-wet bloc known as ACTT, Abilene Committee on Taxation and Trade. A second anti-alcohol group, known as the Taylor County Committee for the Protection of Our Children, took out full-page ads suggesting that a "yes" vote would mean "more winos" "go-go dancers, "honky tonks" and "bar brawls." ACTT countered with ads headlined "Hysteria vs Logic," noting that there were already 43 "private clubs" where drink was available in Abilene and suggesting the city could drink up sales tax revenue. ACTT also lined up a California sky-writer who planned to spell "VOTE WET" in the Abilene skies on election day. (Windy conditions scrapped the last minute advertising stunt.)

Early results showed the decision to be nip and tuck, but late in the evening two election boxes from ACC Hill came in with the measure failing there by a 6 - 1 margin. Box 45, set up in a corridor of Moody Coliseum on the school's campus, recorded 89 voters opting to go wet while 589 chose to keep things dry. It was all over except for the wets crying. Although a majority of southside boxes voted for alcohol sales, the northside went 60 to 40 against. When the election results were announced at the HSU - Centenary basketball game at the Taylor County Coliseum, the largely Baptist crowd provided a prolonged ovation.

Few were more interested in the election outcome than Dallas Perkins, the mayor of legally wet Impact. With the results hanging in the balance, high winds blew down a power line that put the Perkins' home in the dark. He went to bed unaware that Impact's monopoly remained intact for now.

FEBRUARY 18, 1914

Way, Way Ahead of Their Time

Standing atop a moving rail handcar near Elmdale, Abilene mayor E.N. Kirby placed a telephone call to the offices of the *Abilene Daily Reporter*. In 1914! With Kirby moving along the T&P rails at a steady clip, both parties clearly heard the other and both parties were even a bit astonished that the experiment worked. It worked because of an invention by George Neel of Elmdale. Neel's idea was to run a wire along the railroad ties and to use the train's steel wheels—the handcar wheels in this case—as a medium to complete the connection. With Neel and Tom Russell pumping the handcar up and down the tracks, Kirby first called the paper, then rang up Wooten Grocers before phoning two friends to show off what surely had to be the world's first mobile phone.

FEBRUARY 19, 1947

Big Day For Roscoe

Farm implement dealer Roscoe Blankenship walked into the city secretary's office after lunch on February 19, 1947, to file as a candidate for Abilene mayor. Hours later, at its annual banquet, the Chamber of Commerce honored a surprised Blankenship by naming him as the chamber's first Citizen of the Year. He won the mayoral race unopposed; no one was willing to take on the popular civic leader.

Roscoe Blankenship

Fishy Fishing

While on a picnic outing at Lytle Lake, a group of Abilene schoolchildren came across six sticks of dynamite near the dam. The explosives, hidden beneath a rock, appeared to be new. Abilene Gas and Electric Company owned the lake and maintained a nearby storage house where they stored explosives, but a check revealed all of its dynamite was untouched. The dynamite discovery seemed to explain recent appearances of dead fish floating in the lake. Two and two were put together and a night watchman was posted to the lake.

FEBRUARY 20, 1927
Long Distance, Deep Pockets

At 7:30 a.m., Southwestern Bell Telephone began accepting calls from Abilene to Great Britain. Calls had to be placed through the operator and each call would be assigned a number, with the backlog handled in the order received. However, the backlog was non-existent, as the cost of the call was $84 for the first three minutes and $28 for each additional minute. Adjusting for inflation, a five-minute call to the old country in 1927 would set you back $2,084.

FEBRUARY 21, 1934

The Hardins' Gift

Bonds used to finance construction of the new campus buildings for Abilene Christian University in the late 1920s were retired in 1934 by a gift from John and Mary Hardin of Burkburnett. The Baptist couple donated $160,000 to the school which, in turn, honored the generosity by naming the main building "Hardin Administration," memorializing Mr. Hardin's first wife Cordelia and her mother, who were members of the Church of Christ. In time, John and Mary Hardin would have their names attached to Baptist schools—Hardin-Simmons and Mary Hardin Baylor College.

FEBRUARY 22, 1917

Steamrolled

A Thursday night basketball contest proved a raucous affair as the Simmons Steamers took on the Baylor Bears before a capacity crowd jam-packed inside the new Marston Gymnasium on the Abilene college campus. The Steamers (an early day nickname for the Simmons squad) played with speed and efficiency throughout the nip and tuck contest. The Simmons fans, up on their feet throughout, suffered from a collectively elevated tension as the two Baptist squads battled for denominational bragging rights. At the halfway mark, Simmons held the slimmest of leads, 12 - 11. Late in the game, things ratcheted to a fever pitch as the Waco five wrestled their way to a two-point advantage, 20 - 18. With only seconds remaining, Simmons drew even and the devout crowd rocked and reverberated with a passion dangerously approaching actual dancing. With the clock ticking down to zero, the pious and prayerful watched in glorious rapture as a Simmons basket offered up a miraculous conclusion, 22 – 20.

A second game, played the following day, solidified Steamer superiority, as the Simmons squad bested the Bears once more, 21 - 15. The defeated grizzlies headed for the Brazos, muttering that baseball season was coming.

FEBRUARY 23, 1941
The 45ᵗʰ Rolls In

At 6:30 a.m., more than 300 trucks drove away from Lawton, Oklahoma in a pouring rain—that turned into a heavy snow—for the 200 mile trip to Abilene and the relocation of the Army's 45ᵗʰ Division. They traveled in two columns—the east column passed through Wichita Falls, Throckmorton and Albany and the west column came through Vernon, Haskell, Stamford and Anson. The Oklahoma Highway Patrol escorted the 1,700-strong advance detachment to the Red River. Across the bridge, the awaiting Texas Highway Patrol took over in leading the massive convoy south. Three flat tires, one fender-bender, and some minor scrapes and bruises received when a troop truck skidded off the highway north of Albany could not slow down the Abilene-bound procession. (Traveling at 30 miles per hour, they could not be slowed down much more anyhow.)

The west column came into Abilene along Grape Street while the east group rolled in on Ambler, with the two joining up on South 14th at Butternut to continue the final few miles out of town to nearby Camp Barkeley. Hundreds of Abilenians stood happily along the streets

Abilene welcomes the 45th Division

to greet the U.S. Army with hoots, hollers and waves. Five days later, Abilenians thronged outside once more, this time to watch an even more impressive parade as 1,500 more trucks arrived, bringing more troops to town. Wearing their most alluring smiles, Abilene girls cheerfully watched as 10,000 eligible young men arrived on their doorstep.

ALSO ON THIS DAY IN 1951...
Vienna Boys' Choir Performs

The 32-member Vienna Boys' Choir arrived in Abilene following a long bus drive from El Paso. The world famous altos and sopranos performed at Radford Auditorium on the McMurry campus, offering a concert entirely in German.

Pizza Arrives

Still standing at 733 S. Leggett Drive is the building where Abilene first encountered pizza. Richard's Restaurant opened across from the city's first suburban shopping center, Elmwood West, in 1954. Richard was Richard Rivers, a former WWII combat pilot who partnered with his next door neighbor, Alden Cathey, to open up the restaurant serving a wide variety daily from 11 a.m. to 11 p.m. With space for 200 diners, Richard's offered a contemporary setting complete with orange table-tops, dark brown Fabrilite upholstered booths, Mayan and Javanese masks hung in wrought-iron frames, and a pink brick planter dividing the foyer from the dining area.

The menu offered Texas steaks and chops along with chicken and seafood dishes. Soups, salads and an appetizer list, including oyster cocktails, were offered as were Mexican and

Richard's Restaurant in 2021

Italian dishes. Among the Italian selections was a Napolitan pizza and a salad for $1.25. Richard's was the only menu in town to carry such an exotic option, at least for a few months, when Milano's and Casey's began serving up pizza slices as well.

Three months after opening, Richard's Restaurant was sold to Jack and Riley Simmons. It closed in 1956 and the building became the Elmwood West Club, complete with an indoor swimming pool.

FEBRUARY 25, 1933

Mr. Radford Gets a Surprise

After 50 years in the wholesale grocery business, James Radford not only amassed a personal fortune but a wide assembly of friends. Those friends and admirers conspired to surprise Radford with a banquet

James "Jim" Radford

in honor of his 50-year effort to build up Abilene, which began with his arrival in 1883. On Saturday, February 25, 1933, Mrs. Radford and her two sons escorted a quite surprised Mr. Radford into the second-floor ballroom of the Hotel Wooten. The location itself spoke of his widely held admiration, as the hotel was owned by his largest grocery competitor, Horace Wooten.

The crowded room roared with applause as the soft-spoken Radford humbly accepted the civic accolade. Clifton Caldwell presented a large plaque made from a cross-section of a mesquite that stood at North Fourth and Cedar. It was inscribed: "1883-1933 To J.M. Radford, faithful citizen, foremost builder, this plaque is presented in appreciation of 50 years constructive service by you and the progressive company you founded and with the affection of the citizenship of Abilene." Master of ceremonies Judge Wagstaff likened James Radford to a great tree, unshaken by any storm. The 72-year-old Radford spoke to the hushed crowd, reminding all, "A man passes the road but once, and he ought to leave it better than he found it."

Four months later, on July 4th, Abilene builder James Radford died suddenly at home in the arms of his wife.

FEBRUARY 26, 1948

Bingo Makes a Short Break

Longtime Abilene Zoo resident and local lion celebrity Bingo enjoyed a short break from the confines of his barred enclosure at the Fair Park menagerie. The 16-year-old feline lunged against his door, causing a faulty latch to give way and causing a shared moment of surprise between Bingo and zookeeper J.D. Burns. As the door swung open Burns quickly tried to push it shut but found he was no match for the big cat, who not only exited but managed to claw Mr. Burns' shoulder on his way past. Unwilling to let a lion—celebrity or not—loose in the middle of town, Burns managed to lure Bingo back into captivity by going on top of the cage and presenting himself as a possible snack. Bingo stepped back into his pen to closely examine this possible light meal, allowing Burns to reach down and slam the door shut. Again, man and beast looked at one another (or so I surmise) with Bingo offering a lionized-look that said, "Well played, Mr. Burns. Well played." (For the end of this tale, see December 21.)

FEBRUARY 27, 1881

Presbyterians Get Going First

When a group of Presbyterians gathered for worship near the temporary Texas and Pacific depot on Sunday, February 27, 1881, the town lot sale that would create Abilene was still two weeks away. The Buffalo Gap family of William Adolphus Minter saw the promise of Abilene and moved to the T&P tracks in anticipation of Abilene coming into existence. The Minter family and a handful of others met under a tent at the site staked off at North First and Pine Street. The service began at 11 o'clock

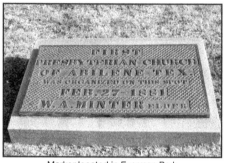
Marker located in Everman Park

and was led by Rev. William Waldo Brimm of the Dallas Presbytery, who aptly read from the third chapter of Luke, where it is recorded that Lysanias was the tetrarch of the biblical Abilene. Brimm offered a sermon based on Jeremiah 6:16, urging the few congregants to walk in the old ways and find rest for their souls. Brimm continued to travel to Abilene, preaching once a month until May.

FEBRUARY 28, 1967
Civic Building Boom

Abilene's five banks jointly took out a newspaper ad reminding readers that this day was "a most significant day in the future of Abilene and Taylor County." It was the day to decide on issuing $13.3 million in bonds, the largest package presented to the city and county electorate. Two county propositions were on the ballot along with four city issues. The county hoped to raise $3 million for a new courthouse and another $1.75 million to build a coliseum near the airport. On the city wish list: $2.5 million for street improvements, $685,000 for park improvements, $3 million for building a civic center, and approval to spend $2.5 million to enlarge the airport. More than 14,000 voters arrived at the polls (surpassing the 1962 record turnout for the city charter election) with every proposition getting a thumbs up. The widest win margin went to street maintenance, while park improvements barely cleared the bar by 157 votes.

The Leap Day Club

Courtesy of the *Abilene Reporter-News*, 44 Leap Day babies celebrated their quadrennial birthday at the Hilton Hotel. Hosting the group was editor Frank Grimes, who penned a poem for the occasion.

> The year is 'thirty-six,
>
> The day is twenty –
>
> Too late for clever tricks,
>
> Too soon for verse of mine.
>
> But may we wish you luck,
>
> Long years of happiness,
>
> A world of health and pluck –
>
> A life of gentleness!

The birthday honorees were mostly strangers, arriving from 22 area towns; however, all quickly bonded over their unique, shared natal day. The oldest attendee was J.W. Smith of Tye, celebrating his "eighteenth" birthday, while the youngest was Herbert Barrier of Colorado City, who was enjoying his first celebration in four years. The Ray Maddox Orchestra serenaded the group, with soloists singing "Love's Old Sweet Song" and "When I Grow Too Old to Dream." The newspaper's managing editor, Max Bentley, served as master of ceremonies, telling the group that they are four times as rare as the average person, who has one chance out of 365 to be born on any day, while this group had only one chance out of 1,460 of arriving on February 29.

Bentley announced that the newspaper planned a second banquet four years out and suggested, "Maybe we can have the president of the

The initial gathering of Leap Day babies at the Windsor Hotel gathering

United States here to welcome you then. His name, by the way, will still be Franklin Delano Roosevelt." Enthusiastic applause followed Bentley's prediction. After enjoying a five-course meal, the three-tiered birthday cake was cut and four lucky honorees found prizes—a silver ring, a thimble and two dimes. The evening concluded with the singing of "Auld Lang Syne" followed by hugs and handshakes and many offers of "I hope to see you in four years."

Leap Day Leap

After 57 years serving as a pastor—32 of them leading First Baptist Church—Rev. Millard Jenkens decided to leap into retirement on Leap Day Sunday of 1948. Three days later a formal reception took place and included a selection of Jenkens' favorite hymns sung by a seven-man church group. Songs included "Joshua Fit the Battle of Jericho," "Old Time Religion," "Come Thou Fount," and—in a genre leap—"Darling Nellie Gray."

Millard's ecclesiastical stats:

Sermons preached	7,801
Members received	12,446
Funerals conducted	2,699
Weddings performed	1,270
Missions organized	5
Prayer meetings held	1,560
Revivals preached	119
Hospitals started	1

MARCH

No More Weather Flag Waving

Effective this day, Abilene weather observer William Green received a national directive to stow all weather flags and cease running them up the rooftop flagpole to convey weather conditions. The National Weather Bureau in Washington issued the edict as a money-saving measure. It seems supplying wool flags to weather stations across the U.S. was too costly and it was noted that displaying such flags to convey the weather was largely ineffective, given the constantly changing conditions. However, the local weather bureau was instructed to continue to maintain one flag—white with a black circle in the center—the flag to indicate an approaching "norther" or cold wave. Farmers needed to know if such a change was in the air.

MARCH 2, 1914

Thanks, Docs

On this day, Sallie and William Estes were surprised by the birth of triplets. William cried tears of happiness one minute and tears of worry the next. As a brickmason, he feared he could not feed three extra mouths, as he and Sallie were already raising six children in a small house on Locust Street. There was much discussion as to what names should be given to the two boys and a girl. Early thoughts were to name the girl for her mother and the boys politicized to Woodrow Wilson Estes and William Jennings Estes. In the end, the Abilene trio were named in honor of the three physicians who assisted with the unusual birth. Son Jack was named for Dr. Jack Estes while Jim was in honor of Dr. Jim Alexander. Dr. Auda V. Cash was memorialized in the daughter being named Cash Estes.

Sympathetic townsfolk donated $32.20 to help with the added family expense brought on by Jack, Jim and Cash. Tragically, mother Sallie Estes died nine days later due to complications from giving birth, and in July, infant Jim passed away. Unable to care for Jack, Cash and the other children, Mr. Estes sent them to live with relatives and friends. Jack and Cash went to live with a family friend, Fannie Stockton on Pecan Street, and were raised thinking that Fannie was their mother. In 1954, Jack Estes was reading the "40 Years Ago" column in the Abilene newspaper and was stunned to see a reprint of the 1914 article noting the triplet birth. The article named his parents, something he had been unaware of for four decades.

MARCH 3, 1881
Abilene Barnett

Writer A.C. Greene put it best, "The name Abilene is not a common one. You have to be marking some special occasion to name a baby Abilene. You have to be expressing exuberance, be excited about the future and already possessed of loyalty for a place which won't officially begin for nearly two weeks." He was writing about the birth of a baby girl, born to parents A.M. and Fanny

Headstone of Abilene namesake, Abilene Barnett

Barnett on this day. The girl, first to be born in the soon-to-be-born town of Abilene, was named Abilene Barnett. At the age of 12 days, she was one of the witnesses to the lot auction on March 15 birthing the namesake town. Tragically, young Abilene Barnett would only live to be 2 years old, dying in 1883. Abilene is buried in the southwest corner of the City Cemetery next to her mother and older sister, both of whom died in 1883 as well.

MARCH 4, 1911
Lytle Who?

A note addressed to the editor of the *Abilene Farmers Journal* arrived from a man living in Ohio inquiring about the name of "Lytle." Seems the Ohioan was wondering if the creek, cove, gap and lake bearing the Lytle name might memorialize a relative who moved to Texas many years before. Unsure of the answer, editor Joshua Hicks reverted to investigative reporter and left the newspaper office to ask a sampling of old-timers about the common local name. Dropping in on attorney Jim Thomas at his Cedar Street office, Hicks posed the question but no answer came forth, although Thomas did offer up an explanation for the genesis of "Guion." Next up was Judge Wagstaff, found behind his desk at his Pine Street office. However all that the old-timer could produce was, "It was a name used around here before I arrived."

Catching Judge Augustus Kirby just as he was about to board the train, the attorney replied, "I haven't the slightest idea." Jack Wills and Frank Rickard were queried without result. Hicks next approached veteran Abilenian and Chief of Police John Clinton, hoping he might field the question. No such luck. Hicks trekked to the real estate office of Mat Lambeth on Chestnut. A true war horse, Lambeth had been living in Taylor County well before there was an Abilene. Hicks figured certainly such a deep historical repository could solve the riddle. Lambeth vaguely remembered a man who owned a ranch in the area named Lytle but was unwilling to lay his oath on it.

(The Texas State Historical Association believes that the creek, cove, gap and lake are named for early settler John Lytle, who trapped horses in the area to sell to the Mexican government.)

MARCH 5, 1908
Limits on Yellin', Interferin' and Spittin'

Abilene city fathers passed a flurry of ordinances, all intended to regulate social activities, all printed in the newspaper this day. Among the now-banned activities: using megaphones to solicit business, interfering with funerals, and spitting. The fine for "amplifying your voice through a megaphone in order to attract business along the streets and alleyways" was set at a hefty $100. As to funeral interference, the law forbade anyone from "willfully stopping, breaking, confusing or crossing through a procession," further stating that one must conduct themselves in an orderly manner at such events, inferring megaphones were unwelcome in this instance either. Guilty parties would be subject to a fine ranging from $5 to $50.

As for spitters amongst the populace, they were henceforth "forbidden from expectorating on the sidewalk, sidewalk crossings, on the floors or walls of business houses, stores, offices, hotels, restaurants, churches, theaters and streetcars." Violators would be paying a fine of $25. Notably, spitting at the cemetery during a funeral was perfectly legal.

MARCH 6, 1958
A Spot-On Imitation

Conditions were ripe; the weather outside was ominously threatening and the Lincoln Junior High gym had around 200 players and spectators inside for a girls basketball tournament. Seated at the top of the stands, an unidentified young boy, having calculated the circumstances, managed to prank the entire assemblage. From the top row of the bleachers he produced a prolonged and highly accurate imitation of the Abilene tornado siren, resulting in the gym being emptied in a semi-orderly stampede in just under four minutes. The throng raced for safety in the pedestrian tunnel not far from the gym's entrance, leaving one rather self-satisfied boy sitting alone in the stands. Following a phone call by the tournament director to the local weather bureau, all returned and play resumed with hearts beating fast both on and off the gym floor.

MARCH 7, 1939

Abilene Apaches

The two-year-old West Texas-New Mexico baseball league welcomed Abilene into its ranks in early 1939. The eight-team league included the Lubbock Hubbers, Pampa Plainsman, Big Spring Barons, Midland Cowboys, Lamesa Loboes and a lone New Mexico squad, the Clovis Pioneers. The Amarillo Gold Sox were joining the league along with Abilene to make it an even eight. The first order of business for the Abilene team was to come up with a name. The newspaper sports editor offered to accept votes for the top suggestions, with a season pass going to the person whose recommendation garnered the most votes.

From a long list of suggestions, the possibilities were whittled down to three—Oilers, Aces and Apaches. Assistant Abilene Christian baseball coach Arthur Coleman proposed "Aces." Thomas Green first suggested "Oilers" while Dub Pool, a teacher and former McMurry footballer, thought "Apaches" had the right ring. Balloting was heavy, with the majority opting for a hometown team known as the Abilene Apaches.

Opening day saw the Apaches take on the Lamesa Loboes before a crowd of 2,000 at Withers Field. The diamond, built in northeast

Abilene, was named for the team president and manager, Fincher "Tat" Withers. (Withers Field was located at what is today the site of Will Hair Park.) Pre-game ceremonies for the inaugural game included introduction of the Abilene players and the presentation of the season pass to Dub Pool, who watched in disappointment as a ninth inning rally pushed the Loboes past the Apaches, 4-3. Turns out, Dub's pass was not good for long—on July 9, just eleven weeks after their debut— the Abilene Apaches relocated to Borger, becoming the Borger Gassers. (Abilene rejoined the league in 1946, playing as the Blue Sox. In their first game against the Gassers on April 30th, Hayden Greer stole home in the tenth inning, putting those Borger boys in their place, 5-4.)

MARCH 8, 1886
Irish Whiskey

Frances Ames, a local Irishman, entered a southside Abilene saloon and in the space of 30 minutes downed three and a half pints of whiskey. Within another 30 minutes, he was carried out a dead man, buried at the city's expense.

MARCH 9, 1883
Knock it Off

Abilene started in 1881, but the city did not incorporate until March 9 of 1883. The newly formed government immediately set out to straighten a few things up. On this day, Mayor Daniel B. Corley signed Ordinance No. 1, entitled "Offenses Against Official Duty," making it unlawful to impersonate a city officer. Also going into effect, a ten-part ordinance titled "Offenses Against Public Morals & Decency." One can assume that ordinances addressed contemporary problems. That being the case, early Abilene appears to have been a bit libertine. Ordinance #1 stated: "It shall be unlawful for anyone to appear in the streets or public places of the town in a nude state, in a dress not belonging to him or herself, or in an indecent or lewd dress, or to expose his or her person or be guilty of an indecent or lewd act where persons passing might ordinarily see the same." Locals were also forbidden from bathing in Lytle or Cedar creeks between sunrise and sunset. After dark, all bets were off.

ALSO ON THIS DAY IN 1950...
Minter's Celebrates 50 Years

Minter Dry Goods celebrated 50 years of business with an evening gala and recognition of two long time employees, both having served 40 years—Myrtle Adams, head of the ready-to-wear department, and Lena Ries, hosiery buyer.

MARCH 10 1939
The First Lady Drops By

A visit by First Lady Eleanor Roosevelt prompted Mayor Will Hair to proclaim Friday, March 10, as "Eleanor Roosevelt Day." When the Sunshine Special rolled into town, an estimated 3,500 Abilenians thronged to the train station to witness her 7 p.m. arrival. Mrs. Roosevelt rewarded their wait with a smile and a wave before getting into a car for the four-block trip to the Hilton Hotel. A bellboy in cowboy regalia assisted her with her bags as she signed the register, followed by hotel

manager Bill Reidy seeing her
up to her room and proffering
a hotel menu from which she
ordered broiled sweetbreads.
Then, invoking all the powers
due such a hotel manager in
such a situation, he ordered
the switchboard operator to
hold all calls so that the First
Lady might enjoy her dinner
uninterrupted.

     Mrs. Roosevelt's 16-
hour visit was highlighted
by an address at Hardin-
Simmons; the school invited
the First Lady to speak as

Mrs. Roosevelt with Dr. Sandefer
and his granddaughter Diana, 1939

a part of the school's artists program. Numbered among the crowd of
1,800 jammed into the school auditorium were the 44 members of
Abilene's Eleanor Roosevelt Child Study Club, who came as a group to
hear their namesake speak. Dr. Rupert Richardson had the honor of
introducing the well-known guest because HSU President Dr. Sandefer
was in ill health, but 5-year-old Sandefer granddaughter, Diana, presented
Roosevelt with a basket of yellow snapdragons. Following her speech, the
First Lady dropped by to wish Dr. Sandefer well before being whisked
to the West Texas Chamber of Commerce offices for a press conference.
When asked if she thought the country would ever see a woman elected
president, she remarked such a notion as "foolish," adding, "That won't
happen for many, many years. It is difficult enough for a man to gain and
hold the following he must have to accomplish anything as president."

MARCH 11, 1959

Sweating It Out

Near midnight, Taylor County Sheriff John Woodard, accompanied by Police Chief Warren Dodson and three Texas Rangers, walked up the front entrance of the Abilene Country Club to carry out a search warrant alleging that the club manager had property "for the purpose of gaming, gambling, wagering and betting on gaming and gambling boards, tables and other gambling equipment." In a room just right of the club entrance, the raiders located 12 men and one woman gathered around two craps tables. The loud and lively crowd slowly quieted as the police presence dawned.

The sweating over a roll of the dice gave way to actual sweating when a Texas Ranger stood by the door while the other lawmen began taking names. Following a rather rough dismantling of the gaming tables and the confiscation of $4,187 in cash, the crowd dispersed. An hour later, the law officers wrapped up their work and returned to Ranger Wood's car only to find that someone had let the air out of two tires.

In the end, 18 were charged with unlawfully "sweating a gambling game," while the club manager was busted for permitting gambling devices on the premises. Among those facing a maximum penalty of $50 were six out-of-towners, two Air Force officers, and local men whose addresses were along some of Abilene's finer streets—Sayles, River Oaks and Elmwood. The following week, all pled guilty and the Country Club paid the fines on behalf of the inconvenienced members.

MARCH 12, 1927

Gas and Groceries Galore

In 1927, the Abilene population totaled in the neighborhood of 23,000; however, the city was home to an astonishing 87 full-service gas stations and 115 grocery stores. The city inspector for weights and measures, Charlie Cheshire, compiled a list of both since he would be the one to stop by to check the accuracy of grocery scales and gas pumps. Seven mom 'n' pop grocery stores lined a two-block stretch of North Second, and there were five more grocers in the 700 block of Oak Street alone. The greatest choice was on Pine Street, where you could pick from nine stores.

MARCH 13, 1956

Frozen Bird

With temperatures below freezing, an American bald eagle passing through the Abilene area parked for the night on a tree branch on the Lou Davis ranch. Awakening the next morning, Mr. Eagle discovered his claws firmly frozen to his perch. A ranch hand noticed the earthbound bird and gently gathered him up, delivering him to Game Warden J.D. Jones, who phoned the federal game warden in Lubbock for advice. The Fed was unsure of the next move so he dispatched a letter to Washington asking for directions on how to proceed. In the meantime, Warden Jones thought that the Abilene High Eagle cheerleaders might like to meet a real eagle, even suggesting the bird might make a nice living school mascot. Following the avian introductions, the rare bird took up residence at Warden Jones' home where two freshly killed rabbits—offered up as lunch and dinner—went uneaten by the anxious eagle.

Washington thought little of the prospect of the eagle becoming a school mascot, so the eagle was pardoned and set free. However, nine years later, in 1965, Zoo Director Walt Keunzli granted permission for the AHS Booster Club to adopt the zoo's golden eagle as the official mascot. Dubbed as "Champ," the mascot made pep rally appearances and watched the human Eagles play on Friday nights.

MARCH 14, 1911
Theodore Roosevelt Makes a Visit

Former President Theodore Roosevelt was on a cross-country train trip. It began in Atlanta with the aim of arriving in Phoenix for the dedication of the Roosevelt Storage Dam. After stops in Birmingham, Jackson, New Orleans and Houston, the 52-year-old Republican then stopped in San Antonio before detouring north to Waco, Dallas and Fort Worth. Roosevelt's private three-car train departed Fort Worth on March 14, 1911, at 9:50 and headed west to deliver T.R. for a scheduled speech that evening in El Paso. Towns all along the Texas and Pacific track had wired ahead requesting that the former president might consider a stop and a speech.

That morning, in an Abilene court, the district attorney urged the judge to fire off a telegram to the former president requesting him to stop, to which Judge Blanton replied, "He wouldn't listen to me. I'm a Democrat. 'Tis the mayor's place." So Mayor Kirby, who was in the courtroom in his role as lawyer for the defense, agreed and hurriedly dispatched the following: "Your friends and admirers here are legion. Entire citizenship insists that you stop here five minutes. Kindly arrange it. We will not accept refusal. E.N. Kirby."

When Roosevelt's train briefly stopped in Baird to switch engines, his Texas traveling companion was handed a sheaf of telegrams half an inch thick. Included in the stack was Mayor Kirby's request.

Theodore Roosevelt speaking to the Abilene crowd

Approaching Abilene mid-afternoon, engineer Joe Stoude had but little choice to make the unscheduled stop when he saw the track ahead clogged with a crowd of 4,000 Abilenians. Stoude pulled the train to a stop alongside the new T&P depot at twelve past three. More than 1,000 school children had mercifully been let out early in hopes of catching a glimpse of Colonel Roosevelt and both sides of the track from Pine to Cedar were lined up to 30 people deep. Engine 277 slowed to a crawl and issued forth a shriek of white smoke as the 17-strong Simmons College band struck up "Lo, The Conquering Hero."

Enthused Abilenians emitted a sustained ovation when they saw, standing on the rear car platform, the mightiest American of the day flashing his famous tooth-filled grin. Local state senator W.J. Bryan quickly swung up onto the train to stand pointedly next to Roosevelt. With the crowd cheering and chanting, "Hello Teddy!" he held up his hand and spoke.

"My friends, I have but a few minutes to talk owing to our train schedule. But my friends, Colonel John Simpson, whom I knew forty years back as "Hashknife" John, told me it would be a felony to pass through Abilene and not stop. I want to congratulate you on your excellent school system (here the train began to roll west) and your fine crop of babies!"

According to the *Daily Reporter*, amid the plaudits of 4,000 men, women and children the picturesque New Yorker went west waving his arms and flashing his teeth as far as the eye could see.

Teddy Roosevelt was in Abilene for one minute and fifty seconds.

ALSO ON THIS DAY IN 1885...
Tin Can Tying Gets Banned

In an ongoing attempt to get things under control, the town council passed an ordinance prohibiting the "tying of tin cans, or other things, to the tails of dogs, horses, calves, goats or other animals."

MARCH 15, 1881
It's A Town!

Abilene was born on this day when the Texas & Pacific Railway auctioned off the town lots. A T&P official tacked up a city plat on a board at South First and Chestnut showing the newly laid out town. The railroad company set up a crude platform from which the auctioneer could be heard, and he got busy gaveling the town into reality. For weeks prior, newspapers across Texas carried ads touting the sale and the opportunity that lay waiting "in the midst of one of the most beautiful, fertile and healthy sections boasting the very finest grain and stock producing lands of the West," and further proclaiming Abilene would become one of the most important points on the T&P line.

The *Dallas Daily Herald* noted that the Abilene site offered "lands as level as a floor" but predicted that the real city to sprout along rails would be Baird. The T&P tracklayers reached the Abilene location two months before on January 15th with the lot sale ambitiously scheduled for five days later, however it was pushed to March, hoping to raise the advertising buzz and provide time for more hearty souls to arrive. Land hungry immigrants camped beneath

Newspaper ad carried in publications across Texas

tents, wagons and other primitive shelters while casting about for the best business lots and discussing which tree-named street might offer the best home location.

Auction day dawned cold but with warm excitement as the crowd moved in close to find out who would bid and learn which lots would bring the most interest. The northside was marked off into 83 blocks, while 80 more, each 300 feet square, were south of the tracks. Both sides offered 228 business lots and over 800 residential locations. With a town bisected by a railroad, there was much discussion about which side lumber yards and merchants might prefer.

Baird resident Jonathan Taylor Berry plunked down the first cash, paying $350 for two lots out of Block 8 at the northwest corner of Pine and North Second. Cameron and Phillips Lumber won the next bid, choosing a Pine Street location as well and convincing many that the northside was the preferred one. As the auction ended, 139 lots sold for an average price of $175. The following morning, 178 more lots hammered sold with the two-day Abilene land auction wrapping up by noon. The new Abilene landowners shook hands, back-slapped one another and with an optimistic thrill anxiously set about building the "Future Great" city of West Texas.

MARCH 16, 1951

Billy Graham Saddles Up

Evangelist Billy Graham drew a crowd of over 6,000 to his morning service held inside the Rose Field House on the campus of Hardin-Simmons. Graham was casually dressed in a blue sport coat, light gray gabardine pants and donned a short-brimmed cowboy hat given to him by Amon Carter while Graham had been in Fort Worth. Trombone-playing musician Cliff Barrows accompanied the evangelist and led the gathering in singing "Amazing Grace" followed by "In the Garden."

After the service, the youthful preacher lunched at the Windsor Hotel, where he was presented with a cowboy shirt. The Abilene hosts then drove Graham to the HSU stables for a few minutes of horseback riding, and the school president presented a hand-tooled saddle to Graham who responded, "I shall always think of you West Texans and this wonderful school, Hardin-Simmons University, every time I use this saddle." (Which was a nice way of saying, he would likely never think of HSU again.)

A Pachyderm Predicament

Night time drivers traveling along U.S. Highway 80 three miles west of Abilene could see flares ahead and were warned to slow as they neared the problem. All were quite surprised to find that the problem involved having to maneuver past Taffy, an 8,000-pound elephant laying in the middle of the road. Taffy had a starring role in the Heart of Texas Carnival and was en route to Colorado City when, just after 8 p.m., she leaned hard to one side and fell from the back of her truck. Taffy's handler, Jack Barons, tried to coax and cajole her back upright, alternately using sweet-talk and a bullhook. He informed the growing crowd, "When she's ready to get up, she'll get up." After more than three hours of trying to solve the problem, a closer examination was initiated, revealing that Taffy was not simply being stubborn—the 85-year-old pachyderm fell from the truck because she had passed away.

MARCH 17, 1905

Grocery Calls

In response to a growing annoyance amongst local residents, Abilene's grocery men signed an agreement stating that each would stop sending salesmen door-to-door soliciting orders. Instead, they would rely on telephone calls to generate business. The agreement stated, "All we cannot reach over the phones we will take chances on their sending their orders to other stores." Front stoop visits from salesmen went away, replaced by jangling phones interrupting dinner.

MARCH 18, 1915

Slow It Down Buster!

The *Abilene Daily Reporter* editorial page issued a strong appeal to all Abilene automobile drivers to slow down. The paper noted that, "EVERY day accidents that would cause the loss of life or make somebody a cripple for life are narrowly avoided at the intersection of Pine and North Second streets." The editor added, "Men, women, boys and girls who drive autos, we call on you to resolve to never drive on the streets of Abilene again at a speed which is unlawful." At the time, the downtown speed limit was 10 miles per hour. You could crank it up to 15 mph in the residential areas.

MARCH 19, 1918

The Freight Depot

Nearly two and half years after the Texas & Pacific Railway announced plans in 1915 to build a new freight depot at North First and Pine, the building was finally finished in March of 1918. The 260-foot-long building, constructed of concrete and red Thurber brick, was finished in just five months. T&P president J.L. Lancaster came out from Fort Worth to inspect the new building with its 29 trackside doors. Finding all acceptable, Lancaster ordered office records and telegraph equipment out of the old freight building and into the new one.

Lancaster noted that the Abilene drought would be broken soon because whenever he and chief engineer E.F. Mitchell visited any city, a good rain followed, predicting, "Abilene may expect a good rain in a short while." Taking no chances, the next evening prayer meetings across the city pointedly asked Heaven to let loose with a good soaking. It finally rained on May 3, 44 days after the freight depot was completed.

MARCH 20, 1950
Cold Hard Cash

Car salesman R.M. Ziegler, working at Thornton Motors on Oak Street, sold a truck to a Merkel area farmer. Ziegler personally delivered the vehicle, aiming to collect a check for $980 to satisfy the account. The farmer said he had not trusted paper money since Franklin Roosevelt devalued it during the Great Depression. Rather than bringing a check back to the office, Ziegler man-handled two cloth bags containing 605 silver dollars and 750 half-dollars to settle the deal.

ALSO ON THIS DATE IN 2021
ACU Defeats Texas

The ACU Wildcats men's basketball team, seeded 14th, pulled off probably the biggest win in the school's history, defeating the third-seeded Texas Longhorns 53-52 on two free throws by Joe Pleasant with one second left in a nationally-televised NCAA March Madness first-round game. The win earned extensive media coverage for ACU and Abilene.

MARCH 21, 1881
First Marriage, Free Lot

As a representative of the Texas & Pacific Railway, Stoddard Johnston was instrumental in developing Abilene, laying out the streets and giving them their names. He also had the authority to donate a city lot to the first couple who married in the new town. One week after the town lot auction, Anna Rollins and Ira Border exchanged their vows and became the proud owners of a free corner of the new Abilene. Exactly which lot they came to own is not certain; however, the couple lived at North Third and Orange Street for some time and surely they were savvy enough to build on the complimentary Abilene soil.

Last Train Out

Having provided passenger service along the Texas & Pacific rail line since 1881, the last T&P passenger train left the Abilene depot three minutes late at 9:33 a.m. on this day in 1967. The final train had arrived from the west at 9:15 a.m. before continuing on its journey to Fort Worth. Thirty-nine folks climbed aboard at the Abilene stop, many just for the right to lay claim to the minor honor "Left Town on the Last Train." Included in the group was a contingent of elementary school students who clambered aboard for a final choo-choo field trip to Baird. One passenger on the terminal ride noted that her grandfather had arrived in Abilene on the first train 86 years earlier in 1881. A fair-sized crowd of Abilenians came to stand along the platform and watch as history and 39 semi-celebrities headed out of town towards the morning sun aboard the last train out.

Piffle Kerr Takes the Bait

The visiting Hilltoppers of Dallas University bested the Wildcats of Abilene Christian in both tilts of a baseball doubleheader at the all-dirt diamond. The first game tallied up 8 - 3 with the ACC squad racking up seven errors while, in the late match-up, poor base running figured into the equation.

With a chance to even the score in the eighth inning, Piffle Kerr came to the plate and with a mighty swing managed a long hit over the head of the center fielder. Running hard, Piffle rounded first and headed for second under the false assumption that the Hilltopper second baseman

Earl "Piffle" Kerr

was standing on the baseline when, in fact, he was several yards into the outfield where he turned in an Oscar-winning performance, acting as though his foot was on second and awaiting a throw. Piffle took the bait and wound up far astray from his intended target. By the time he noticed his mistake, Piffle was tagged out on what had looked to be a stand-up triple.

"Piffle" Kerr's given name was Earl Elmer and he came to ACC from Lubbock to study education. His graduation page in the 1926 Prickly Pear yearbook noted that the lesson to be learned from Piffle was, "Don't let mistakes discourage you; profit by them" and went on to remind all how he ran into center field while trying to reach second base a year earlier.

MARCH 24, 1942
Birdie on Number 17

Local lumberman Ross Jennings teed up on Number 17 at the Abilene Country Club, took a beautiful backswing, came around swiftly, managing to perfectly top the ball so that it dribbled only a few yards down range. Attempting to make some distance with his second shot, Jennings lined up his three-wood, unleashed a forceful stroke and cleanly sent the ball aloft…where it solidly struck an unsuspecting field lark passing overhead. Ball, bird and a fair number of detached feathers fell to the fairway. The bird did not survive the surface-to-air missile. Jennings managed par.

MARCH 25, 1943
Uproar at the Zoo

~~The City Parks Board~~ passed a stay of execution, granting four South African and Nubian lions, along with two Alaskan bears, a 30-day reprieve. Two weeks earlier, the board had voted to condemn the Abilene Zoo carnivores to death by a one-man firing squad. The president of the City Parks Board offered three reasons for the death-row sentence. *1. The cost to feed the meat-eaters was exorbitant. 2. Refuse from the cages at Fair Park flowed into Catclaw Creek, creating an unpleasant odor downstream. 3. Should the park be bombed by WW2 enemies, the wild animals might be set loose on the city.* The resulting uproar could be heard all over town.

Fair Park Zoo exhibit of Alaskan bears and Nubian lions

Bob McDaniel, the man assigned the unenviable task of killing the lions and bears, protested that a city the size of Abilene could surely afford to maintain the animals and he would prefer to not serve as executioner. Instead, he began to feed the inmates at his own expense. Retired zookeeper George Baggett offered to return and care for his former charges at no expense, while H.A. Pender, who had donated two of the lions, asked for mercy on behalf of the city exhibits. Officers at the Abilene Army Air Base offered to provide meat, bread and bones free of charge.

The public outcry did not fall on deaf ears. Following the stay of execution, the board opted to reverse course altogether, commuting the bears and lions to a life sentence and authorizing $1,000 be spent improving the zoo. However, not everyone was happy. The formerly free-roaming peafowls found themselves now confined to a cage.

Epileptic Asylum Opens

The State Epileptic Asylum in Abilene was scheduled to begin receiving patients on March 16 but a high wind on the 14th blew the newly completed standpipe over, leaving the facility without a supply of water. A temporary, smaller water tower was hastily erected and on March 26 patients arrived from San Antonio as well as from the State Lunatic Asylum in Austin and the Insane Asylum in Terrell. By the end of the day, 104 patients arrived in Abilene. In all, around 200 patients suffering from epilepsy came to Abilene by summer. At the time, the very misunderstood affliction, considered a psychiatric condition, saw

The State Epileptic Colony administration building and cottages

sufferers being placed in asylums. In 1925 the State Epileptic Colony was renamed to Abilene State Hospital. A third name change took place in 1957, becoming the Abilene State School. Now known as the State Supported Abilene Living Center, the facility continues to offer care.

MARCH 27, 1965
Chet Huntley Comes to Town

Two-thousand Abilenians crowded into Rose Field House on the Hardin-Simmons campus to be a part of the largest Chamber of Commerce banquet in its then 57-year history, besting the 1963 crowd who came to hear Norman Vincent Peale. The throng gathered at 7 p.m. to hear well-known and widely admired NBC newsman Chet Huntley, the New York half of the Huntley-Brinkley Report. Hounded by autograph seekers, Huntley had little time to eat before Chamber president C.E. Bentley invited him to the podium. In his 45-minute speech (that was locally televised) the veteran broadcaster touched on the Republican Party, Vietnam and the failures of communism.

MARCH 28, 1944
Jimmy Bickley is Back Home

Having left Abilene six months before, 22-year-old Jimmy Bickley once again woke up in his parent's home at 1041 Willow. The twelve-week odyssey he had just endured was an experience the military commanded him to be silent about. Second Lt. Bickley had been the co-pilot on a B-24, known as "On the Ball," which, after a bombing run over Germany, failed to return to its English base. The War Department reported Bickley and his crew missing on January 7. Their whereabouts remained unknown until Jimmy and three others showed back up in London seven weeks later.

Granted two 21-day leaves, Bickley spent three weeks in Abilene and then moved on to Santa Monica, California, where a girl figured in his post-war plans. Jimmy spent his time in Abilene enjoying home-cooked meals, speaking at his alma mater, McMurry, and visiting his extended family in Merkel. News reporters who sought to learn more of his ordeal were handed a military order notifying them that Lt. Jimmy Bickley was forbidden from revealing any details of the 50-day period in which he was missing.

After the war, Bickley was able to tell about the events of January 7, 1944. The crew of "On the Ball" completed its bombing run over Ludwigshafen, Germany, and were over Brou, France, when 20-millimeter rounds hit the nose of the plane as well as the Number 2 engine and cockpit. With the plane on fire and three of the crew dead, the other six bailed out. Bickley's parachute floated him down to a French farm, where the family hid him from German troops. The French underground then moved him from safe house to safe house, helping him make his way across the Pyrenees to Spain and on to Gibraltar. He flew from Gibraltar back to England on February 24.

After his Abilene visit, Lt. Bickley returned to active military duty and remained in the service following the war. While stationed in Labrador in December of 1947, Jimmy survived a second military plane crash when the C-54 transport he was on went down in flames near Goose Bay. The accident killed 23 servicemen. Jimmy Bickley was, again, one of six who survived. Jimmy Bickley died in 2002 at the age of 80.

Twelve Hours With the Red Sox

Greeted by over 500 fans, the Boston Red Sox arrived at noon on board their special train car. The crowd was keenly interested in catching sight of Tris Speaker, the Texas boy who had made it to the big leagues. With press in tow, the 28-member squad crossed North First Street to the Hotel Grace for lunch. Before their scheduled 4 p.m. game at West End Park, the Sox divided into seven cars and were given a tour of the town.

Businesses closed at 3:30 and more than 2,000 filled the grandstands, lined the diamond, or looked on from their buggies and automobiles as the visiting pros took on the United Commercial Travelers, a team made up of locals but reinforced with two Sox players—an outfielder and utility pitcher. Tris Speaker came to the plate five times and did not disappoint, managing a triple, two doubles and two singles to insure the Sox turned in a respectable 19 – 7 shellacking.

Following the game, a dance was staged for the fellas and they attended a late movie at the Vendome that told the story of the 1910 World Series. After a full 12 hours in Abilene, the Boston boys climbed back aboard their train car at midnight, waving goodbye as they headed for Fort Worth.

ALSO ON THIS DAY IN 1965...

New Zoo Gets Going

A small crowd braved the cold wind and misting rain for the groundbreaking ceremony held at the site of the new zoo in Nelson Park. Taking turns with the silver shovel were Mayor Lee Byrd, Parks Board chairman Jack Stroube, Oscar Rose, City Manager H.P. Clifton, Willis Cox and Zoo Director Walt Kuenzil, who dug a spadeful for Mrs. Morgan Jones Sr., who made the largest donation for the effort—$15,000—covering the cost of the flamingo and water bird exhibit. The new Abilene Zoo opened on July 2, 1966, with a crowd of over 5,000 streaming past the gate.

The Abilene Zoo, 1970

MARCH 30, 1932

Digging for Dollars

Suspicious activity occurring next door to the Farmers & Merchants Bank on South First Street led Abilene police to do some digging. What they found was...well, digging.

Police had a building, just east of Citizens Bank, under surveillance when two of the suspects showed up, opened the padlock and entered the empty building. Officer Ruck Sibley and Detective Wilburn West waited until they shut the door, then walked up and knocked. Ed Rice opened the door just as Rupert Black, covered in dirt, emerged from a tunnel at the rear of the building. The officers found a shaft about eight feet deep that entered a tunnel extending nearly 50 feet in the direction of the bank. They also found oil drums filled with dirt and a variety of short-handled digging tools. The digging duo soon implicated two other tunneling pals who were rounded up and also placed under arrest. The four told police that an unknown man, who wanted a tunnel where he could store bootleg liquor, had hired them at a rate of $5 a day. Skeptical police were not buying the story and brought conspiracy charges against the quartet.

Measurements showed that the boys tunnel veered north and, had they broken through the floor, they would have been disappointed to find themselves inside the J.C Penney store next to Citizens Bank, and not in the vault. Officers soon learned that the vacant building next to a second bank, the F&M Bank, also had been leased to the group. The four were arrested in a plot to rob two banks—Farmers & Merchants as well as Citizens National Bank—by attempting to tunnel beneath the vaults. In the end, charges were dropped against one digger while two of the conspirators faced trial together. The jury was unable to reach a unanimous verdict and a mistrial declared. The fourth man was tried days later and found to be not guilty. The mistrial case was never re-heard.

Preach On

Seven Abilene pastors combined in a joint proclamation, stating that some who profess Christianity have a tendency "to walk in a worldly way" and that such behavior needed a spotlight shone upon it. Sensing it was their ministerial duty among their respective flocks, they requested that the newspaper print a list of certain dangers and stumbling blocks facing Abilene church-goers, to-wit: dancing, card playing, attending the theatre, skipping church and drinking whiskey. As to dancing, it was stated that no Christian engages in this pastime without compromising his Christianity, not to mention that police reports from large cities noted a very high percentage of fallen characters engaged in dance. In addressing the problem of whiskey drinking, "those who do imbibe, murder their influence and surrender their moral right to church membership."

MARCH 31, 1943
Some Darn Good Chutin'

Hardin-Simmons graduate and former Cowboy Band drum major Owen Baggett found himself drifting beneath a parachute, on the verge of earning a distinction believed to be unique in Air Force history. Just minutes before, Baggett had been co-piloting a B-24 on a

Owen Baggett, drum major for the HSU Cowboy Band

bombing run aimed at destroying a railroad bridge in Burma. Attacked by a squadron of Japanese fighter planes, Baggett's plane filled with smoke and the crew obeyed the order to bail out. While under his parachute, Baggett watched his plane explode. He then realized that the Japanese pilots were turning around to strafe the crewmen floating helplessly downward. Hit in the arm by Japanese machine gun fire, Baggett watched as the enemy swung around for another pass. The pilot slid his canopy back and as he came closer, Baggett reached down and grabbed the .45 automatic strapped to his leg. As the Japanese plane neared, Owen fired four shots and then watched as it stalled and spun into the ground, earning Baggett the distinction as the only person to shoot down an enemy aircraft using a pistol.

Baggett spent 30 months as a POW imprisoned near Singapore. He retired with the rank of colonel in 1973 and he passed away in 2006.

APRIL

The First Drive-In Theater

Abilene's first drive-in theater opened just west of town along Highway 158 [the northwest corner of South 14th and Willis Street]. Carroll Jones and Chuck Williams brought the novel movie experience to Abilene with their Skyline Drive-In. The screen was parallel to the highway and faced north with enough space in front to accommodate 400 cars. Audio for the movies was broadcast from a large central speaker, rather than individual speakers for each car, prompting neighbors to quickly lodge complaints with city hall about the nightly noise. The first movie cast up on the 30-by-40-foot screen was "Tall in the Saddle" starring John Wayne.

One year after opening, George and Ruth Likins bought the Skyline, renamed

The Elmwood Drive-in along Willis Street at South 14th

it the Elmwood Skyline, and began offering a watermelon garden and picnic tables where you could sit, watch the show and enjoy your melon. They also permitted one local entrepreneur the concession to knock on car windows and offer to sell you a hard-boiled egg. The Likins operated the theater until 1965 when they cashed in, selling it for $225,000 and making room for the Bank of Commerce to occupy the corner.

APRIL 2, 1936
The Optimist, Not Always So

The student newspaper of Abilene Christian College, known as *The Optimist*—and in publication since 1912—on occasion reflected news characterized as less than optimistic. Notably, on this day, when the "love/not love" affair between campus beauty Wilma Kendrick and the dashing Howard Utley was detailed in print for campus readers. The Kendrick-Utley affair had been an outwardly observable romance since the first of the year, alas, the newspaper reported: "At the first of this year Miss Kendrick openly declared that her affections would be directed solely at Mr. Utley if he so desired. But Utley fell for someone else and left Wilma out in the cold again. However, the cold settled on her shoulders which she now turns toward Mr. Utley at every opportunity." Touché.

APRIL 3, 1974
Judge Ely Gets A Boulevard

In January of 1974, the City Council unanimously voted to honor Walter Raleigh Ely Sr. by changing the name of an east Abilene thoroughfare from Stadium Way to Judge Ely Boulevard. Ely was a longtime local attorney and judge who served in the 42nd District Court and who was named by Governor Moody in 1927 to serve on the Texas Highway Commission. Judge Ely was on the commission for eight years, serving as chairman for four years, and is credited with reorganizing the scandal-ridden department, establishing a state highway network, and beginning the roadside park system.

Coinciding with Judge Ely's 96th birthday, a reception and luncheon took place at the Abilene Civic Center, followed by a dedicatory ceremony at E.S. 11th Street and Judge Ely Boulevard where the new sign was unveiled. Walter Raleigh Ely died on January 31, 1978, two months before his 100th birthday, with his name living on, still figuring in on the way to the stadium.

Judge Walter Ely, right, admires his sign

APRIL 4, 1927

Without or With Offense...

Bernard Hanks, publisher of the *Abilene Daily Reporter*, dropped a piece of paper on the desk of editor Frank Grimes. On it was a couplet from Lord Byron's poem "Don Juan." Hanks asked, "What about running that under the masthead?" Grimes agreed and the quote first ran on this day in 1927. It read, "Without or with offense to friends or foes we sketch your world exactly as it goes." Frank Grimes, a Byron scholar, noted that the apropos phrase was "a hope, a goal, an aspiration and a policy." The Byron quote now appears on the editorial page.

APRIL 5, 2002
Local Luminary: A.C. Greene

"Every man has a village in his heart…" For A.C. Greene that village was Abilene. (The initials were for Alvin Carl although he legally changed his name to A.C. in 1953.) In his evocative 1969 memoir, "A Personal Country," Greene fondly recounts that "Abilene is my village. It is the place I know best, the spot I have kept against change, although the town that made my village is very different, and so am I." The influences and experiences of Abilene inspired much of A.C. Greene's writings. He became a widely known literary figure in Texas, authoring numerous books and serving as a journalist and editor for the *Dallas Times Herald*. Greene often related Texas anecdotes, infused with humor, and offered perspectives on life topped with common sense.

Greene graduated from Abilene High School and got his start as

A.C. Greene, 1969

a reporter for the *Abilene Reporter-News* in 1948 before operating a local bookstore and teaching journalism at Hardin-Simmons. Greene left Abilene in 1960 and, although he never returned to live in his hometown, he often noted how deeply Abilene lived inside of him. With his grandmother serving as the librarian for

Abilene's Carnegie Library, Greene naturally developed a love for books.

In 1988, Greene underwent a heart transplant, receiving the heart of a 31-year-old woman who had died from cancer, and two years later he wrote of the experience in a book titled, "Taking Heart." On April 5, 2002, A.C. Greene died from cancer and was buried on the Green Ranch in Shackelford County. The A.C. Greene Award is annually awarded at the West Texas Book Festival.

<h3 style="text-align:center">APRIL 6, 1957</h3>

Abilene Public Schools Stadium

Abilene voters went to the polls on Saturday, April 6, 1957, to decide if a $750,000 bond should be issued by the school district. The funds would finance construction of a new football stadium, replacing Eagle Field, the 25-year-old stadium at Fair Park. The new stadium became a reality by a scant 42 votes. A light turnout—with 907 voting in favor and 865 giving the project a thumbs-down—revealed that four of the eight ballot boxes opposed the bond, but precincts 4 (ACC fire station) and 7 (Elmwood fire station) pulled in enough "yes" votes to float the bond.

Abilene Public Schools Stadium
near completion, 1957

The site for the new field—with the less-than-exciting name of Abilene Public Schools Stadium—became a bone of contention between the school board and the city commissioners. Nearly a year after the bond passed, the school board had not decided on the site. City commissioners pushed for the stadium to be next to the fairgrounds. The school board politely suggested they mind their own business. The board was leaning toward a 40-acre tract belonging to Ruth Jones and her family. A sales contract between the school district and Mrs. Jones was already in place but in the end the site was not selected. (In 1967 Mrs. Jones would donate much of the property to the City, becoming Redbud Park.) Additionally, James Radford offered to donate a 75-acre site east of Cockerell Drive but drainage issues nixed that idea.

Eleven months after the bond election, the school board finally voted 6-1 to purchase the 49-acre site west of the fairgrounds, the one touted by the city commissioners all along. Unfortunately, it was not for sale. Brothers John and Louis Wise owned much of the property and did not wish to sell. The school board instigated condemnation proceedings in order to acquire the property, at which point the Wise brothers decided to accept $67,500 for their property.

By the time construction bids were accepted, the estimated cost from 1957 had gone up. In order to shave off added expense, the school board opted to forgo paving the parking lots. That convenience would come much later.

Houston architect Milton McGinty drew plans for the stadium. Ten years prior McGinty designed the football stadium for Rice University, and McGinty's vision for the Abilene stadium was a miniature version of that field with similar looking ticket booths and press box.

Two and half years after the voters' approval, the Abilene Public Schools Stadium was ready for play. The initial gridiron contest took place on September 11, 1959, as the state's fourth ranked Abilene Eagles took on second-ranked San Antonio Jefferson on a chilly night with the temperature in the 50s. Thirteen-thousand fans, many arriving at 5:30

when the gates opened, paid the $1.50 price of admission. With just over a minute remaining, Jefferson needed to make the two-point conversion to tie the contest. Abilene fans roared as the pitchout was fumbled and AHS' Dave Parks fell on it. The new stadium was christened with a 14-12 Abilene win.

ALSO ON THIS DAY IN 1957...
ACC Ties a World Record

At the Texas Relays in Austin, Waymond Griggs, Bill Woodhouse, James Segrest and Bobby Morrow, who ran the anchor leg, tied the world record for the 440-yard relay, covering the track in a blistering 40.2 seconds.

APRIL 7, 1897
The Waters of Lytle Lake

A Mr. Dickens of California joined J.M. Ingle two miles east of Abilene as they put their drag-line scrapers to work building a dam across Lytle Creek. Paying for the project was the Lytle Water Company, spearheaded by Fred Cockrell, company president. The aim was for the company to supply a permanent water supply for the city. Included in the 17-part agreement between Lytle Water and the City of Abilene was a provision that the water company would furnish free water to regularly fill two public troughs, water to sprinkle the streets, to irrigate the city cemetery, and provide no-cost water to all public buildings used by the city. One year after completion of the lake, the windmill and water tanks were removed from the yard of the Texas and Pacific Hotel on North First Street since abundant water was now in place.

APRIL 8, 1956
Diamond Jubilee

Turning 75 was the cause for a week-long celebration known as the Diamond Jubilee, bringing Abilene citizens together in a variety of events, parades and contests. The Sunday edition of the *Abilene Reporter-News* topped out at 277 pages and included eight special sections covering everything from the city's history, families, and economy to neighboring towns and Dyess Air Force Base.

The Pioneer Parade kicked things off on Monday as 15 bands, 11 horseback groups, and vehicles ranging from hearses to tandem bicycles moved along the downtown route. Dedication of the courthouse

Cast members of "Saddles to Jets"

monument to the Taylor brothers followed the parade, and an evening concert at Fair Park Stadium by the Anson High School band was presented just before the first performance of "Saddles to Jets," a play recounting Abilene's history, featuring a cast of over 1,000 and a climactic explosion of a pretend nuclear bomb. (The Tuesday night crowd of 3,500 were disappointed as the bomb failed to explode when technical director Harry Graf made the theatrical decision to forego the simulated blast because a group of roaming children were too close for comfort.) Tuesday offered an art exhibit, carnival rides, a luncheon honoring editor Frank Grimes, and a fiddler contest.

Wednesday was Oil and Soil Day, with the fairgrounds providing space to honor the local oil industry along with farmers and ranchers. The beard-judging contest for Brothers of the Brush awarded prizes for oldest, blackest, whitest, reddest, most repulsive, fullest, most distinguished and most novel beards. The novelty prize went to George Hine, who shaped his whiskers into a "7" on one cheek and a "5" on the other.

Thursday was Baseball and Antique Auto Day. The Blue Sox opened their season against Lubbock, winning 7-6, while a parade of 85 antique cars motored through downtown. Friday was Youth and Education Day and still another parade—this one featuring junior high bands—followed by a baton-twirling contest next to the depot that was dominated by three Anson twirlers. Open house at Dyess served to punctuate the week as thousands came out to see the aircraft display and watch the Air Force Thunderbirds perform their acrobatics.

APRIL 9, 1956
The Taylor Brothers Get Their Due

Ninety-eight years after the Texas Legislature created 23 counties out of Bexar and Travis, including Taylor County, the identity of just exactly who Taylor was, was firmly established. In 1858, the legislature dictated that the new counties be named for the principal waters draining within the boundaries or for a deceased person. In naming Taylor County, however, the lawmakers failed to specify the

Monument to the Taylor brothers in front of the old Taylor County courthouse

identity of Taylor. Following exhaustive research by Jewel Scarborough
in 1956, it was determined that the legislature honored Edward, James
and George Taylor for their heroic actions. The trio of Tennessee brothers
were defenders of the Alamo, losing their lives in that 1836 fight. Mrs.
Scarborough took her research to State Rep. Truett Latimer, who drafted
legislation to properly recognize the honorees. The unveiling of a granite
monument, fitted with a bronze plaque—sculpted by Lincoln Borglum—
took place at the Taylor County courthouse square on a cold, windy day
in April of 1956, solidifying the honor.

APRIL 10, 1891
The Lights Came On

For the first time, electricity illuminated Abilene, marking the slow
banishment of the flickering and fluttering light from coal oil lamps.
The Abilene Electric Light and Power Company, formed by R.W. Kindel
of Weatherford and four Abilene investors, secured the contract to
provide electricity to the city and to build a power plant. Kindel oversaw
the installation of the Wood arc dynamo and incandescent dynamos
purchased from Edison General Electric Company, capable of lighting
1,300 bulbs. With darkness falling, the dynamos went into service on
Friday, April 10, 1891, accompanied by a celebration featuring a band
and speeches. As additional wire arrived, the system expanded to serve a
growing subscription list of residential customers, with each assured that
the danger of shock was low.

A Rare Honor for Rare Courage

Abilenian Cora Caldwell traveled to Camp Wolters near Mineral Well on this day so she might attend an extraordinarily rare occasion, one honoring the actions of her 36-year-old nephew, Sgt. George Keathley—a posthumous awarding of the Medal of Honor. Following high school, George enrolled at Texas A&M in 1933 but, unable to afford the cost of attending, withdrew from there in 1937 and took a job with the Soil Conservation Service before joining the Army in 1942. He served as a staff sergeant in Company B of the 85th Infantry Division. Keathley's death occurred on September 14, 1944, in a bloody battle fought on Mt. Altuzzo, Italy.

With his company pinned down and all commissioned and superior noncommissioned officers killed, Keathley took over, crawling from casualty to casualty offering first aid to the living and collecting ammunition to distribute to those still able to fight. Issuing orders and shouting encouragement, he repeatedly drove back the German assault.

When a grenade exploded next to him, causing what would be a mortal wound to his stomach, Sgt. Keathley stood up, pushing clip after clip into his rifle, holding the German troops off for another fifteen minutes. Inspired by his actions, the remaining troops pushed back the German offensive.

Medal of Honor recipient George Keathley

Before falling, Keathley requested of Tech Sgt. Charles Dozier, "Write to my wife and tell her I love her and I did everything I could for her and my country."

At the ceremony, widow Geneva Keathley accepted the medal presented for her husband's conspicuous gallantry and intrepidity.

In 2007, George Keathley's Medal of Honor was given to Texas A&M where it is on permanent display at the Sanders Corps of Cadets Center. Keathley Hall, built in 1964 as a residence dorm, honors this former Aggie and heroic nephew of Abilene's Cora Caldwell.

ALSO ON THIS DAY IN 1971...
Coody Masters Golf

Thirty-three year-old Abilenian and professional golfer Charles Coody edged past Jack Nicklaus and Johnny Miller to win the 35th Masters Golf Tournament, finishing two strokes better than the second place pair. Besides earning the coveted Masters green jacket, Coody picked up a check for $25,000 and quipped that "it would be used to pay some bills."

APRIL 12, 1933
Daredevil Roland Climbs the Wooten

Once was enough for the "Human Fly" Henry Roland. The 39-year-old daredevil from Cleveland made his living by scaling tall buildings, often paid by local merchants sponsoring his feats. Five years earlier, Roland visited Abilene where he deftly scaled the Hotel Grace and the nine-story Mims Building. Returning in 1933, Roland attacked the outer walls of Abilene's tallest building, the 16-story Hotel Wooten. He began his ascent at 2:15 and successfully reached the rooftop less than an hour later. Promised an encore at 7:30 that evening, a large crowd began gathering early to witness the repeat performance. By 8 p.m., the crowd concluded Roland skipped town and would be a no-show, sending the disappointed Abilene crowd home. Sadly, four years later, Henry Roland fell to his death while performing in Tennessee.

APRIL 13, 1919
Chickens Run Afoul

Before newly elected city officials took their seats in April of 1919, the last act of the retiring City Commission was to finally settle a longstanding and hotly debated topic in town—passing a chicken ordinance. The public debate concerning chickens was tightly drawn along two lines. The Pro-Poultry crowd squawked that they needed chickens for their egg-laying ability, while Anti-Cluckers wanted beautiful gardens and had run out of patience with free-range scratchers ruining any decent chance for a colorful flower bed. The *Abilene Reporter* editorial page often opined on the issue, consistently siding with the Anti-Hen & Rooster faction.

The final ordinance not only tackled the chicken issue but wisely sought to head off any future controversies by including ducks and turkeys in the sweeping ban. Specifically, the named fowl were, henceforth, labeled a "nuisance" and prohibited from roaming haphazardly about the public streets and private yards of Abilene. Scofflaw birds would be subject to impound and released only upon payment of a 50-cent fine. For any chicken, duck, turkey—and, it could be assumed by extension, pheasant and goose—too slippery for Abilene law enforcement to lay hands on, officers were authorized to implement a shoot-to-kill policy. (No timeframe for the acceptable length of chase prior to unholstering was stated.) Further, the ordinance was effectively immediately.

In 1957, Abilene commissioners expanded support for the anti-fowl stance, sanctioning any chicken, duck or other fowl to "crow, quack or emit noises deemed a breach of the peace and quiet of Abilene, Texas." However, in 2015, the City Council backed the personal rights of in-town roosters, opting to allow them to cock-a-doodle-do without government interference.

APRIL 14, 1956
Dyess is Dedicated

Serving as the climax of Abilene's 75th birthday Diamond Jubilee was the formal dedication of Dyess Air Force Base. General Francis Griswold, vice-commander of the Strategic Air Command, spoke from the parking ramp, telling the thousands in attendance, "What we see around us today is the result of your vision and diligence." Griswold wrapped up his remarks with, "We learned long ago that the best and most efficient bases are those located near communities where the people are friendly and understanding." (Perhaps a sentiment worthy of permanent display at the gate to Dyess, don't you think?) Abilenians not only pitched in to purchase needed land to make the base a viable possibility but also donated to build the VIP Quarters and the base swimming pool.

General Francis Griswold, vice-commander of the Strategic Air Command, arrives to speak at the dedication

APRIL 15, 1899
Globe Lightning

Just after 4 o'clock in the morning Abilenians were roused from their sleep by a deafening explosion during a heavy rainstorm. Well before dawn, W.E. Hughes was walking from his home on Cedar to his meat market on Pine Street and watched as a luminous, rolling ball of fire moved rapidly westward, followed by a terrific explosion that destroyed a rented residence in the 100 block of Orange Street. T.M. Wingo occupied a room on the northside of the house while Mr. and Mrs. Coke Harkrider and their infant son William slept in a room on the south end. The ball of fire seen by Mr. Hughes entered along the electrical wires, setting off a series of blasts blowing out all the windows and breaking bottles throughout the house. Boards propelled out the front window with such force that the front fence was pushed over and all the wires inside were burned while the parlor was set on fire and a section of the roof collapsed.

The explosion was attributed to "globe lightning" that traveled along wires. Mr. Wingo, sleeping on an iron bedstead, suffered serious injuries but felt that his wool mattress saved his life. The Harkriders were unhurt.

APRIL 16, 1945
Secret Sororities and Frats Are Out

Abilene school trustees unanimously voted to accept a recommendation from the junior and senior high PTA groups to ban all sororities and fraternities among Abilene students. Further, to insure compliance, all incoming high school students would have to sign a pledge card indicating that they did not belong to such an organization nor would they join one—with at least one parent required to sign as a witness. Students refusing to sign would be ineligible to participate in any extracurricular activities, hold a class office, participate in athletics, theatrical productions, graduate with honors, or receive medals and scholarships.

Leaders of the nine targeted sororities and fraternities issued an open letter to the community pointing out all the good they did in the community and hoping to reverse the decision. It was to no avail. The board's action marked the end of Tri D, Double A, Khoda Deru, Lambda Beta, Sigma Phi Omega, Semper Sorosis, Phi Sigma, Delta Sigma and Alpha Sigma Chi…at least until the next year when they were replaced by YMCA-sponsored Tri-Hy-Y clubs such as Zenith, Corkers, Harmonix and La Pluma. 17 new clubs had formed by 1947.

APRIL 17, 1907
Ministerial Menaces

Norris Griffin and Will Reese, both lads hailing from Tuscola, were standing trial in the county court of Judge Overshiner. Representing the pair was Abilene attorney Harry Tom King, who was seeking to defend the boys against the county attorney's charges. The prosecution alleged that on the fourth Sunday of March, young Norris and the budding Will disturbed public worship at a Tuscola church by engaging in loud and unacceptable whispering. Fifteen ear-witnesses, including the pastor, presented their testimony, with the case lasting most of the day. (At one point Judge Overshiner halted the proceedings to perform the wedding of

Mr. E.P. Perry and Miss Willie Reynolds with the trial attendees serving as witnesses and with no one whispering loud enough to trigger arrest.) The jury finally rendered a verdict at 4 o'clock in the afternoon, finding Norris and Will not guilty of worship interruption.

A month later, Eli Pruitt and Cris McGehee faced the same charge, disturbing public worship by their audible antics at a Buffalo Gap church. Once again, Harry Tom King represented the accused and, once again, he won an acquittal for the worship rattlers.

APRIL 18, 1958
Carnegie Library Checks Out

Fifty years after Abilene's Carnegie Library began going up, she came tumbling down. Construction on the two-story, south-facing building on North Second began in 1908 and cost $17,500. The building (including a dirt-floor basement) was ready for opening by mid-1909.

Back in 1899, the Federation of Women's Clubs had assumed responsibility for finding a permanent home for the nomadic Abilene library books that had already moved on four occasions. In 1906, Federation officers Mamie Thompson, Ella Cockrell and Hattie Sayles felt that industrialist Andrew Carnegie might want to help and placed a request to the steel magnate for $20,000. Carnegie agreed to grant $17,500, stipulating that the library must commit to spend 10-percent of that amount annually

The Carnegie Library along North Second Street

on new books. All agreed and plans were drawn to replace the old Stith home at North Second and Cedar with a red brick library.

Following the razing of the old library in 1958, a $700,000 mid-century modern building took over the same spot, opening on January 18, 1960. However, not all of the old Carnegie building has been lost. Brick from the library was re-used and still graces the home at 677 Westwood. (Note: In 1908, Ballinger received $17,500 and Stamford $15,000 for their Carnegie Libraries, which they have stubbornly refused to demolish.)

APRIL 19, 1910
A New Depot

The long-held Abilene dream of a new depot took the first step toward reality. With the old 1898 depot offering up a less than impressive welcome to travelers, all felt it was time to pressure the T&P decision-makers to sweep away their wooden depot and ramshackle outbuildings for a modern bricked version. Following much imploring and subtle arm-twisting, the railroad came around to Abilene's point of view and drew plans for a new train station.

St. Louis contractor Hughes and O'Rourke won the bid for the project. They were already in the neighborhood constructing the Big Spring depot so their crew headed east to begin work on a 170-foot long station that would sport a two-story tower with an eight-sided roof. Just as the last shack fell to the ground in April 1910, a freight train arrived delivering a concrete mixer for use in pouring the new foundation for the iconic Abilene building.

APRIL 20, 1922
Golf and Golfers Arrive

With the finishing touches complete, Abilene's first golf course prepared for the inaugural round. The Abilene Country Club welcomed Syd Cooper of Dallas and his 18-year-old son, Harry, who came out west to put on a demonstration. The familial duo spent the afternoon inspecting the course (protected by a five-foot high wolf-proof fence) that had been designed a year earlier by the senior Cooper. The following afternoon a gallery of around 100 followed the pair as they battled for the first win on the newly completed links. Young Harry managed to cover the course in 79 strokes, besting his dad by six swings. Following the indoctrination round of Abilene's first golf course, club members pulled out their own sticks and scythes to give the links a go.

Early-day golfing at the Country Club

The next year, Harry (soon nicknamed "Lighthorse Harry" for his quick pace of play) turned pro and began a career that included 31 PGA Tour wins, twice coming in second at the Masters Tournament, and ranking number 16 on the all-time tournament win list.

APRIL 21, 1885

Editorial Gunplay

The editors of competing Abilene newspapers had their fill of one another and decided the best way to settle their difficulties might be to fill the other with lead. Editor of the *Abilene Reporter*, Charles Gilbert, and W.L. Gibbs, editor of the *Magnetic Quill*, continually took opposing sides on most every subject – fencing, labor unions, sheep grazing. Their troubles came to a head late afternoon in front of the First National Bank with both men attempting to prove the pistol is mightier than the pen. Drawing their handguns, the two editors took aim, firing generally at the other. Five bullets whizzed across the street with Gilbert grazed across the forehead and Gibbs suffering a blow to his arm. Neither man was seriously injured but both were arrested. Five months later, the *Magnetic Quill* closed up shop as the *Reporter* stowed its weapons and pressed on.

APRIL 22, 1939

Hmmmm

Without context or explanation, the student newspaper of Hardin-Simmons printed a list titled, "H.S.U. Library Reading List On Venereal Diseases." Possible topics for students to read up on included: "Are We a Nation of Prudes?" from Collier's Magazine, "Bedbugs Transmitting Syphilis" and "Combating Syphilis Among University Students." Reader's Digest offered "Combating Early Syphilis," while the February 1938 edition of Survey included, "Are You Afraid of Syphilis?"

Conjecture as to the origin and necessity of such a list falls on Dr. Arnette, HSU professor of zoology, who months earlier lectured students

about the connection between prudency, ignorance and spreading
venereal diseases. Arnette pointed out, "Some people blush at undressed
lumber and even make pants for their table legs."

High and Fairly Dry

Nine inches of rain in less than a week brought the creeks out of
their banks and an overnight deluge on this day helped create a sea at
the junction of Lytle and Cedar creeks beneath the railroad bridge. An
unfortunate family, camped at that spot, moved into their wagon and
perched on the highest point they could reach but found the rising waters
quickly minimizing their sanctuary. They fired guns to attract attention,
and the fire boys came to the rescue, tied a rope to the family hack, and
pulled the fairly dry family ashore.

APRIL 24, 1950
The Clack Sisters Are
Unceremoniously Retired

At the end of a difficult school board meeting, the Clack sisters,
Miss Bobbie and Miss Tommie, were out of a job. Prior to adjournment,
member Roy Leach suggested that one of the new schools in Abilene be
named in honor of the longtime educators. His suggestion became a
reality 42 years later.

Bobbie Clack began teaching English at Abilene High School in
1923, following 13 years at the lower grade levels, and Tommie Clack
took on her AHS English position in 1917, having taught in other

districts since 1903. After 40 years in the district, Miss Bobbie got on the wrong side of the superintendent (who felt she had embarrassed a group of boys) and he indicated that he did not intend to renew her contract for the 1950 school year. Miss Clack appealed the decision, asking for an open hearing before the school board. AHS principal Joe Humphrey spoke in defense of Bobbie, heartily recommending that she

Miss Tommie Clack

be re-employed for the upcoming school year. The board then heard from Bobbie. The superintendent stuck to his guns but did offer a path less harsh than refusing to renew the contract, recommending instead that the board immediately consider a policy dictating mandatory retirement for teachers when they reach age 65. The board unanimously adopted the policy. Only two teachers in the district fell under the new rule, Bobbie, age 66, and her sister, Tommie Clack, age 67.

Between them, the Clack sisters had 84 years of teaching, and were beloved by thousands of former students. In 1992, the Abilene school board honored the Clack sisters by naming a new middle school in their honor.

Miss Bobbie Clack

One and Done

A crowd of 1,800 gathered at the Taylor County Coliseum anxiously waiting pop star B.J. Thomas to take the stage. Just days earlier, the popular singer took home an Oscar for his chart-topping hit song "Raindrops Keep Falling On My Head." Thomas' Abilene concert day began with a 4 a.m. arrest followed by six hours sitting in jail in Rockford, Illinois, for being intoxicated at a hotel where he threatened a bellhop and two police officers. After a local fan there paid his $25 bond, Thomas began his trek to West Texas.

His Texas International flight from Dallas to Abilene was two hours behind schedule but he finally arrived, sped to the coliseum and took the stage. The patient crowd gave Thomas a thunderous welcome and he launched right into his first number, which turned out to be his last number as well. Following the song, Thomas dropped his hands to his side and said, "I've been up too long." Then the 27-year-old singer turned and walked offstage. It soon became obvious that his departure was not a joke.

In the days following the greatly shortened concert, KRBC-Radio refused to play any B.J. Thomas songs until he apologized while KNIT cut back on Thomas' airtime. In 2019, Thomas returned to Abilene, performing at the Paramount Theatre, where he apologized for the 49 year old slight.

APRIL 26, 1946

Play Ball!

The Abilene Blue Sox first took to the diamond before a home crowd on this day in 1946. It was the opening contest in a 140-game schedule set for the eight-team West Texas-New Mexico league and the Friday night game saw the Sox take on the Clovis Pioneers, with the ump crying "Play ball!" at 8 p.m.

The squad had a working agreement with the National League Brooklyn Dodgers in cooperation with their Fort Worth farm team, which explains the name and the Dodger-blue socks worn by the team. The league limited rosters to 15,

Blue Sox Stadium was located at
South 14th and Barrow Street

allowing for only four veteran league players and requiring a minimum of five rookies. Team payroll capped at $2,200 a month.

The Blue Sox were owned by 25-year-old *Reporter-News* sports writer Howard Green, along with George Steakley and Dr. James Bridges, a former Camp Barkeley medical officer. Green's boss at the newspaper, Hal Sayles, convinced a group of local businessmen to contribute the money needed to buy a ball park site along South 14th Street and build a stadium with seating for 3,500.

As game one of the '46 season got underway before a sellout crowd, it proved a lively affair with 22 base hits and Sox shortstop Pete Spatafore getting ejected after the ump took offense. The Sox brought in eight runs in the eighth inning to get by Clovis 19-14. For the season, the home team would go on to notch 97 in the win column, losing 40, while bringing home the pennant for its opening season. The Abilene Blue Sox folded in 1957 and the stadium demolished to make way for a shopping center. H-E-B grocery store now occupies this site.

The Abilene Aces Take the Field

The West Texas Baseball League formed in 1920 with six teams but was out of business two years later. Then, in 1928 the group reconstituted, fielding six more teams: San Angelo Red Snappers, Coleman Bobcats, Midland Colts, Lubbock Hubbers, Hamlin Pied Pipers and the Abilene Aces. (Thomas Best of N. 17th Street suggested "Aces" as for the club name, winning a season pass worth $44.25.) The Aces home opener saw them take on the Pied Pipers at Gardner Field—so named for team owner Alvin Gardner of

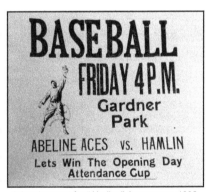

Advertisement for "Abeline" Aces game, 1928

Wichita Falls who purchased the former Abilene Christian College ball park site for $10,000. It was located on South First between Portland and Miller Street.

Advertisements in the *Abilene Times,* touting the afternoon game, misspelled the home team's name; however, that slight did not hurt play as the Aces led from the start, scoring four in the first and helped along in the second inning when Bobby Turgeon sent the horsehide over the left field fence. The Aces bested Hamlin 15-11.

The league championship for the '28 season was a five-game series between the Aces and the Red Snappers. The fifth and deciding game went San Angelo's way—Snappers 8, Aces 3. The Aces last season was the following year.

ALSO ON THIS DAY IN 1895...

You Can Call Me Now

Charlie Roberts brought telephone service to Abilene in 1895. The Abilene Telephone Company erected poles and strung wires along right-of-ways granted by the city in exchange for the city having free use of the poles and the right to string electric lines onto the upper arms. Mayor D.W. Wristen approved the agreement and Mr. Roberts began to enlist subscribers to his convenient new phone service, reminding all that he could save you a long walk. In addition to his telephone company, Mr. Roberts owned a collection agency. Conjecture has it that collecting debts may have been the motivation to start up the phone service.

APRIL 28, 1958

A Feat of Flying

Rather than abandon a fellow crewmate, First Lt. Jim Obenauf stayed with his burning B-47 bomber and, with the canopy gone, flew mostly blind in sub-zero weather in order to save the life of his unconscious navigator, Major James Maxwell.

The four-man crew, assigned to the 341st Bombardment Wing at Dyess AFB, took off from Amarillo at 10:30 p.m., headed to Denver on a training run when an explosion rocked the aircraft at 34,000 feet. With the fuselage on fire, the pilot instructed his crew to bail out. Major James Graves pulled the handle to blast the canopy off the top but the pilot and co-pilot seats failed to fire, so Graves followed a second crewman through the nose escape hatch, both parachuting to safety.

Co-pilot Jim Obenauf climbed down to follow the others out but noticed that Maxwell was unconscious, his oxygen mask blown off. Confronted with the difficult choice of saving himself by bailing out or facing what appeared to be certain death by staying with the plane in an attempt to save his fellow officer, Obenauf returned to his seat. Miraculously, without the canopy, and with winds whipping at over 200 miles an hour, the temperature at -20 and debris blinding him in one eye, the young airman managed to fly over 300 miles to reach the Dyess runway and make a perfect landing from the co-pilot's back seat position. For heroism in saving the life of Major Maxwell, Jim Obenauf was awarded the Distinguished Flying Cross as well as the Kolligan Flight Safety Award and, in June of 1959, was a contestant on the popular CBS game show "This Is Your Life," where he was given a 1959 Edsel station wagon and a color television set.

APRIL 29, 1924

New School Opens, But Bring a Chair

Construction of a new high school along South First Street began in 1923, which proved to be a fortuitous move since, just as the new one was nearing completion, the old one caught on fire. By April of 1924 the new school lacked a few final touches and was awaiting arrival of the furniture. Then, around 9:30 p.m. on Friday, April 25, Mrs. Cecil

Armstrong pulled into her drive on South Fourth and smelled smoke. Mrs. Armstrong convinced her husband, who happened to be a fireman, to follow his nose and investigate. It led him to the old school. Every piece of fire-fighting equipment rushed to the scene, but the damage to the interior proved extensive.

The school building—built in 1909 on the same property as the new one, at the back of the lot on South Third and Peach—was too small for the rising student population. With the old school out of commission because of the fire and the new one not yet complete, school officials convened on Monday and decided to move into the new building early. Students were asked to assemble at the site to move salvageable items to the new school. However, in order for everyone to have a seat on Tuesday morning, the principal requested all students to bring with them a kitchen chair from home. It turned out that by day's end, enough chairs were salvaged to negate that request, but news spread slowly and so the next morning, Tuesday, April 29, 1924, a fair number of students came to school lugging a kitchen chair up the sidewalk. The students were the first to walk the halls and the class of 1924—who attended class there for just four weeks— took the title of First Graduating Class from the new school.

Abilene High School, 1924

First Presidential Visit

As Texas Republicans prepared to go to the primary polls deciding between President Ford and former California governor Ronald Reagan, Ford made an Abilene stop in hopes of swaying local voters. It was the first visit by a sitting president. Abilene was his last Texas stop before the primary scheduled for the next day. Ford spent three hours downtown shaking hands and asking for support among the Key City crowds, although the president had some serious competition for Abilene's attention. The Doobie Brothers were in town and set to rock the Taylor County Coliseum.

Air Force One flew to Abilene from Lubbock, touching down in the rain at Dyess Air Force Base just before 5 p.m. where the president was greeted by over 1,000 airmen. At the Civic Center, Mayor Fred Lee Hughes named Ford an honorary citizen and proclaimed he was exempt from paying any local taxes. Ford quipped that Hughes, the local Buick dealer, should not trade in this Ford just yet. At the Jaycee-sponsored reception, 23-year-old Diane Boles courageously asked Ford if she might kiss him, to which he wisely agreed. A crowd of 2,000 heard a short stump speech in the auditorium before Ford moved across the foyer to the exhibit hall where 4,000 more waited to see and hear the president. He skillfully played to the hometown folk by praising former ACU quarterback-turned-Dallas-Cowboy Clint Longley (who had yet to sucker-punch Cowboy icon Roger Staubach or it is doubtful Ford would have cashed in on Clint's Abilene connection).

By 8 o'clock Ford was back at Dyess. Waiting for him aboard Air Force One were a dozen copies of the *Abilene Reporter-News* supplied by circulation director Al Miller. The presidential plane lifted off at 8 p.m. and at 8:30 Miller received an in-air phone call from President Ford thanking him for the papers. Ford kept Miller on the line for three minutes, telling the surprised newspaper employee how pleased he was with the Abilene reception and praising Abilene for having such an attractive Civic Center. Chances are, Al Miller voted for Ford, but Reagan won the Texas primary. (If you are curious, the Doobie Brothers drew a crowd of 5,600.)

MAY

Mattie Alexander Dies at 103

At the age of 103, Mattie Alexander, one of Abilene's most colorful residents, passed away. On Mattie's birthday one month earlier, a local radio station treated her to a limousine ride around town. When asked what she wanted to see, she replied, "Heaven."

Mattie was born in Canada in 1887 and orphaned soon after, her mother dying two weeks after giving birth, while Mattie's father, a well digger, died in a cave-in two weeks before she was born. An Irish circus performer known as Madame Amy took Mattie in, raising her alongside her own daughter who was born the same day. The two girls, Mattie, who was black, and Evelyn, who was white, were raised as twins. At the age of 14, Evelyn was killed while practicing a high-wire act.

Mattie grew up among the circus where she tried the tightrope but gave it up to work with the trained elephants and chimpanzees. In 1916, Mattie took a job with Ringling Brothers Circus riding a pachyderm named Queenie under the big top. Arriving in Abilene in 1969, Mattie worked for Maxine Perini before retiring in 1978 and beginning a new career leading exercise classes well into her 90s. Mattie Alexander is buried in the City Cemetery.

MAY 2, 1931
Hollywood Picks a Beaut

When the staff of the Simmons newspaper, *The Brand*, decided to hold a contest to select the top campus beauty in 1931, editor Lewis Jobe thought, "Who better to judge the top Simmons beauty than a Hollywood star?" Jobe wrote to heartthrob Gary Cooper asking if he would do the honors, and to everyone's surprise, Cooper agreed. Photos of 20 campus lookers were forwarded to Tinseltown and a few weeks later Cooper wrote, "This is the most difficult thing I have ever had to do. It is my sincerest thought that I never saw a bunch of intelligent beauty where it was so hard to choose the best." In the end, he picked a beaut from Bogolusa, Louisiana—Miss Carol Johnson.

For the 1932 contest, Douglas Fairbanks Jr. was tapped to make the selection, opting for Esther Parrish of Ballinger as the top campus eye-catcher. Frederick March was awarded the honor 1933, granting the top spot to local head-turner Dorris Garrett.

Hollywood bombshell Mae West served as judge for the fourth annual pageant of beauties roaming the Simmons University campus. When the school editor initially wrote Mae West in 1934 asking if she would serve as the one-woman selection committee, she wrote back, "I will be glad to try my hand with your beautiful young ladies. When the photographs are ready, mail them to me and I will try to do as well for you as Mr. March, Mr. Fairbanks and Mr. Cooper. Come up and see me sometime. Best wishes, Mae West."

West submitted her final decision, choosing dark-eyed, brown-haired Eleanor Byarlay from Kalamazoo, Michigan. Her reply included a stinging postscript, "Say, are your students as terrible looking as the pictures show or is it the photographer?"

MAY 3, 1895
Snakes Gotta Go

Mayor Daniel Wristen issued a stern warning to Clyde Hathaway about his snake collection. It seems Mr. Hathaway was in the habit of collecting rattlesnakes and keeping them in slight contraptions at his home, much to the annoyance of his neighbors. Clyde was an electrician who was tasked with maintaining telephone lines, thus providing him ample opportunity to turn up his reptilian treasures.

Two recent escapees managed to slither away from Hatahaway's home and caught the attention of his neighbors, Mr. and Mrs. James Cunningham, who were out for a walk when they were on the receiving end of a snake strike. The quick-acting mayor promptly issued an order that the snakes be removed post haste or face extinction. Mr. Hathaway complied, relocating his slithery pets to an unknown locale.

In 1899, Mr. Hathaway was one of the founding members of the Abilene Association of Bee Keepers. Hard to keep a good man down.

MAY 4, 1962
Scrambled Studebaker

Abilene police impounded a 1955 Studebaker station wagon found abandoned near the gate to Dyess Air Force Base. A check of the license plate revealed the car should be a Studebaker coupe, not a wagon. The plates were registered to Mae Jackson living at 942 Mulberry; however, when an Abilene detective knocked on the door, he found that the present resident had lived there 12 years and had never heard of Mae Jackson. Digging deeper, the police found state records indicating that the serial number of the car belonged to a 1946 Cadillac owned by a Dallas man. Not easily put off, investigators next looked up the car's engine number only to find that it belonged in a 1954 Oldsmobile owned by a Houston woman. In the car's backseat was a postcard addressed to a Dyess airman who turned out to be unknown to base officials. Having exhausted all leads, Abilene police shelved the file on the orphaned Studebaker with multiple personalities. Should you be missing such a confused car, please contact the Abilene police theft division.

MAY 5, 2007
Dinosaur Bob

One unhappy Abilene resident felt that Dinosaur Bob had outstayed his welcome. The smile-inducing, lifesize sculpture of long-necked Bob, a dinosaur who liked to chase cars—at least in the imagination of children's book author and illustrator William Joyce—had been loaned to the Grace Museum by Austin artist Bob "Daddy-O" Wade. The city granted a one-year permit allowing Dino Bob and a full-size VW Beetle to take up a spot atop the museum's parking garage roof along North First Street. The anonymous complainant felt that 12 months was

Dinosaur Bob looming over Cedar Street

more than enough viewing time and contacted the city attorney asking why Bob was allowed to stay past his lease? So, in accordance with civic enforcement, Bob was told to come down and head on his way.

Thankfully, Abilene's iconic equivalent of the Statue of Liberty was able to find new digs (just around the corner) atop a building owned by the National Center for Children's Illustrated Literature on Cedar Street. Dino Bob's lease on that perch has no expiration.

MAY 6, 1954
Willing Test Subjects

Over 600 Abilene second-graders joined with thousands of others nationwide volunteering to receive Dr. Jonas Salk's trial polio vaccine in hopes of validating its effectiveness against the dreaded disease. Parents were asked to sign up if they wished their child to be among the group administered the test. Participation in the attempt to erase the paralysis-inducing disease was heavy, with some schools reporting 98 percent of students taking part.

Taylor County was one of 10 Texas counties selected as a test group. In his role as County Medical Director, Dr. A.G. Arrant enlisted 30 nurses and doctors to give the inoculations as well as take blood from first- and third-graders used as controls in the test. The injection was the first of a series of three that the students received. School PTA groups helped with the testing by handing out lollipops and ice cream to the children. One Lamar Elementary lad announced, "It didn't hurt at all." Another boy noted, "I got scared, but it didn't hurt a bit. But I went ahead and cried anyway."

A year later, second-graders nationwide received the approved vaccine. The number of polio cases dropped from over 35,000 in 1953 to only 161 by 1961.

MAY 7, 1916
What a Gas!

A gas pipeline laid from Moran to Abilene first brought the modern convenience to town and its arrival was reason to celebrate. The plan was for the gas to flow 34 miles from Moran to the end of a 4-inch pipe standing 15 feet in the air and located just across from Radford Grocery at South First and Oak Street. Much of Abilene gathered after dark for the big occasion. Fred Wood, the 21-year-old Chamber of Commerce leader, was tapped to impressively set the escaping gas alight and do so in true over-the-top Chamber of Commerce fashion. Fred planned to aim fireworks towards the end of the pipe, with the resulting pyrotechnics brightly marking a new way of life for Abilene homeowners. As gas escaped at 90 pounds of pressure, Fred armed himself with 15 Roman candles. Pointing the first one toward the pipe, he lit the fuse and let fly, but hooked it. So, he reset and let fly once more. Another miss. And again, and again, and again. Only hissing gas filled the night air. After a full round of misses, an impatient bystander passed a match forward, and BOOM…the sky lit up with a dream come true—a gaseous Abilene.

MAY 8, 1888
Abusive Language

Mayor Daniel Wristen approved a city ordinance aimed at putting a halt to abusive language on the streets of Abilene. The City Council ordained that "any person in the presence or hearing of another, curse or abuse such person, or use any violently abusive language to such person concerning him or any female relatives, under circumstances reasonably calculated to provoke a breach of the peace, he shall be deemed guilty of an offense" and such an offense could cost a convicted swearer anywhere from a $5 to $100.

Spring Clean Lacks Pep

Entering day three of a city-wide clean-up effort, health officer Dr. Auda Cash complained that citizens were displaying insufficient pep for the endeavor. Encouraging all to take up broom and brush, Cash pointed out that the soon-to-arrive locating committee—scheduled to survey Abilene as a potential sight for Texas Technological College—would not be impressed if things in Abilene didn't neaten. He further noted, tidying the streets, alleys and lots not only demonstrated civic pride but tamped down the chances of disease-carrying rodents who were on the verge of gaining the upper hand. City workers collected trash heaps compiled by citizens peppy enough to lend a hand, and many homeowners took up a brush to whitewash their fences and the trunks of their trees. (The once common practice of whitewashing a tree was intended to reduce the effect of heat on the trunk.)

The locating committee made its visit but opted to award the new college to Lubbock. Abilene's consolation? For the most part, things around town looked a bit more presentable, and the uninspired could put their feet back up.

ALSO ON THIS DAY IN 1937...
Traffic Troubles

Police chief T.A. Hackney made a plea for Abilene drivers to change their ways. The chief warned motorists to quit chasing after fire trucks and reminded all that the flashing red light at Pine and Ambler was the same as a stop sign. Hackney also admitted that, although the speed limit in town was 20 mph, tickets were not issued unless you were caught putting the pedal to the metal and speeding at over 30 mph.

County Seat Redux

By 1913, the Taylor County courthouse was nearly 30 years old and in need of much repair. However, given the condition of the cracked and crumbling 1885 courthouse, prudence dictated that building a better and bigger one was the wiser choice. The idea was put before county voters in March and the bond issue passed rather handily, with 63 percent voting to build. But, the idea was not so highly favored amongst the Buffalo Gap electorate. Of the 94 voters who went to the polls there, only three voted for a new courthouse. It seems the 30-year-old indignity brought about when Abilene stole the county seat back in 1883 still smarted. On the day of the 1913 courthouse bond election, a group of 443 counterinsurgents nestled in the Gap signed a petition demanding that the former county seat once again claim the title.

The issue was put before voters on Saturday, May 10th. In the lead up to election day, the fight was regularly front page news. Banner headlines read: "VOTE FOR ABILENE SATURDAY" – May 7. "BIG COUNTY SEAT RALLY FRIDAY NIGHT" – May 8. "ABILENE WILL APPRECIATE YOUR VOTE" headlined the May 9th edition. And, the morning after the election, spread across page one, "ABILENE WINS BY 969 MAJORITY" (120 votes were cast at the Buffalo Gap polling station with a solitary Gapper opting for Abilene). The next day, the paper carried another front page story, this one headlined, "COMMISSIONERS ARE DISCUSSING NEW COURT HOUSE."

MAY 11, 1888
First Graduates

The Abilene High class of 1888 included six graduates—the first students to earn their diplomas from the school. Walking the stage at the Maltbie Opera House on Pine Street were five girls and one boy, Tarleton Middleton, who, it was reported, liked all the girls. The female graduates included Ella Cole (daughter of the school superintendent), Quay Minter (a charter Abilenian who arrived with her family when she was 12 years old), Minnie Kershaw and Neva Taylor (both would become teachers in Abilene) and Ella Jeanette Porter (last surviving member of the class, passing away in 1966 at the age of 94). As for Mr. Middleton, he settled in Oklahoma where he was in the cattle business with his brother.

MAY 12, 1959
Missiles at the Ready

A trip to Furr's Supermarket at the Merchant Park Shopping Center—or perhaps to TG&Y, Thornton's or to fill up at Clinton's Texaco—offered an added buzz this day. Displayed in the parking lot at North 12th and Grape Street was a U.S. Army Nike-Ajax surface-to-air missile. Tilted skyward, the nearly 33-foot long white missile was a big draw for shoppers and offered a taste of the armaments to be stationed near Abilene starting in 1960. (Not to be confused with the twelve intercontinental Atlas missiles and their silos which encircled the city later.) If you did not make it by Merchant Park Center to see the impressive site, you could catch it on display the next morning at Abilene High or at Lincoln Junior High after lunch. Your last chance to see the interceptor missile was to run by Elmwood West or River Oaks Shopping Center the following day.

In 1959, the Army selected two sites, one near Lake Fort Phantom and a second location 12 miles southwest of town, near View, for Ajax locations. Over 300 Nikemen were hired (as well as a few German Shepherds who went to work as sentries) to operate the two sites, each consisting of six launch pads, barracks, mess hall, assembly buildings and ready-quarters manned around the clock. Sitting atop each of the launch pads were two Nike-Hercules missiles, the upgraded model from the Ajax version, ready to shoot down possible in-bound enemy aircraft. Cuts to the Defense Department budget in 1966 closed the two Abilene missile launch sites, having stood vigilant for six years.

MAY 13, 1928
The Telephone Building

Going up on the corner of North Fourth and Cypress Street, the largest telephone building between Fort Worth and El Paso was receiving its finishing touches in early 1928. Groundbreaking for the two-story structure (with a basement to boot) took place in October of 1927 and the interior details were now wrapping up as the telephone machinery was installed. The roof of the building was constructed so that a third floor could be added, and it was in 1965, along with a remodel that replaced the original exterior red brick exterior with the brown brick still in place.

In conjunction with the new building, Southwestern Bell was switching over to dial phones in 1928—no more ringing up the operator. Prior to the new system going into effect, phone crews were sent out to schools to provide dialing demonstrations.

Abilene Courts

In 1925, as paved highways began to link the nation's cities and towns, Mr. W. B. Burns of Big Spring saw opportunity in the tourist court business. Burns opened Abilene Courts in 1930 offering more than just a campsite for tourists; rather, his motor court would be an apartment hotel for the convenience of tourists. Investing $30,000, he oversaw the completion of 20 apartments with oak floors, ceiling fans, private baths and overstuffed furniture. Sixteen of the apartments were two rooms—bedroom and kitchen—and a bath, while four were one room. Kitchens were outfitted with a dinette table, four chairs, sink and an ice box.

Abilene Courts along the Bankhead Highway

The rooms faced a gravelled inner courtyard with an ornamental bird bath in the center. Travelers could tuck their autos into the eight-foot wide garages adjoining each apartment. Mr. and Mrs. Burns moved to Abilene with their two young daughters, living in an apartment near the arched entrance. The Abilene Courts were partially razed in 2020. (Heck! Weren't we all partially razed in 2020!?)

MAY 15, 1922

Mr. Frisky and Miss Tiny Start the Zoo

Walking along a downtown Abilene street, insurance man Willis Cox met up with Chamber of Commerce secretary Grady Kinsolving and handed him a box. Cox knew of Grady's dream of starting a zoo in Abilene and he wanted to do his part to kick things off. Inside the box was zoo resident number one, a squirrel with an irritable disposition, named Mr. Frisky. The bushy-tailed rodent was soon joined by a squirrelette, Miss Tiny, and the Abilene Zoo had all the ingredients for expansion.

MAY 16, 1913

High School Honor

Writing under his official title "Visitor of Schools," University of Texas professor J.L. Henderson advised the Abilene superintendent that Abilene High ranked high indeed among schools in the southern states. At the annual meeting of the Commission on Accredited Schools for the Southern States held in Richmond, Virginia, a review of all southern high schools was conducted. The commission named 135 to their list of "best schools." Twenty-eight of the 135 were Texas schools and Abilene High was among them. Henderson encouraged the superintendent to continue and maintain the high standards which had garnered the honor; specifically, for three-fourths of high school teachers to be college graduates, for no teacher to be in charge of more than six classes per day, and the average class size to be 30 students or less.

The Paramount is Prepped

Mayor Thomas Hayden and the four city commissioners arrived early Saturday morning, joining officials from the Paramount-Publix Company to ceremonially make the electrical connection starting the giant electric sound projectors for the first time. Mayor Hayden then offered his prepared address to an audience of three—Barry Burke, divisional manager of Publix; W.E. Drumbar, district manager; and Al Fourmet, the Paramount manager—telling the men that "Paramount-Publix has added materially to Abilene's beauty, appeal to visitors and its ever-growing skyline by the erection of this handsome place of amusement." The grandiose movie palace was set to open two days later. Mr. Horace Wooten spent $400,000 on the Cypress Street theatre—adjoining his soon-to-be-opened Hotel Wooten—and leased the building to Paramount-Publix.

Touted as "West Texas' most perfect theatre," the Paramount bigwigs oversaw final touches and helped train the 40-person staff with last-minute instructions. Resplendently dressed male ushers were schooled in how to accept — never take — tickets and in the art of seating guests by asking, "How far down please?" Doormen were advised that on opening night

Opening night of the Paramount Theatre

they would be in contact with such dignitaries as the mayors of Albany, Cisco, Baird, Clyde and Merkel.

Before the grand opening, the staff tested the 90-foot marquee which held over 1,400 bulbs along with a neon sign installed by the Texlite Electric Sign Company. The state-of-the-art air-conditioning system was put through its paces, ensuring it would keep the auditorium at a comfortable 70 degrees. Mr. Mende, a floral artist from Chicago, oversaw the installation of thousands of pink, yellow and La France roses, magnolia blossoms, red bougainvillea and garlands of Spanish creepers which he hung from the balcony—all artificial along with faux cypress trees made in Italy. The Magnascope screen, made of rubber and filled with tiny holes to ease the sound flow, and by far the largest in the city at 24 feet high and 29 wide, was tested as well. The projection equipment underwent a trial run to insure a smooth showing of the world premiere of "Safety In Numbers." On opening night, 60 cents bought you a seat on the lower floor to watch the Buddy Rogers film and the added features—a short comedy, "All Teed Up," a color classic titled "In Gay Madrid," and a song novelty, "I'm Afraid to Go Home in the Dark."

MAY 18, 1951
Shelby Junius Treadaway is Honored

The bypass highway just east of downtown Abilene was the brainchild of the veteran district engineer for the State Highway Department, Shelby Junius Treadaway. (He definitely spelled it Treadaway, and pronounced it with three syllables, Tread-a-way, not elided to Tread-way.) Shelby Treadaway graduated from Texas A&M College and is credited with building the first farm-to-market road in Texas, connecting

Beaumont to Houston. In 1936, Treadaway
arrived in Abilene to work at the local office
of the State Highway Department where he
quickly realized there was a need for a bypass
road, pressing the issue repeatedly to the
Texas Highway Department.

The notion to attach Treadaway's name
to the road was first put forward by Abilene
paint dealer Frazer Edmonds and the idea
gained traction from an editorial by Frank

District Highway engineer
Shelby Treadaway

Grimes. On May 18, 1951, the City Commission and Mayor Ernest
Grissom unanimously ordained the name change, turning Magnolia
Street into North Treadaway Boulevard and parts of Short, China and
Willow streets into South Treadaway Boulevard. (A wide tree-lined street
is often designated as a boulevard, and although Treadaway Boulevard is
wide, the trees seem to be missing.)

Not long after the road signs went up, and on the heels of being
named Engineer of the Year by the Texas Society of Professional Engineers,
Treadaway moved to Austin where he remained until his death in 1967.

MAY 19, 1948
Monkey Business

Two Abilene policemen responded to a call from Joe Showalter of
Sammons Street who was reporting that a monkey was running around
in his front yard. Officers Cliff Cunningham and Floyd Willis arrived just
before 7 a.m. and strategized that a lariat was their best bet for corralling
the wayward simian. Following a number of throws, the roping proved

a success and the Abilene offices maneuvered the little fella into the back seat of their squad car where, as you might expect from a frightened monkey, he crazily jumped all around. The back window was down about four inches and as the officers began to drive away, the tethered monkey squeezed out and up onto the top of the car. Driving slowly, the officers headed to 2133 South Fifth where Walter and Blanche McKeg had earlier reported that their pet monkey was missing.

ALSO ON THIS DAY IN 1966...
Shotwell Stadium is Christened

A crowd packed the second-floor Windsor ballroom for a noontime luncheon and to be part of Pete Shotwell Appreciation Day. Coach Shotwell was a hometown favorite who coached Texas youth for 50 years, nearly 30 of them in Abilene. Known to many as "Pete," others called him "P. E." or "Shot." However, absolutely no one called him by his given name—because very few even knew it. Born in 1893 as the fourth child out of a clan that would grow to 15, even his family called him by his initials, but they knew what the "P" and "E" stood for.

At the luncheon, Coach Shotwell humbly received the accolades and was

Coach Prince Elmer
"P. E." Shotwell

astonished to hear the announcement that, as a thank you, the group was sending him and his wife on a tour of Europe, along with $3,000 spending money.

But the biggest surprise came when it was announced that the school board had unanimously voted to honor Coach Shotwell's career by renaming "Abilene Public Schools Stadium" to "P. E. Shotwell Stadium." Abilene school board president Morgan Jones made the announcement and read the 150-word resolution. Many in attendance tuned out the resolution as soon as Jones read the first three words, instead looking at one another and smiling across the tables, digesting the revelation so carelessly tossed out, *"Whereas Prince Elmer Shotwell has…"*

Prince Elmer, who knew?

ALSO ON THIS DAY IN 1987…
The Paramount Opens Again

On May 19, 1987, two former Paramount Theatre managers, Wally Akin and Frank Sheffield, ceremoniously flipped the switch that once again lit up the Paramount marquee. For eight years, the darkened sign held just six letters spelling out "CLOSED." With a refurbished 75-foot marquee, now holding red letters reading "SOLD OUT," the sidewalk in front of the theater was bathed in the glow of 308 bulbs literally illuminating life along Cypress Street and, as it would prove over the following years, symbolically sparking life back to downtown Abilene, a pivotal moment in the history of Abilene.

The re-lighting of the Paramount sign took place 57 years to the day after the theater's grand opening in 1930. Built by Abilene businessman Horace Wooten, the ornate, Spanish courtyard-themed movie palace closed in 1979, and although more than one entrepreneur attempted a new scheme—including a Texas version of the Grand ol' Opry—it appeared that the old girls glory days were in the past. Thankfully, no.

MAY 20, 1959
23-Degree Parking

Parallel parking in downtown gave way to head-in angled slots this day. Motorists had been forced to maneuver into the parallel spots since 1946, but that scheme now gave way to a new concept in metropolitan parking. North Third Street between Cypress and Walnut was the first stretch to convert to the innovative, shallow, 23-degree parking rather than the common 45- and 90-degree spots found in most cities. City Traffic Director Charles Clinard noted that the new parking model provided a convenience for drivers and created an average of two extra spots in any block. The new parking was popular. The new parking meters were less well-received.

MAY 21, 1956
What a Blast!

Roused from his bunk at 3:45 a.m., Abilene oilman and consultant to the Federal Civil Defense Administration, 55-year-old French Robertson, took up his spot on the deck of the USS Mt. McKinley positioned 32 miles from the Bikini Atoll in the South Pacific. Robertson was one of 32 civilian observers invited to witness the pre-dawn blast of Cherokee, a thermonuclear hydrogen bomb dropped, for the first time ever, from a B-52 Stratofortress. Donning thick goggles, which could not be seen through in normal light, Robertson was directed to keep his eyes closed for 10 seconds following the blast.

Robertson reported the explosion sounded like rolling thunder and once he could take a peek, he saw a brilliant white light covering the entire area followed by a heat blast three minutes later. The massive bomb created a cloud that rose over 20 miles and produced a fireball initially measuring four miles wide which grew to a purple-orange mushroom cloud over 100 miles across. Robertson had already witnessed three atom bomb tests carried out in the Nevada desert, the largest equivalent to 30,000 tons of TNT; however, the H-bomb test he saw this day over the Pacific Ocean was estimated at 3.8 million tons of TNT.

MAY 22, 1946

Poof Goes Mr. Pigeon

Certainly not on par with witnessing the momentous blast as seen by French Robertson (see above), Dr. Cyrus Ray happened to be looking out the window of his seventh floor office in the Mims Building and witnessed an explosion—specifically, an exploding pigeon. With a bit of free time on his hands, Dr. Ray was gazing out the window admiring a pair of pigeons cooing and enjoying the springtime morning atop the Majestic Theater. Dr. Ray watched as the male bird took off (as a doctor, he apparently could identify male and female pigeons from some distance) and fly across the alley to take in the view from the roof of Minter Dry Goods.

Having had his look, the unsuspecting pigeon lifted off and headed back across the alley. Conjecture suggests he was en route to again nestle near his feathered female friend, when, shockingly, a small explosion flashed into a white ball accompanied by the slight sound of a "poof." A few feathers floated earthward but the boy bird disappeared, seemingly vaporized. Scientifically curious, Dr. Ray rushed outside, joining Mims barber Charles Dick and haircut customer A.K. Doss, still caped and in mid-cut, to see what had occurred. No sizable trace of Mr. Pigeon could be found, and the mystery was never resolved.

MAY 23, 1916
Oil!

Considerable excitement arrived around 10 o'clock on the morning of May 26 as word reached Abilene that oil was flowing from a locally-sponsored drilling operation six miles south of town. Investors quickly headed to the site near Potosi to see the crude rise to the surface. Over 50 Abilenians held stock in the exploration company formed to search for oil. It was the oil committee of the Chamber of Commerce who, months earlier, decided that there was economic potential if it could be shown that oil reserves lay beneath Taylor County soil. There was a strong hunch that such was the case so the company, formed out of the committee recommendation, was incorporated as Hunch Oil & Gas Company. Chamber secretary Fred Wood noted, "Whenever a gambler goes to place a bet, he always has a hunch he is going to win it."

Hunch Oil investors approached Indianapolis oil man Frank Fox, who previously financed and drilled a dry hole near Potosi in early 1916. In order to entice Fox to try again, Hunch Oil raised $11,000 from the sale of stock in the new company. Fox agreed to drill down to 2,600 feet on the farm of Mrs. R.H. Anderson. The well site was ceremoniously staked at 2 p.m. on March 13 by Hunch stockholder and Abilene physician, Dr. J.M. Alexander. Fox had staked the earlier location using a dead branch to pinpoint the

Stock certificate issued to Kirven Kade Legett for shares in the Hunch Oil and Gas Company, 1917

drill site; superstition held that such a move doomed the location to be dry. In hopes of securing a producer, Fred Wood chopped down a sappy young mesquite to fashion the greenest stake possible. Hardware store owner Cross Payton held the stake as Alexander pounded it into the dirt, remarking, "Hope the well won't be as hard to drive as the stake."

With the excitement of oil coming from the ground, hundreds began flocking to the site. Visitors were cautioned to be aware of three things—do not leave the gate to the pasture open, do not strike matches near the well, and do not get overly excited—Abilene may or may not have a big field underfoot.

One week later a rainstorm blew through the area, toppling the 82-foot tall wooden derrick. By 1920, the first well to bring up oil in Taylor County was producing six to eight barrels a day. The well produced only for a short time but outlived the Hunch Oil and Gas Company which was out of business by 1918.

MAY 24, 1930
An Extremely Rare Medal

Seven years after graduating from Simmons College in 1923, John Newsom decided to offer an annual prize beginning in 1930 to a Simmons ministerial student who maintained a high grade point average for all four years and who preached no fewer than 104 sermons in his time at the college. However, at the June 1930 graduation, the Newsom Medal was not awarded as no student met the criteria. Ditto for the winter graduation in 1930 and spring 1931, and winter 1931 and spring 1932. By this point most everyone had given up on any student ever winning the elusive Newsom honor, but, miraculously, at the May graduation of

1933 it happened. Arthur Travis of Abilene was granted the first John Newsom Medal. It has never been awarded since. Congratulations to Rev. Travis.

MAY 25, 1948
600 Get a Chance to Watch the Clock

Mr. Gilbert Pechacek, chairman of Abilene, Inc., the industrial development arm of the Chamber of Commerce, announced that U.S. Time Corporation would soon take up a lease on an Abilene building and employ up to 600 in the production of alarm clocks, wristwatches and the famous Ingersoll pocket watch—the original $1 watch offered by the old Waterbury Clock Company, predecessor of U.S. Time. A building at 709 North Second was leased for a five year term with plans of a workforce that would make the plant Abilene's largest employer by nearly double. (The second largest employer at the time was Lankford and Sons, at 380 employees who produced trousers for military personnel and later, uniforms and sportswear.) By 1963, U.S. Time provided jobs to 850 at two Abilene plants. In 1969, U.S. Time changed the company name to Timex. The local Timex operations ceased in 1977 and today the original Timex building is home to a church.

MAY 26, 1905
Municipal Waste

The days of Abilene outhouses were numbered as the city septic tank was nearing completion. With only a few plumbing connections necessary to put the whole system into operation, excitement was generally high and local plumbers busy from dawn to dusk. (The few landlords who balked at the expense of plumbing their properties were reminded that when it comes to public health, local governments do indeed possess emergency powers.) A city ordinance made it unlawful for Abilenians to receive or remove waste by way of "privy, cesspool, urinal basin, water closet, slop sink or slop drain" unless same was connected to the new sewage system. Toilets were required to have flush tanks with a minimum five-gallon tank and each flush must dispense at least three gallons.

Police Chief John Clinton proudly toured interested parties, showing off the huge septic tank composed of 22-inch-thick brick walls set on a concrete floor and soon to be topped by a concrete top laid on railroad iron and thick enough to withstand any pressure.

A Local Luminary: Earsie Avant Brown

Born at 441 Cherry Street in 1899, Earsie Brown would live nearly her full 89 years in that family home. Earsie's father, Taylor Avant, was especially well known in Abilene at the turn of the century for his ice cream creations known as Hokey-Pokey—square-cut delights wrapped in cellophane which he sold for a nickel. The Hokey-Pokey Man peddled his ice cream from a one-horse wagon, announcing its arrival by tinkling bells.

Earsie attended Mary Allen Seminary in Crockett before returning to Abilene where she first worked as a laundress. In 1933, Earsie met and married Dave Brown, creating a name combination that became synonymous with good food in Abilene. During the Great Depression,

Dave and Earsie opened up
a café on Willow Street in
a rented house. With no
money to turn on the gas
and lights, they set up tables
and chairs in the front yard.
Dave cut the bottom out of a
washtub to make an outdoor
smoker, walked along alleys
to gather cooking wood,
and invested $1.50 in meat

Dave and Earsie Brown in front of their cafe

that he smoked al fresco. The savory smell drew people in on Friday
and Saturday—the only days they could afford to stay open. Earsie took
charge of the beans and potato salad while Dave handled the steaks
and barbeque, cooked in a secret sauce containing ten drops of a never-
revealed liquid.

Known far and wide, Dave and Earsie's appetizing reputation drew
in Camp Barkeley entertainers such as Joan Blondell, Jimmy Durante and
boxer Archie Moore. Following Dave's death in 1966, Earsie continued
to operate the famous Abilene eatery until January of 1973. This Abilene
luminary died in 1988 and is buried next to her husband in the Abilene
City Cemetery.

Vigilante Justice: Tom Barnett is Dead

Convicted of the murder of Alex Sears, Tom Barnett was sentenced to spend the remainder of his days in prison. However, the number of days was cut seriously short when, just after 1 a.m., a mob of around 50 men took the law into their own hands, storming the Taylor County jail and bringing Barnett's days to a premature close. The armed and masked men made their way into the rooms of jailer Ben Peevey, demanding the keys to the cell doors. Peevey refused and was roughed up in return. Going from cell to cell demanding to know if Barnett was the occupant, they finally turned him up on the third floor when one inmate ratted, "Here he is, boys." The group spent half an hour trying to force open Barnett's cell door as he sat in silence; exasperated, one suggested, "Let's shoot him." A fusillade rang out and Barnett was struck 15 times. The mob quickly fled the scene.

An exhaustive investigation failed to determine the killers of Tom Barnett.

MAY 29, 1946

Carter G. Woodson Honored

The Abilene school board met in the office of the superintendent and acted on a recommendation submitted by the PTA and William Johnston—principal of the city's segregated school—who suggested a name for the 450-student campus. The board accepted the recommendation and named the school in honor of writer and historian Carter G. Woodson. The nationally-known Woodson was the second African-American to receive a doctoral degree from Harvard and he was a public advocate for improvements in black education and also for the establishment of Black History Month. More than 35 schools bear the name of this one-time leader in education.

With the school board's decision, the Abilene campus would no longer be known as the "negro school" but would have "Woodson School" spelled out across the top of the single-story, red brick building at 520 North Ninth. In 1946, the school had 13 teachers who taught in less than ideal conditions with grades 1 – 4 averaging 46 students in a class. The 55 students in third grade sat three to a desk. Woodson School had 12 classrooms, a library and cafeteria, but there was no gymnasium, auditorium or vocational programs and there was not a single projector in the building. Principal Johnston worked to establish a band program in 1946 but was hampered by a lack of funds to purchase instruments. The junior and senior high students moved to their own campus in 1953, also named for Carter Woodson. Both schools still stand.

MAY 30, 1930
A Local Luminary: Benno Schmidt

Benno Charles Schmidt graduated from Abilene High School this day and began a path leading him to the highest echelons of government and service. Born in Abilene to Margaret, 35, and Benno Sr., 40, a traveling salesman for the Wooten Grocery Company, the trio lived on North Third. From their home young Benno would walk to school at Central Ward and later to Abilene High, where he served as class vice president and was on the debate team. Just one day shy of his turning 13, Benno lost his father, attending his burial on Benno's own birthday. In order to support her son, Mrs. Schmidt went to work as the director of the county welfare association and mom and son took in Margaret's

widowed sister-in-law. The two women
imbued Benno with a thirst for education
and a grounding in faith through the
First Christian Church. In 1930, Benno
left Abilene for Austin where he would
graduate from the University of Texas with
a law degree, then join the faculty there
before moving on to teach at Harvard Law
School.

Benno Schmidt

Following service in World War II, Benno got a call from New
York financier Jock Whitney inviting the 33-year-old Abilene boy to join
his investment firm. Benno would remain at J.H. Whitney & Company
for 52 years, rising to managing partner and leading the firm's efforts
to invest in upstart biotechnology companies. Benno found the whole
concept of betting on new companies to be an adventure, so he dubbed
the investment strategy "adventure capital," shortened to "venture
capital." This Abilenian not only coined the term but led the way in
providing venture capital to move new ideas and companies forward,
managing to hit some serious financial home runs along the way.

Benno served as board chairman for Memorial Sloan-Kettering
Cancer Center and on the boards of CBS and the Whitney Museum,
among others. President Nixon appointed Schmidt to lead the nation's
War on Cancer, and Benno would go on to serve as a health-policy
adviser to several Presidents.

Benno Schmidt credited his success in life and business to the
foundational tenets instilled by his mother and aunt inside a supportive
Abilene home on North Third Street. This local luminary died in New
York in 1999 at the age of 86. (P.S. One of Benno's five sons served as
president of Yale University from 1986 to 1992.)

MAY 31, 1968
Woodson High School Closes

Twenty-two graduating Rams received their diplomas in the Woodson High gym, the last group to graduate from the segregated high school. The ceremony got underway at 8 p.m. with valedictorian Joy Frances McGee presenting a welcoming address and salutatorian Larry Gindratt offering a tribute to the recently-slain Martin Luther King Jr. The class motto, "We Shall Overcome," spoke of the ongoing struggle for equal civil rights. Former Woodson graduate, and the current school band director, Howard Carver, gave a farewell address to the class and

Students in front of Carter G. Woodson High School, 1955

the school. Principal D.W. Porter then presented the class to Abilene superintendent A.E. Wells who distributed the diplomas. Crossing the stage alphabetically meant that the last student to graduate from Abilene's Carter G. Woodson High School was James Alton Winn.

JUNE

Underground Economy

The Brenham Weekly Banner reported that "a new industry had been inaugurated at Abilene—the shipment of prairie dogs"—noting that 200 of the scampering cash-rodents were set for shipment to St. Louis.

Jerkwater Town: KRBC vs KRIC

A civic tiff between Abilene and Beaumont was settled. Radio stations in both cities applied to the Federal Communications Commission wanting to change their frequency on the radio dial. Abilene's KRBC and Beaumont's KRIC were both transmitting over 1450 kilocycles on the AM band and both stations applied to boost their power and go out over the airwaves at 1470. The situation attracted statewide attention when, in a hearing before the Commission in Washington, KRIC's attorney referred to Abilene as a "jerkwater town." *Reporter-News* editor Frank Grimes came to the city's defense, daring Beaumont to match the bright future of Abilene and offering Beaumont a ten-year head start. The *Beaumont Enterprise* shot right back with an editorial titled, "Abilene? Abilene? Where's That?" ending with, "Maybe that Beaumont lawyer did speak hastily. But don't get your blood pressure up that way; you'll black out. And in the wide open space in which you live out there, it might be days before they find you."

The FCC announced its final decision, granting the application of KRBC to claim 1470 on the dial and vindicating this jerkwater town.

JUNE 3, 1890
False Alarm

Well after dark, the boys of the fire department rushed to their wagon, hurriedly hitched up the horses, and raced off to the west where a fire was glowing. A moonlight dash to the scene near Elm Creek proved to be only a pleasure ride as the fire boys found the flames were coming from the kiln of Mr. Morse who was firing bricks.

JUNE 4, 1920
Acrobatic Art Oakley

Abilene aerial acrobat Art Oakley was the star performer at the Dallas auto races. The 24-year-old daredevil made a mid-air leap from one airplane to another, walked on the wings and hung by his knees from the landing gear. Art claimed to be the only person who ever successfully transferred from a moving train to a plane in flight, a stunt he performed for a movie. The Oakley family lived on Mulberry Street in Abilene but Art and the "Oakley Aerial Escadrille" spent a considerable number of days performing at fairs and races across the country. Art had learned to fly in 1917 while serving with the Army Air Corps. Giving up barnstorming in 1921, he settled in Ardmore, Oklahoma, where he established an airport and taught Wiley Post how to fly. Abilene's Art Oakley died in 1963 at the age of 67.

JUNE 5, 1897
Ben Anderson Leaves His Mark

Construction of the dam across Lytle Creek in 1897 was underway when Ben Anderson decided to leave his mark at the job site. In the fresh mortar between stones used in the lake spillway, Ben carved his name and the date. If you know where to look, his notation remains visible more than a century hence.

Ben Anderson, June 5, 1899

JUNE 6, 1944
Wartime Jubilation

Abilene was roused from sleep early on this Tuesday as word was received that the Allied invasion of France was underway. At 2:27 a.m., the Associated Press notified all newspapers they were awaiting a news release from the Allied Command which would confirm the German troops along the coast of France were under attack. Six minutes later the news flashed as bells rang in newsrooms across the country, "The Allies have landed in France."

Using a pre-arranged system, Abilene newspaper staffers were called in to work where they picked up phones to make calls, waking city officials with the news so the synchronized plan to announce the news to a sleeping Abilene could be set in motion. Fire engines and police cars were dispatched throughout town while factory whistles readied to blow, and the lone radio station, KRBC, went back on the air.

At the appointed minute, 3:10 a.m., the cacophony was let loose, sirens wailed, whistles screamed, and lights began to come on throughout town. Telephone lines to the police and newspaper were quickly swamped and radios tuned to learn the long-awaited news. The D-Day edition of the newspaper was on the streets before sunrise. Throughout the day people streamed to churches whose bells tolled in jubilant peals. First Presbyterian rang out hymns, while the organist at the small Episcopal Church propped open the door of the Orange Street sanctuary and played, "Onward Christian Soldiers." Hundreds of Abilene families felt the encouragement of community support as they nervously awaited news from sons who were in the fight.

Taylor County Votes Dry

Following a long and often contentious run-up, the local option election to decide if Taylor County would be wet or dry finally arrived. Drys outvoted Wets by 170, with the ban on alcohol to take effect at the start of 1903. Saloonkeeper Ike Brown filed suit against the manager of the prohibition election who "maliciously aroused and stirred up the people of Taylor County" thus bringing damage to his business in the range of $10,000. Although he and other Taylor Countians no longer had easy access to alcohol, not all was lost. On the same day, next-door neighbor Callahan County voted wet. Abilene would remain a dry city for the next 75 years.

JUNE 8, 1911

City Commissioners Ban Hitching Horses to Trees

The Abilene Board of City Commissioners passed an ordinance making it "unlawful for any person to tie or hitch any horse or other animal to any tree, awning post or lamppost in any street in the City of Abilene." Scofflaws in violation of this edict could receive a fine of $25.

JUNE 9, 1911

Mayor Vetoes Ban on Hitching Horses to Trees

In his four years as mayor, E.N. Kirby had yet to veto any action taken by the commissioners. However, on this day, Kirby wielded his veto pen striking down the ordinance passed one day earlier, prohibiting anyone from hitching horses to a tree, etc.

In explaining his unprecedented action, Kirby noted that property owners could subject their own trees to whatever stress they deemed acceptable. Further, if the commissioners wished to ban horse hitching to city trees, then the city should provide posts, since failing to hitch one's horse altogether was also a violation. Finally, Kirby pointed out that at least half of the women in Abilene would be arraigned in short order for violating the ordinance as written, urging the commissioners to reconsider the matter. They did, and three weeks later, Kirby signed into law a revised ordinance. Section 1 now made it unlawful to tie your horse to any "ornamental tree." Section 2 defined ornamental trees as being any tree except the mesquite. Hitch away ladies.

JUNE 10, 1951

Hail of a Storm

Rip-roaring winds and heavy hail arrived after 4 p.m. on an otherwise quiet Sunday. C.E. Sitchler of the National Weather Service described the hour-long windstorm as being "of hurricane proportions." Although not a tornado, wind gusts were clocked at 120 mph and for one sustained five-minute period it howled at 75 mph and a 30-second gust of 109 set an Abilene record. Hailstones as large as baseballs smashed windows, dented cars and punched holes in roofs.

Several families were left homeless after their houses blew off their foundations. Telephone service was out along with electrical power as much of Abilene was covered in downed tree limbs. Hendrick Hospital lost 85 percent of its windows while ACC and HSU suffered hundreds of broken panes. The McMurry campus was littered with uprooted trees and homes along Sayles Boulevard suffered toppled chimneys and bent over rooftop TV antennas. Blue Sox field on South 14th lost a section of the outfield fence, while at North Third and Treadaway a warehouse blew down, exposing 60 new Kaiser-Frazer automobiles to the hail and wind.

Rainfall totals were undetermined because the wind either toppled gauges or blew the water clean out of them. The city reported that Lake Fort Phantom rose 1.5 feet and Lake Kirby was up nine inches, bringing it to an all-time high. The entire 40-man police force was called out, along with highway patrolmen and local National Guard troops, to help secure businesses and aid stranded citizens including over two dozen golfers stuck in the municipal golf clubhouse, several with hailstone-induced bruises suffered as they raced for shelter.

JUNE 11, 1913

Approval of the New Courthouse Plan

Architect George Burnett of Waco won the design contest for the new Taylor County Courthouse after the county commissioners and a three-man advisory citizens committee gave his idea the nod. Burnett submitted a Greek design with a French Renaissance influence. The three-story building was set to be 140 feet long and 80 feet wide with a three-door portal entrance on the west front. The budget for constructing the new county building was $130,000, with the architect fee being $4,550. Two years later, in May of 1915, the new courthouse opened for public inspection, followed by the relocation of county offices a week later. County Judge Ed Overshiner was pushing to move county offices from the temporary quarters at the Hotel Grace into the new building on Thursday the 13th; however, other county officials balked at moving on the 13th considering such a move as unlucky, further it was considered bad luck to move in on a Friday. Saturday was the day set for the relocation in order to allay all superstitious fears. Judge Overshiner promised a free marriage license to the first couple applying at the new courthouse. During Saturday's move-in, Arthur Hay and Miss Ollie Trantham stepped up to the county clerk's desk, claiming the gratis license.

JUNE 12, 1931

Amelia Makes a Dent

A startled crowd of 1,500 watched as famed aviatrix Amelia Earhart crashed from 30 feet onto the Abilene airport parking lot in her failed bid to takeoff for Oklahoma City. Three especially chagrined spectators stared helplessly as Amelia's auto-giro fell into the lot on top of their cars. W.L. Bailey looked on as the spinning propeller smashed the windshield of his Hudson, while W.O Scott and Charlie Killian each witnessed injury befalling their automobiles, a Ford and Chevrolet, christened with newly dented roofs.

Miss Earhart was in Abilene as part of a transcontinental tour touting the safety of flying an auto-giro (a winged plane with a top-mounted helicopter propeller). She had already flown from New Jersey to Los Angeles and was now making her way back east. Amelia and her mechanic were unhurt following the crunching crash. She quickly stood up in the open cockpit craft and announced to

Earhart's crashed auto-gyro at the Abilene airport

the gawking crowd, "I underestimated my distance. Probably a small whirlwind caught the rotor." However, a week later the Commerce Department—in its early aviation oversight role—reprimanded Miss Earhart for her carelessness and poor judgment in taking off from the Abilene airfield.

Robert English Starts the
Black Chamber of Commerce

A 26-year-old reporter for KRBC-TV organized Abilene's Black Chamber of Commerce. After earning a degree in mass communication from Abilene Christian University in 1971, Robert English began a 10-year stint as a news reporter. Seeing the need for Abilene's black-owned businesses to have their own distinct advocacy group, he organized the Black Chamber of Commerce in 1975, directing the organization as a volunteer. English later left KRBC to become the media director for The Bridge, a job-training center, but also found time to organize the Abilene Black Ensemble, a performing arts group and he worked to bring black authors and poets to Abilene. In the midst of launching a statewide magazine, "Texas Black Monthly," in 1987, English passed away at the age of 39.

Abilene is Happy. The Lake is Full.

Workmen had barely walked away from their task of building the dam across Lytle Creek when the heavens opened up and a lightning-filled storm brought a lake-filling rain in a matter of hours. Behind the 800-foot dam, water began backing up for a mile starting late on June 14. By the following day a grand lake was in place, prompting long lines of carriages to head east from town as residents had to see for themselves the reservoir that assured a ready supply of water and a safeguard against fires. *The Abilene Reporter* headlined IT IS NOW LYTLE LAKE and opined that it was the "most beautiful lake in the broad state of Texas." (Perhaps due to the excitement, the newspaper masthead mistakenly indicated the year as 1896 rather than 1897.)

The edition noted that "Abilene is happy today. Happy smiles chase each other down the faces of thankful people and warm handclasps with hearty words of congratulation pass between our people at every meeting." However, not everyone was happy. During the deluge, a bolt of lightning struck the Methodist parsonage, punching a foot-wide hole in the roof, allowing water to sprinkle—but certainly not fully immerse—Elder Chapman.

JUNE 15, 1915
The Pool's Open

Over 3,000 assembled at 7:30 p.m. for the opening of Abilene's first swimming pool and most remained right up until closing time at 11:30. The much-anticipated pool—or natatorium, as it was known in 1915—was a private concern built at Fair Park [Oscar Rose Park]. Stock was sold to provide capital for the Sanitary Natatorium Association, which owned and operated the pool. The $3,500 natatorium was built at what was known as the Sayles tank, the former livestock watering hole on property west of the Sayles home at South Seventh and Sayles Boulevard. The concrete pool was 75 by 100 feet, sloped to a depth of 9 feet, and held 400,000 gallons that was changed twice weekly, the discharge used for watering the park.

On Saturday, June 15, 1915, the bathing public was welcomed to test the waters. Before the throngs could dive in, Simmons president Dr. Sandefer made a short speech noting the need for such a city asset. As the Abilene Concert Band filled the night air with music, the waters awaited those who ponied up the 25-cent price of a plunge. Towels were available—as were bathing suits if you did not own one personally—along with 42 dressing rooms providing a spot to slip into your trunks. Fears of drowning were themselves drowned out by the presence of swimming instructor Professor Lee Koen, who also offered 15 lessons for $5. In 1923, the stockholders of the Sanitary Natatorium dissolved the company, forcing Abilene bathers to find other cooling spots.

JUNE 16, 1946

Key City of West Texas

Abilene became "The Key City of West Texas" today. Five weeks earlier, the Advertising and Publicity committee of the Abilene Chamber of Commerce launched a contest for the selection of a slogan speaking to the city's character, with a $25 award going to the one making the winning suggestion. More than 200 entries were received. The committee opted for one submitted by Mrs. Jack Smith, who proposed "The Key City of West Texas." The idea may have stemmed from the frequent wartime use of the term, as headlines often noted that the Allies or Axis powers were targeting "key cities" in the European fight.

The original Key City logo

Ten days after the selection, the slogan first appeared in a newspaper ad for the shoe department at Ernest Grissom's store. A year later, the first group to adopt Key City in their name was the newly formed Key

City Owls Motorcycle Club. ("The Key City of West Texas" quickly
shortened to simply "Key City.") In 1948, Cecil Phillips renamed his car
lot at 1590 Butternut from Phillips Motors to Key City Motor Company
with the tagline, "Your Key to Better Cars in the Key City," making it
the first business to bear the name, albeit, one with a short duration;
Key City Motor Company lasted less than a year. By 1949, two Abilene
businesses took on the name, "Key City Realtors" and the "Key City
Vocational Institute," where veterans learned cabinet making. By 1960,
everything from answering services to wrecking yards had adopted the
Key City name.

JUNE 17, 1978

End of the 75 Year Drought

In one of the largest election turnouts in Taylor County history,
voters narrowly approved the sale of alcoholic beverages in Abilene,
specifically in Precinct 1, which mostly included the city. The election
marked the end of the 1903 action that first parched the county. Over
23,000 voters went to the polls, and the Wets outvoted the Drys by
a mere 131 votes, half of one percent of the total ballots. (The largest
voter turnouts had been the '68 and '72 presidential elections, the 1968
governor race and the 1976 election on the same wet/dry issue when
over 24,000 turned out. The Drys prevailed that day by 1,614 votes. See
February 17.)

The forces pushing for a change organized under a group called
Update '78 while the anti-alcohol group, CBC or Citizens for a Better
Community—and who had prevailed two years earlier—pushed for the
status quo. Learning from their prior defeat—largely from the polling

boxes on Abilene's college campuses—Update '78 leaders strategically pushed for a June election, when many Abilene college students were not in town. (Also, in the 1976 election, Dyess AFB happened to be on alert status, preventing many airmen from casting their ballots.) Passage of the proposal finally allowed the sale of alcoholic beverages from package stores and across-the-counter servings of mixed drinks. The need to drive to Buffalo Gap or Impact to wet your whistle came to a halt. Opponents asked for a recount but their hopes evaporated; the official number put the margin at 122 votes. Abilene was wet by a drop.

JUNE 18, 1932
Will Rogers Drops In

More than 100 Will Rogers fans showed up at the Abilene airfield hoping to catch a glimpse of their favorite humorist as he stepped from the westbound American Airways plane. Sure enough, first off the plane was a shirt-sleeved Rogers. Pulling off his well-worn hat, he entered the small terminal building to the applause of his Abilene admirers, greeting them with a warm "Howdy folks," before heading over to greet his longtime friend and world champion cowboy Bob Crosby.

Rogers had been in Chicago for the Republican National Convention and was returning to his home in Beverly Hills before he had to turn around and head eastward a week later, back to Chicago and the convention for his own Democratic party, of which he once quipped, "I am not a member of any organized political party. I am a Democrat."

Juneteenth

An all-day celebration took place on Juneteenth 1934. The festivities kicked off with a parade leaving from the African-American school at North Eighth and Magnolia [N. Treadaway] and passing through downtown before ending at Macedonia Baptist Church. In the afternoon, the Black Eagles took on the Lampasas Panthers in a baseball game held at the old ACC field on South First Street. In the evening, everyone gathered for a dance staged at the Lytle Lake pavilion. In keeping with the custom of electing a Juneteenth queen, votes were cast and counted with Loraine Stephens and Alice Turner receiving the same total. Thus two queens were selected for 1934.

Make Tracks to Mack's

One hundred and ten lucky folks were treated to a preview taste at Mack Eplen's Drivateria in a foretaste of what all of Abilene would soon come to savor. Destined to become an Abilene icon, offering great food and several delivery choices—drive-in, dine-in, take out in our insulated bags, or phone it in by ringing up Orchard 3-8151.

Mack Eplen's along North First

Eplen first began serving his creations to Abilene diners in 1936 and by 1958 had the recipe for culinary success down to a science. The drivateria (a portmanteau of drive-in cafeteria) would rise to local notoriety by offering Square Burgers. The meat and the buns were uniquely square, you could opt to add pickles, tomato, relish, chili, smoke sauce, mayonnaise, or any combination therein.

For the lunchtime crowd, "Meet me at Mack's" was a common invitation, but the earliest slogan employed by Mr. Eplen was an appeal to "Make Tracks to Macks." The restaurant known simply as "Macks" (despite Mr. Eplen having a stable of Abilene restaurants bearing his name) not only served charcoal broiled burgers (Mack preferred hickory wood charcoal) along with malts and shakes, but the blue and white building with a huge "Time to Eat" sign served a pivotal role in the Abilene dating scene. To spend a Friday or Saturday night driving around Mack's was the pre-smart-phone equivalent of texting, Snapchatting, Facebooking, and internet dating sites. Driving along First, Shelton and Green with your buddies was the preferred platform for flirting with a passing parade of date possibilities.

ALSO ON THIS DAY IN 1958...
Miss Abilene Becomes Miss Texas

Eighteen-year-old Abilene beauty Linda Daugherty was chosen as Miss Texas and would represent Texas in the upcoming Miss Universe and Miss United States contests (not to be confused with the separate Miss America pageant). Dark-haired, hazel-eyed Linda received an all-expense-paid one-week trip to Los Angeles and a guaranteed screen test by Paramount Studios. Linda made it to the semi-final round of Miss United States, but Miss Louisiana took home the tiara.

Future 'Davy Crockett' / 'Daniel Boone' Recovers From Stabbing

Hardin-Simmons freshman Fess Parker was rushed to Hendrick Memorial Hospital in serious condition following an altercation that resulted in a knife wound to his neck. An earlier automobile accident led to the quarrel between 21-year-old Parker and a 37-year-old Abilenian at a home on Ross Street. Abilene police arrested the slasher, charging him with assault. Parker recovered from his wounds but left Abilene, transferring to the University of Texas the following year. In 1954, Walt Disney cast Parker in the role of Davy Crockett in the television series of the same name, and in 1964 the former HSU Cowboy took on the Disney role of Daniel Boone.

Fly Fighting

Abilene set out on a fly fighting crusade. Druggists reported that fly paper was in short supply, and screen wire dealers were pleased with the uptick in business. Warmer weather generated the buzzing menaces in profusion, bringing a dent to health and general happiness. Citizens were urged to take measures: get rid of manure piles, screen in all porches so flies will succumb to the outdoor heat, mix two pounds of resin with one pint of castor oil and paint the result onto old newspapers, placing them throughout your house. The Abilene newspaper carried this exhortation: "The great menace to the health of our people today is not the water from Lytle Lake but in the filth in the alleys, barns and privies of this town.

Your willful neglect to clean your premises may cost the life of some member of your family or your neighbor's family." (So wear your mask! Oops…sorry, wrong pestilence.)

JUNE 23, 1938
First Boaters on Lake Fort Phantom

Before the Fort Phantom dam across Elm Creek was finished, the waters began to back up, creating an ever-deepening lake. Recent rainfall brought the level up to a boat-floatin' level in June of 1938, motivating Lee Roy York and Ben Franklin Cox to be the first to float on the murky waters. The duo launched their 12-foot motor boat on Elm Creek near the brick plant in north Abilene. Lee Roy, 22, ran a poultry business and just happened to be the son of the mayor, while Ben, 28, worked with his father at Cox Typewriters. Three hours after they set their craft in the water, they reached the dam, earning them the honor of "First on the Lake."

JUNE 24, 1994
Hole-in-Won

Abilene Buick dealer and former mayor Fred Lee Hughes offered a new 1994 LeSabre to anyone who made a hole-in-one at a charity golf tournament at the Abilene Country Club. Indeed, on the par-3, 179-yard 10th hole, a golfer managed to pull off that rare feat. The golfer was none other than Fred Lee Hughes himself! "I'm going to give it to Wanda, my wife," he quipped, "because she needs a car."

JUNE 25, 1889

The Cornerstone of School Number One

The cornerstone of Abilene's "magnificent" new school building was set in place on this Tuesday evening. The Masonic fraternity carried out its traditional role after marching from its lodge rooms to the school site at South First and Peach. The stone, hiding a time capsule filled with relics, was dedicated using corn, oil and wine before local attorney Kade Legett addressed the crowd. Legett pointed out that "the children of our time must soon become the architects of the living temple of the Republic and,

if we expect them to discharge this trust with efficiency and fidelity, they must be educated and enlightened." Following Legett's speech, a prayer was offered and the cornerstone mortared in place. Inside the capsule was: The History of the Gleaners (a group of ladies from First Presbyterian Church), a copy of the *Abilene Reporter* and the *Taylor County News*, lists of lodge members, one dollar in change, and a half pint of corn.

Original Abilene High School along North First, 1890s

The school opened in 1890 and was razed in 1924.

Answering the Call

By noon, 43 Taylor Countians had enlisted in the National Guard Company, heeding the call made two days earlier at a rally in Everman Park when Judge Wagstaff spoke to a crowd of 3,000. Wagstaff called for local men to serve their country by enlisting to fight the Central Powers in World War I. First to sign up was Curtis Kean.

JUNE 26, 1951
Abilene's Heart

The funeral for an unknown woman, thought to be about 40, was held at the Kiker-Warren Funeral Chapel. More than 300 strangers answered the call to give the anonymous woman a decent funeral and burial with donations totaling $458, more than enough to provide a casket and marker at the burial plot donated by Elmwood Memorial Park. Two weeks before, the woman registered at the Hotel Wooten as "Ruth Brown," but police determined that was not her actual name. After checking in, she drowned in the storm-swollen waters of Catclaw Creek. Over 5,000 Abilenians came by the funeral home to see if they might be able to identify her, and an artist's drawing ran in the newspaper—all to no avail.

Evidence indicated that around 4 a.m. she took off her shoes near the North Third Street bridge over the creek, setting them next to her purse, which contained no identifying papers. Her body was found later that morning near the State Street bridge at Cobb Park.

The newspaper editor wrote of the community's response to

tragedy, adding, "We like to think of this as one of Abilene's noblest gestures. It was wholly spontaneous, it needed no urging, and it came from the heart." Six Abilene men volunteered to carry the casket to its resting place. Her bronze burial marker reads: Ruth Brown   unidentified 1951. Her identity remains unknown.

JUNE 27, 1958
"Is Your Refrigerator Running?"

A Miss Hardy, living on South 12th Street, once again fell victim to a prank phone caller. Earlier calls sent deliveries of food and other articles to the Hardy home. One caller even sent an unnecessary ambulance racing to the Hardy house. On this day, a Child's Ready Mix truck showed up with a load of concrete, not a load she ordered. Abilene police detectives announced they would like to make the acquaintance of the caller. A good place to start might have been Abilene High School. Miss Hardy taught history there. (And if the title to this day's happening does not make sense to you, ask your grandparents.)

JUNE 28, 1960
Local Hero: Gene Garrett

Quick action by 23-year-old Gene "Jesse" Garrett saved two men from certain death and very nearly cost Gene his own. Work taking place 18 feet deep inside a tank at the Grimes Filtration Plant on East Highway 80 was the scene of the near tragedy. Two employees of the Dallas Water Tank Service Company were sandblasting inside the tank when gases seeping beneath their face masks caused them to be overcome by toxic fumes. Before passing out, one man managed to yell for help. Up on the surface, Garrett heard the cry and had the presence of mind to run to the office to relay the emergency before racing back to the access hole. Refusing to wait on the fire department, Garrett donned a facemask, tied a rope around himself so that two others could lower him through the small

Gene Garrett

opening. Reaching the bottom, Garrett quickly lashed ropes around the unconscious men, who were then hoisted to the surface. Still in the tank, Garrett was overcome by the fumes and a second rescuer, Robert Griffin of Abilene, went in to save Garrett.

Asked if he considered his own safety before taking action, the shy young man, speaking from a hospital bed, grinned and—looking embarrassed—nodded his head "no." Gene Garrett died in Abilene in 2017 at the age of 80.

JUNE 29, 1985
The Stand-in Star Arrives

A crowd that would later be estimated anywhere from 10,000 to over 50,000, gathered along the Dyess flight line to witness the arrival of "The Star of Abilene," the first B1-B Lancer to be delivered and stationed at the base. Turns out, the sinister-looking jet, appearing just before 2 p.m., was not "The Star of Abilene" but rather the understudy. The name, suggested by 15-year-old Cooper High School student Darleen Miller, was first revealed when the crowd read it on the side of the plane. At the time, the USAF had just two operational B1s. The day before, the bomber tagged for Dyess flew from California to Offutt AFB in Nebraska but, upon landing, a metal plate in the air conditioning system came loose, with bolts making their way into one of the engines.

Not wanting to disappoint a crowd—that included Senators Lloyd Bentsen and Phil Gramm, Representative Charles Stenholm, the Chairman of the Joint Chiefs, and the mother of base namesake Ed Dyess—the remaining B-1B, earmarked for testing and still located at Edwards AFB in California, was hastily decaled with "Star of Abilene" and dispatched as a stand-in for the real "Star."

General Bennie Davis, commander of the Strategic Air Command, piloted the stealthy gray-green bomber, approaching from the east at 1:40 p.m. Davis brought the needle-nosed bomber directly over Abilene—with the wings in their swept-back position he streaked overhead at 630 mph before making three low passes at the base. The four-engined, $400 million plane delighted the crowd with an earth-shaking crescendo before thundering to a perfect touchdown right on time. Following repairs, the real "Star of Abilene" arrived a few days later.

In 2003, after 17 years, 7 months and 23 days, "The Star of Abilene" was retired; it is on permanent display near the main gate.

The Star of Abilene at Dyess AFB

The Abilene Club Closes Up, Sorta

Since opening with a formal flourish on June 29, 1930, the Abilene Club operated as a private club in the Hotel Wooten. After 32 years, it closed on June 30, 1962, only to reopen the next day as the members-only "Downtown Abilene Club." Originally, the Abilene Club offered a relaxation spot tucked away on the third floor of the brand new hotel. The green-carpeted rooms included a reading room, ladies card room, billiard room and gymnasium and was the annual site for the liveliest New Year's Eve party in town.

By 1962, unpaid bills—some due to the IRS—brought about the demise of the original club and the birth of its replacement. With tongue firmly in cheek, the charter for the new Downtown Abilene Club stated: "The purpose is the support and maintenance of an educational undertaking, to wit, a club in the City of Abilene, Texas for the improvement and development of the human mind through reading, discussions, exchange of ideas, lectures, information, social contacts and all other means that will contribute to such educational improvement and development of the members of the club." However, everyone knew that was simply a convoluted and wordy way of stating it was a hideaway spot, where for $12 in monthly dues the membership was able to circumvent state liquor laws. By requiring each member to pay up front for individual bottles of liquor and then combining them, the club dues only bought the setup and services. Liquor by the drink, with a wink to a dry Abilene.

JULY

Halftime Stats

With six months of 1937 in the books, the Taylor County win/loss record looked like this: the County Clerk issued 210 marriage licenses, while in district court there were 87 divorce filings prosecuted to a close. Births for the county came in at 450, besting those checking out by 2 to 1, as death knells rang in at 225. The most common culprit being pneumonia, although appendicitis claimed five, while half a dozen Taylor Countians exited with tuberculosis.

Lyndon Lands on the Lawn

In the midst of a tight runoff race with Coke Stevenson to determine the Democratic nominee for the 1948 Senate seat, Congressman Lyndon Johnson arrived in town aboard the "Johnson City Windmill," a Sikorsky S-51 helicopter. Following a couple of low passes over town, the dragonfly-looking helicopter set down at 5:30 p.m. on the lawn west of Abilene High School on South First Street. In a stunt he performed

before almost every landing, Johnson tossed his Stetson out the window
(offering a $1 reward for its return) symbolically putting his hat in the
ring.

Lyndon Johnson greets a crowd from the Johnson City Windmill

A sizable crowd assembled, likely drawn more by the sight of
a helicopter touching down in the middle of town than for hearing a
political speech. With the rotors off, children rushed in close to put their
hands on the helicopter, while LBJ managed to gain the attention of
some adults and briefly outline his "People's Platform for Preparedness,
Peace and Progress." Over three weeks, Johnson crisscrossed the state
in his attention-getting ride, speaking numerous times each day. While
in Abilene, he made three speeches—numbers 170, 171 and 172 of his
tour—before the Johnson City Windmill lifted off, soaring north to
Anson and speech number 173. (Johnson defeated Stevenson by 87 votes
statewide. However, he won Taylor County by more than 1,500 votes.)

Taylor County is Partially Organized

Eastland County served as the judicial seat for Taylor County until an election was held on July 3, 1878. On this day, voters elected a county judge, district clerk, sheriff, tax collector, treasurer and county clerk. Buffalo Gap, the only town in the county, was named as the temporary county seat, with Texas Governor Richard Hubbard directing that an election be held within 30 days to make it official. The election was never held.

Colonel Parramore

With the passing of James H. Parramore, the Abilene newspaper generously noted, "One of the greatest hearts the West has known is stilled forever. It were more glorious to have lived a life like his, with his good deeds and the impress of his clean heart on the lives of others, than to have been a very king." Described as quiet, unassuming and deeply principled, James Parramore was a successful cattleman, staunch early promoter of Abilene, and a deeply devout Baptist who played a vital role in the upbringing of Simmons College and the early civic efforts to raise Abilene into a center of trade.

As the final days of his 77 years began to slip by, seated daily next to his bed was his longtime friend and cattle business partner, Clabe Merchant. From the bedroom of the

James Harrison Parramore

Parramore home on Orange Street, the two old friends listened as, just blocks away, Abilene held a celebration to mark the winning of the West Texas campus for Texas A&M (only to later lose it). This Abilene pioneer is buried in the city cemetery.

JULY 5, 1965

Satan on the Loose

Just after midnight, Satan made a break for it, dashing off to join a pack of roving dogs near the city shop on East Highway 80. It was the first day on the job for the 2½-year-old German Shepherd and rookie member of the Abilene police K-9 corps who, for unknown reasons, was named for the devil. Satan pulled away from patrolman M.C. Vincent, dashing off to mix and mingle with the civilian canine crowd passing nearby. Vincent called and gave chase, all without success in returning the patrol dog to work. Six hours after being AWOL from the police force, Satan rejoined and was forgiven for his absence, with Vincent and Satan agreeing it all amounted to a case of first-day jitters. Soon enough Satan settled into his role alongside the rest of the K-9 troop—Bruno, Tonka and Saber.

JULY 6, 1939

Bearing Bears

Motoring to Abilene from Sacramento, California, Dr. W.L. Williamson hauled a cage in the back of his pickup containing two 5-year-old bears. On the front of the cage was a sign reading, "Look out for these bears. They are meaner than Gib Sandefer!" Williamson explained to any curious questioner, "Gib Sandefer is the meanest man in Texas." Actually, Williamson and Sandefer were good friends who enjoyed needling each other. Sandefer, business manager for Hardin-Simmons athletics and devoted animal lover, regularly aided zoo donations and secured the two bruins for the Abilene zoo, bearing (pun intended) only the cost of transportation. The 350-pound bears, former residents of the Sacramento Zoo, moved into their Abilene cage next to the lions, who were also in Abilene due to the Williamson-Sandefer friendship.

JULY 7, 1966
Houdini Slips By

A newly arrived California sea lion did not take long to escape his confinement in the brand new Abilene Zoo. Around 2 a.m. night watchman Earl Anderson called Walt Keunzli, rousing the zoo director from his slumber, to report that after counting the seals half a dozen times, Anderson only came up with four. Number 5 had apparently managed to scale the wall of his enclosure and make a waddle for it. Anderson issued a zoo-wide APB for the fugitive and soon spotted him taking a moonlight swim in the nearby zoo lake.

The recapture plan included using one of the other sea lions to lure Houdini out of the lake and back to his full-time job. However, the sex-appeal ploy did not work and the slippery seal was still out-and-about. Just after midnight on Saturday, several startled motorists spotted Houdini attempting to cross East Highway 80 and bearing westward (presumably to the Pacific). Corralled by the late night crowd, Houdini was retrieved by Mr. Anderson who brought the escapee back to his pen. A month later Houdini was shipped back to his former home in South

Houdini on a late night swim at the Abilene zoo lake

Dakota but not before inspiring his fellow cellmates. In September, five sly defectors, including two Harbor seals who had just arrived, made good on their own their escape plan. The breakout was set in motion after one seal stealthily used his mouth to turn the knob on the door below the feeding platform and then waited for the wind to swing the metal door inward. The conniving quintet snuck away from their confining pool and then wisely split up. The two smaller Harbor seals, left to their own devices and obviously unfamiliar with the layout, never managed to exit the zoo grounds. One of the older California sea lions was found hiding in a culvert, while a second bewhiskered runaway was spotted, a la Houdini, taking a leisurely swim in the zoo lake. A search by car, on foot, and in a low-flying plane failed to turn up the fifth escapee. It is a longshot, but should you spot him, you can try calling OR 2-9771.

JULY 8, 1982

Abilene National Bank Melts Away

Turns out that a report carried this day in the *Dallas Morning News* was true—Abilene National Bank was in trouble.

Abilene National began operating in 1963 following acceptance of its application for a federal charter. The new bank was organized by local attorney Randall Jackson along with real estate investor Marshall Boykin, car dealers Max Fergus and Carroll Rogers, oil man S.C. Herring, and local pediatrician Dr. Stanton Barron. The bank made its home at North First and Willis Street.

In 1976, a group from Lubbock bought controlling interest in the bank and sent Don Earney to town to run things. Earney led the bank in an explosive growth of assets, soaring from $20 million to $500 million in six years and, in 1980, overseeing building a new six-story home for the bank just north of the original location. However, the 1982 report in the Dallas newspaper suggested that the bank's heavy reliance on loans to the oil industry placed it in serious jeopardy. The story resulted in over $50 million of deposits withdrawn and Earney taking out full-page ads in the *Wall Street Journal* and newspapers across Texas arguing that allegations the bank was on the verge of failure were false. But they were true. On August 6, 1982, Abilene National Bank was taken over by Mercantile Texas, a Dallas-based holding company.

The original bank building and the old 1980 six-story building still stand.

JULY 9, 1904
The Alexander Sanitarium

Abilene brothers, and doctors, James "Jim" Minor Alexander and Sidney McLemore Alexander, bought the large, two-story home of banker E.F. Elkins on North Sixth Street in order to fit it up as a hospital. Surrounded by four acres of lawn, the Alexander Sanitarium boasted every modern medical appliance of the day, and the Abilene locale was touted as offering the best climate in the state to aid the suffering in their recovery.

In 1918 Dr. Jim Alexander converted the sanitarium into a school for training nurses and moved the hospital to a larger, purpose-built building erected next door. Dr. Sydney Alexander died in 1928, with Jim continuing to operate the facility until 1934. Dr. Jim Alexander died in Abilene in 1954.

JULY 10, 1931
Dr. B.J.

Abilene native Bobby Jack Estes was born on this day in 1931. Leaving home in 1948 to attend Vanderbilt University at the age of 17, he earned his degree in 1952. In Tennessee he met and married a local girl, Lale Murrey. Bobby Jack became Dr. B.J. in 1956 after earning his MD degree from Baylor College of Medicine. Dr. B.J. and Lale moved to Abilene in 1957 where he joined the practice of his uncle, Dr. Jack Estes. Dr. B.J.'s own father, Bob, was an Abilene dentist and another uncle, Dr. Gene Estes, was in charge of the medical lab. Jack, Bob and Gene's father was, himself, a longtime Abilene physician, Dr. J.M. Estes.

Over the course of his career, Dr. B.J. delivered hundreds of babies and treated thousands more, often standing vigil beside a hospital bed. If patients could not pay, they still received treatment. On his afternoon off, Dr. B.J. took his doctor's bag to an Abilene elementary school, treating students and even their parents at no cost. Tirelessly committed to those under his care, he was known for ending each patient visit by asking, "Is there anything you need?" If the answer produced a spoken need, he then tried to meet it.

Besides giving time and treatment to his patients, Dr. B.J. supported and volunteered for a long list of community efforts and in helping First

Central Presbyterian Church. In 1997 he was awarded the highest recognition from the Taylor-Jones-Haskell County Medical Society—the Gold-Headed Cane Award for "Outstanding Service to His Fellow Man through the Arts and Sciences of Medicine." He was also named Family Physician of the Year by the Texas Academy of Physicians and awarded the Golden

Dr. B. J. Estes

Deeds Award by the Abilene Exchange Club for his "exceptional record of meeting community needs."

Dr. B.J. and Lale lived on Elmwood Drive where he annually planted a huge vegetable garden, sharing the produce with friends, neighbors, his office staff, and with strangers. Dr. B.J. Estes also grew roses, sharing those miracles of beauty with others, just as he shared himself with Abilene. If you were fortunate enough to call him your doctor, you knew you were in capable hands. Dr. B.J. passed away at the age of 89 in 2020.

JULY 11, 1985
What Are the Odds?

Mother and daughter Judy Davis and Brenda Steele left Abilene for a week of summer vacation on the beaches of the Dominican Republic. Taking their beach towels down to the ocean's edge, they were soon joined by a man who spread his towel nearby. He smiled and asked, "Where are you ladies from?"

"The U.S." they replied.

"What state?"

"Texas."

"Ha, same here. What city?"

"We live in Abilene."

"Are you kidding?! I live in Abilene!"

"Where do you live?

"I live on Gilmer Street."

Mother and daughter looked at one another. "We live on Gilmer Street! Which house?"

The man gave his address and Judy and Brenda met the man who lived two doors down for the first time, 2,000 miles from their common home.

JULY 12, 1950
Project Abilene

The State Highway Department dubbed the highly-complex, one-million dollar restructuring of a local highway interchange as "Project

Project Abilene

Abilene" and the multi-faceted scheme was nearing completion on this day. The multi-pronged engineering feat called for the construction of a British-style traffic circle at East U.S. Highway 80 and Magnolia [North Treadaway Boulevard], creation of two railroad underpasses beneath the T&P mainline, a four-lane overpass above the Wichita Valley Railroad and a bridge over Cedar Creek.

Pre-dating the interstate highway system, the Abilene highway hub served to send travelers east and west along U.S. Highway 80, direct them north on U.S. 83 or south on Highways 83 and 84. Signage directed motorists both north and south along Highway 277 or towards Austin and Houston along Highway 36. The idea was that from the Abilene traffic interchange, a traveler gained access to highways leading to all points in the continental United States. In the late 1990s, the circle was replaced with a four-way intersection.

JULY 13, 1956

Bowling Rolls Big Time

Although bowling first arrived in Abilene in 1938 when David Dahlgren opened the Bowling Palace on Cypress (*Ladies – Bowl Each Day and Keep That School Girl Figure!*), things really took off on Friday, July 13, 1956, when the ribbon on the new 16-lane VFW Bowling Lanes was cut by Brigadier General

Top scorers in the 1955 Women's City Bowling Tournament, l to r, Betty Bridges, Helen Moran, Marty Dooley, Lola Cole, Becky Hodges

Charles Westover. Located on Kirkwood, just behind the VFW Post, the new lanes launched Abilene on a bowling craze. By early 1958, the VFW announced that it would double, adding 16 more alleys in 1958. In April, the Sands Hotel broke ground on a 24-lane bowling center next to the hotel on South First, while Jack Henson built 20 more lanes just west of the Sands on Ruidoso Street. Henson Lanes opened in July of 1958, boasting electrically filtered air to remove the cigarette smoke and telescore machines that projected scores over each lane. In October of 1958, former Paramount Theatre manager Wally Akin opened up Plaza Skate and Bowl on Shelton with eight lanes. One more addition to Abilene bowling, Triangle Lanes, opened in 1978, 20 years after the bowling surge of 1958, with a whopping 40 lanes.

The 124 bowling lanes once available at the VFW (later Whitewood Lanes), Sands, Henson Lanes (later Abilene Bowling) and the Plaza Skate and Bowl are all closed, as are the Triangle lanes which closed in 1994 and the building is now home to a church.

JULY 14, 1914
Black Tuesday

Long before the Black Friday tradition of post-Thanksgiving sales, Abilene's four dry goods stores staged a precursor, opening their doors for July Clearance sales at 8 a.m., with shoppers rushing in. Outside of Minter Dry Goods, "Abilene's Progressive Store," a throng awaited the early opening and the chance to snag bargain merchandise such as men's silk shirts for only $2.65. A similar scene played out in front of Anderson-Schultz Company on Chestnut where summer dresses were half price. In the next block, McDavid Brothers (whose slogan was "Price is the Thing") took out ads reminding that your limited income is "no bar to dressing well – Absolutely Not!" Over at Campbell's on Pine Street, the store advertised millinery would be available at "unheard-of prices" and men's undershirts and drawers could be had for 45 cents. Now, that's worth getting up early for.

Southside Stimulus

A crowd of over 5,000 took up the offer of Chestnut Street business owners and merchants to come out for a free dance. The effort, spearheaded by Royce Boyd, manager of the Palace Theater, intended to highlight the stores and businesses south of the railroad tracks, stimulating trade along streets other than north side Pine and Cypress Street, the main thoroughfares for stores, theaters and businesses. Jerry Abbott's five-piece string band provided the music as thousands of Abilenians strolled Chestnut, enjoying the carnival-like atmosphere while cowboy-costumed store employees kept things in order.

The shuffling throng danced in the street, waltzing and square dancing on the corn-waxed asphalt as Bro Mingus narrated the activities in a live broadcast carried over KRBC radio and as his roving reporter interviewed folks along the sidewalk. Hollis Drugstore and Palace Confectionary on the corner of South First and Chestnut had more business at the soda fountain than they could handle. The festivities lasted until midnight with customers stopping in at Hampton's Café, Shultz Dry Goods, Landis Shoe Shop and Piggly Wiggly. Two weeks later, the whole thing was repeated, drawing an even larger crowd who bought tickets to the Gem Theater, ate at the N&M Café, and satisfied their sweet tooth at the Royal Candy Kitchen.

Business owners formed the South Side Trade Association as they continued to invigorate their side of downtown, even implementing credit coupons. For every 25-cent purchase, customers received a penny credit redeemable at any of the South Side Trade Association businesses. The program lasted only a few weeks before being deemed as illegal.

Seventy years later, the area south of the tracks became known as the SODA District—South of Downtown Abilene—and the dream of rejuvenating Chestnut and Oak Street took on a sustained life.

JULY 16, 1960
Wilma Rudolph Flies

The track at Abilene Christian University served as the site for the 1960 U.S. Olympic Trials for women's track and field. For the price of one dollar, you could attend the two-day event set to determine who would occupy 28 spots on the U.S. team. On the final day of the trials, Tennessee State track star Wilma Rudolph thrilled the crowd as she tied the American record for the 100-meter dash, covering the ground in 11.5 seconds and securing her Olympic spot in that event. She went on to set a new Olympic Trials record for the 200-meter, flying from start to finish in 23.9 seconds, a record that held for eight years. Six weeks after leaving Abilene, Wilma arrived in Rome for the 17th Olympiad where she won gold in the 100 and 200-meter sprints, earning the title of "Fastest Woman in the World."

Tree Sitting

By mid-July, 13-year-old Lynn "Eho" Howell was coasting into his third day leading a pack of nine Abilene youngsters vying for the national roosting title—i.e., sitting in a tree. Eho, located in a hackberry at the Magnolia service station on South First, had been the first to go up, scooping up the early sponsorships and raking in $7 a day; in addition to the fifteen cents an hour paid by his mother, three additional advertisers were in for a nickel every hour. On top of the cash windfall, the Queen Café supplied Eho with food and Service Drug offered up cold drinks.

Also aloft was Roy Roberts in a backyard tree on Ross Street; H.B. Altman, Vance Randolph and Norman Carson were among the limbs as well. Altman went into the branches near dinnertime on Friday, July 18, with Carson taking off at noon on Saturday. Vance found a perch in his front yard mesquite on Santos. Buddy Moore inserted himself in the timber but was recalled a few days later by the bane of many a young tree-sitter—his parents.

By the 26th, Eho equaled the mark of a Kansas City tree-sitter who claimed the American record at 223 hours. The crowd around Howell's hackberry was steady, and by this point in his prolonged perch, he had only two rivals still airborne—Walter Wright, treed over at 802 Palm (although his dog, Rip, had long since come down), and Thurman Cline, roosting in the 500 block of Pine. Howell wound up in third place just behind Wright, both succumbing to the July heat. First place went to Thurman who perched aloft for 383 hours and 30 minutes—a full 16 days.

Sunday Ball Banned

Word on the street was that, due to an earlier rainout, a make-up baseball game was set for the upcoming Sunday afternoon. In an emergency session, the Abilene city council leapt into action unanimously passing an ordinance banning any Sabbath-day ball games effective immediately. Specifically, the ban was imposed on "taking an active part in such a contest within the corporate city limits of Abilene, to include playing, umpiring or managing a team." Because time was of the essence, the usual rules governing passage of a city ordinance—that it be read aloud at three meetings prior to taking effect—were suspended and the ordinance was immediately enforceable. The fine for violating the ban was set at $50 to $100.

Board of Development Brouhaha

Stinging words freely flew across Abilene as the debate over a new tax was on the table. The tax—16-cents on every $100 valuation—would fund a Board of City Development and a municipal band, both managed by the Chamber of Commerce. The board would be composed of 15 citizens overseeing the tax funds designated to promote business and industrial growth. The idea, put forth by the chamber, Lions and Kiwanis clubs, labor unions and the Retail Merchants Association, produced a debate that quickly came to resemble a mud wrestling match. The newspaper endorsed the idea but still felt compelled to use newsprint urging both sides to discuss things like friends. It did little good.

The anti-board folks denounced the ideas as "socialism gone to seed" and the equivalent of a law forcing church members to tithe. Some opposed the plan because it was anti-scriptural, quoting, "He that oppresseth the poor to increase his riches shall surely come to want." Another anti-board voter noted that the proponents would have you believe that it was the chamber "who has made the flowers to bloom and put catfish in Lake Abilene." Those backing creation of the board and the taxpayer-funded band pointed out that it was in everyone's interest to grow and develop existing businesses and to attract new ones. (They could find no scripture to prop up their side of the argument.)

The vote took place on July 25. The vote to create such a board totaled 509. Opponents rallied with 628 votes to quash the whole idea.

JULY 20, 1956
Abilene Proposes to Wylie

Abilene School Board chairman Morgan Jones proposed a marriage between his district and the Wylie school district adjoining Abilene to the south. Jones opined that the two would make a nice couple and that a bright future lay before the duo. A municipality can expand its limits by annexation; however, school districts can only unite if both districts agree to be man and wife. Two weeks after the proposition, the Wylie board agreed to have dinner with the Abilene folks at the Windsor Hotel. The date seemed to go well but, in the end, Wylie walked away from Abilene, opting to remain single.

A Local Luminary: John Deuel Gerhart

When John Gerhart arrived in 1943, his proud parents brought him home to their Highland Avenue home where he joined his older brother. John's father, Willis Gerhart, was the beloved 53-year-old rector of The Church of the Heavenly Rest. On a trip to Missouri in 1940, Willis, better known as "Parson," surprised many when he came back home with a 32-year-old bride, the former Eleanor Deuel, and they settled down to begin a family.

John Deuel Gerhart

John attended Alta Vista Elementary and South Junior High, but not high school in Abilene, opting instead to board at St. Stephen's Episcopal School in Austin. Accepted by Harvard, John would earn a degree in English and French history and literature in 1966 while also writing for *The Harvard Crimson*. Moving on to Princeton, John earned a masters degree in Public Affairs in 1969 and a Ph.D. in 1974. This Abilene boy was named as one of that school's most notable 100 graduates of the 20th century.

For nearly 30 years, John worked for the Ford Foundation in its international division where he aided and advised governments throughout Africa. In 1998, John was selected as president of The American University in Cairo where he led a $250 million effort to build a new campus, and his service was recognized by being awarded Egypt's First Class Decoration for Arts and Sciences. John assembled a world-class collection of African art and was a dedicated birder, ranked as the top amateur for the continent of Africa.

This Abilene boy died at the age of 59 and his ashes were interred in the memorial garden at St. Stephen's in Austin. His parents are buried in Abilene.

Weaver Steps Down and Kirby Steps Up

Abilene's tenth mayor, Morgan Weaver, surprised everyone when he submitted his letter of resignation just three months after being re-

Morgan Weaver

elected to a second two-year term. At the close of the City Council meeting, Weaver asked the secretary to read aloud a paper that told of the onerous mayoral duties and how they conflicted with Weaver's own hardware business. A few days later, the ex-mayor and his family left Abilene and civic stresses behind as they set out for a month-long vacation visiting ten eastern cities.

The election to choose a new mayor was set for August 27. Friends of attorney Egbert Kirby put his name forward as a candidate. Voter turnout was light as the mayoral seat was the only issue on the ballot and Kirby was the sole candidate. After Morgan Weaver returned from his vacation, Kirby was sworn in on September 11, 1907. He would be Abilene mayor for the next twelve years.

Egbert Kirby

JULY 23, 1955
Wrong Couch

After attending a wedding in San Antonio, Millie Basore, 20, was on her way back to her home in Ponca City, Oklahoma, when she stopped in Abilene well after midnight to stay with her friend, Barbara Holcombe. Millie pulled up to 1658 Orange at 3:30 a.m. and, not wanting to disturb her hostess, entered quietly, curled up on the sofa, and was soon fast asleep. Unbeknownst to Millie, her friend Barbara had moved to 1647 Simmons Street.

The sound of a crying baby briefly woke Millie from her slumber long enough to groggily muse, "Barbara doesn't have a baby." However, Mr. and Mrs. Bob Russell did. The Russells rose at 6:30 a.m. and discovered Goldilocks sound asleep on their living room couch. After quietly discussing the situation they finally agreed that Mrs. Russell would rouse the sleeping beauty with a gentle nudge. Sleepy-eyed Millie woke to hear Mrs. Russell say, "Hon, I think you are in the wrong house."

JULY 24, 1968
Oscar Rose Park

Abilene's oldest park got a new name. The park along South Seventh Street and Catclaw Creek was first known as West End Park, because that is where it was, on the west end of town. When the park became the site for the annual fair, it took on the new title of Fair Park. And although the Fair moved to east Abilene in 1954, the park continued to carry the confusing name until 1968. That year, Fair Park was renamed to honor Oscar Rose, an Abilene building contractor and the former Parks

Oscar Rose

and Recreation Board Chairman. Rose was surprised at a special award's dinner held at the Petroleum Club attended by the parks board, City Council, and city staff. The gathering was to present Rose with a plaque commemorating his 17 years on the Parks Board, but the real surprise was in revealing that the city's oldest park would now bear his name. When Oscar Rose first went on the board in 1951, the city had three parks and a zoo compared to the 22 parks put in place during Rose's tenure.

JULY 25, 1949
Fast Flying Pigeons

A flock of approximately 100 pigeons arrived early this morning and rather than fly into town, they came in on the train. Welcomed by Railway Express Agent R.C. Burleson, the birds—per earlier received instruction—were to be set free at sunrise the following day. It was not the first time Burleson had welcomed a convention of pigeons to the depot. In fact, in earlier decades, Abilene often received such freighted fine-feathered friends. Seems Abilene, Texas, lies approximately 1,000 miles south of South Bend, Indiana, home to the nationally renowned Mishawaka Racing Pigeon Center.

As instructed, at dawn on the 26th, Burleson and his fellow railway workers opened up the cages, watching as the homing pigeons circled downtown Abilene three times in order to get their bearings before heading northward for the finish line in Indiana.

As a side note, in the early 1900s an unusually speedy pigeon set a record for covering the same 1,000 miles, turning in a time of 14 hours and 40 minutes. The fast flyer won the race twice more and was known in racing circles as King Abilene.

Showcase Square

At 9 a.m., Mayor Kinard and Marion Dubbs—in her role as Miss Abilene 1962—cut the ribbon formally opening Showcase Square for downtown Abilene shoppers. As the ribbon was snipped near the fountain inside the air-conditioned mall, the nine tenants simultaneously cut ribbons opening for business. The grand opening festivities lasted over three days as thousands came downtown, valet parked up on

Showcase Square at Pine and North Second streets

the rooftop garage, and shopped at J.C. Penneys, G.C. Murphy, Steins, Zales Jewelry, Thom McAn Shoes, Walgreens, Western Auto and Lee Optical. The ninth tenant was the food court, consisting of Bob's Snack Bar. The $1.8 million mall was the dream of a former Nazarene preacher, Claude Stewart, who felt that the move to suburban shopping centers left an opportunity for those accustomed to coming downtown to shop.

Eight years later, Showcase Square sold at auction held on the courthouse steps. The only bid was from the lienholder.

Fish, Flies, Floods

For over a year, the waters of Lytle Lake had been drying up. By late July, the lake was all but empty, save water 18 inches deep nestled right up next to the dam. The owner of the lake, West Texas Utilities, decided to drain the remaining water through two 24-inch outlets in order to save hundreds of fish crowding in for space in the remaining wading pool. The plan was to catch the foundering fish and dump them into Lytle Creek on the other side of the dam. Once enough rainfall fell from the skies to replenish the lake, the displaced fish would be returned to their roomier home waters. However, deep mud complicated the operation, resulting in hundreds of fish unable to participate in the relocation program and, instead, becoming unwilling magnets for flies, prompting countermeasures. Veteran pilot Clay Porter of Shreveport arrived soon enough in his Stearman bi-plane equipped with fly-killing agents. Passing over the dry lake at less than 20 feet, Porter showered the lake with a deadly mixture of DDT and chlordane and, for good measure, did so for over an hour.

One year later, a July rainstorm filled the lake beyond capacity, sending water rushing over the spillway at a depth of over four feet, once again relocating untold numbers of fish against their will.

JULY 28, 1918

Officially Lake Abilene

Over many months the *Abilene Daily Reporter* referred to the proposed Elm Creek reservoir project site as "Lake Abilene." Soon the moniker became the common name by which many cussed and discussed the civic undertaking. So, by action of the city commissioners, the name officially entered into the local lexicon. Per the city fathers, it would be Lake Abilene. The commission further decided to break ground on the big dam project (damn big, if you prefer) the following week, setting plans for a 6 p.m. ceremony on a Monday during which Mayor Kirby would take up the handles of a plow hitched to six mules and furrow the first dirt.

JULY 29, 1970

A Big Welcome to Town

Don Lyman and Joe Corbin moved to Abilene from Delaware ahead of bringing their families to West Texas. The two family men wanted to properly welcome their wives—Nancy and Bunny—and their children to their new hometown so they rented a billboard along East Highway 80 near T&P Lane. The board read, "*Nancy, Bunny and children, welcome to Abilene. We love you, Don and Joe.*"

Lyman drove his family to Abilene and made sure to get stopped by the red light next to the billboard. He told his wife and children, "Well, look around and see how you're going to like your new home." He had to sit through the red light twice before one of his children noticed the oversized welcome.

JULY 30, 1927
Where the Pavement Ends

McClung Construction began work paving the approach to Abilene from Elmdale on State Highway No. 1, also known as the Bankhead Highway. Late arrival of some equipment delayed the work but soon cement, sand and steel were all in place ready to smooth the final stretch of the Taylor County section. A crew of 150 men began linking the 5.8 miles between Abilene and Elmdale, mixing and pouring concrete in a well-choreographed process, although work was delayed for half an hour after it was discovered that the night before a needy motorist had helped himself to 25 gallons of gas intended to run the pump. The 18-foot-wide road went down at the rate of a mile per week; needing three weeks to cure, the road was expected to be finished in time for Charles Lindbergh's upcoming visit, during which he would be paraded from the airport into Abilene along the freshly-laid concrete.

Perhaps in anticipation of the smooth road, a city ordinance passed the day before, raising the speed limit in Abilene from 18 to 20 miles per hour.

JULY 31, 1911

The Storm of Storms

Abilene bore the brunt of perhaps the worst storm to hit the city. Four inches of rain fell in two hours, winds pushed through at over 60 miles per hour, and hailstones large enough to knock a man unconscious fell throughout town. Windows were shattered, roofs were demolished, and animals lay dead in the streets. The dark cloud unleashed damage and misery about 6 o'clock on that Monday afternoon and lasted until 8. One person, young Tom Milner, was killed when a barn crumpled. At Lytle Lake, the Cunningham home was lifted up, carried 75 yards and tossed into the water, with Mr. Cunningham inside. He escaped, but just barely.

Roofs were lifted off, smokestacks and chimneys toppled, signs blew away and windows shattered all across town. An entire row of buildings on South Second Street was leveled

Buildings along Pine Street after the storm

while the banana stand across the street remained standing. The hands on the courthouse clock blew off, while passenger cars along the Abilene & Southern railroad were propelled down the track smashing into an engine. Lytle, Catclaw, Cedar, Elm and Rainy creeks breached their banks. Abilene optimism led many to look past the damage and agree with local businessman Jim Radford, "With the abundant rains we have had, I am inclined to regard the whole affair as something to be thankful for."

AUGUST

Momentous Military Meeting

Seeking to leverage an aeronautical Abilene asset and boost
economic possibilities, the Abilene Chamber of Commerce dispatched
a quartet of civic leaders to Washington D.C. to make a sales pitch.
Comprising the Abilene group was Mayor Ernest Grissom, Chamber of
Commerce president J.C. Hunter, Chamber manager Joe Cooley and the
chairman of the Chamber's National Defense Committee, W. P. Wright.
The civic leaders arrived at the Pentagon for a conversation with United
States Under Secretary of the Air Force John McCone and Major General
William F. McKee, Assistant Vice Chief of Staff. (McCone would go on
to serve as C.I.A. Director in the Kennedy and Johnson administrations
and McKee would rise to become a four-star general.)

Soviet strategic deterrence brought on by the Cold War created
a movement to increase the number of Air Force wings, and that
anticipated development sparked a Chamber of Commerce idea: to
offer the government the deactivated Abilene Army Airfield. Such a
move would mean coming full circle—since the old military airfield at
Tye had been donated to Abilene in 1948 by the government with the
thought that it would become the municipal airport. At the Pentagon

meeting, the Abilene promoters received assurances that when the Air Force increased, the Key City would be given every consideration. The glimmer of hope glowed a bit brighter when McKee asked for additional information about the city to be sent to his office. Expectations soared even higher when an Air Force delegation arrived in Abilene three weeks later to look over the airfield and the city.

The day after the inspection visit, the Abilene City Commission agreed to deed the government the old air field for $1 should it decide to locate a base there. On top of that, W.P. Wright assured the Air Force team that future Abilene-based airmen would be regular recipients of some mouth-watering barbeque. The Armed Forces Day luncheon instigated by the Chamber in 1952 would later morph into the "World's Largest BBQ" as Abilene strives to keep Wright's promise.

AUGUST 2, 1938
Is the Tank Empty?

Not long after sunset, Winnie Rae Bond, 9, and her 8-year-old cousin Dorothy Walls breathlessly ran into their grandmother's home at 502 Vine Street, excitedly reporting that they had just seen a black-suited, black-hatted man sitting atop the nearby 85-foot-high water standpipe and watched as he fell back, disappearing. The cylindrical water tower was situated atop a small knoll known as Standpipe Hill, located at South Fifth and Meander Street. Mrs. Bond quickly alerted the man in charge, Happy Scogin, a water department employee who lived just around the corner from the tower on Amarillo Street.

By the light of the moon, Happy climbed the ladder to investigate but turned up no evidence that someone had recently been at the top. The next morning, Water Commissioner George Morris heard the girl's tale and authorized Happy to empty the 85,000-gallon tank to see if the mystery man had unfortunately fallen inside. Neighborhood fire hydrants were cranked open and a small crowd gathered to watch the water drain out over the next three hours. Once the precious Abilene water was out of the metal tank, a large valve was opened at the base of the tower and Happy began shoving himself inside through the small opening. A few minutes later Happy emerged headfirst, mud-streaked and—living up to his name—with a big grin, reporting that no one had fallen in. Capitalizing on the bright side, Happy revealed that he was able to remove an old tin bucket that had found its way inside the Abilene reservoir.

AUGUST 3, 1949

Houston School

On this day, Houston School opened on the corner of North Sixth and Cottonwood Street with 215 students in grades one through six. The eight-classroom brick building was much nicer than the ramshackle structure previously used along North Eighth Street and known as the Americanization School (the school board voted to change the name from Amercanization to Houston in May of 1947.) The school was in an area known to many as "El Barrio de Los Sancudos," named for the pesky mosquitoes found in profusion in nearby Cedar Creek. Houston School served many Abilene Hispanic students until closing in 1979.

AUGUST 4, 1930
Sabbath Sin at the Cinema

Two months after arriving in Abilene to manage the new Paramount Theatre, Al Fourmet decided it was time to test a local Blue Law prohibiting movies from being shown on a Sunday. Tossing open the doors to the theatre after Sunday lunch, the Paramount drew a large crowd to see a film titled "Grumpy." Not long after the reel began to roll, Al Fourmet was arrested in the lobby for violating the 1921 ordinance. A trial held the next day resulted in a $50 fine levied against Al. His response was to announce the movie planned for the following Sunday, "The Silent Enemy," which prompted a second arrest. On the third Sunday, it was a Buster Keaton movie that propelled Mr. Fourmet on his third trip to jail. In all, he faced charges on seven occasions, was tried three times in city court and twice in county court. Before all charges could be prosecuted, Mr. Fourmet threw in the towel and agreed to shutter the cinema on Sundays. In return, all charges were dropped.

AUGUST 5, 1917
Company I Encamps

In July, more than 160 local young men stepped forward, volunteering for service with Company I of the Texas National Guard. In March, Governor James Ferguson called for volunteers across the state to step forward and serve as the United States prepared to enter World War I. Over 70 of the Taylor County enlistees listed Abilene as their hometown with the balance hailing from Anson, Potosi, Baird, Merkel, Hawley and several other nearby communities.

Company I—attached to the 7th Texas Infantry—encamped at Fair Park for six weeks beginning on Sunday, August 5, 1917, under the command of Abilenians Captain Robert M. Wagstaff and his cousin, Lieutenant Ted Sayles. At 12:01 a.m. on the 5th the men were automatically drafted into federal service.

Company members assembled at the courthouse at 10 a.m. Sunday, answering roll call before marching in four columns down South First Street, turning south for seven blocks to reach the camp. A truck provided by the local Overland auto dealer delivered personal effects and lockers to the park. Two of the fair buildings became barracks (each man had to provide his own blanket and folding cot, with Abilenians donating extra cots for those who did not own one). The poultry barn

Members of Company I

became the mess hall while showers at the park swimming pool provided bathing facilities. The center of the fair racetrack became the drill field. At the park entrance, a guard kept civilians shooed away although they were allowed to swim in the park pool from 3 to 5:30 p.m.

Lacking uniforms and proper military equipment, the area boys learned military drills using broomsticks for guns while wearing overalls and blue shirts. Reveille came at 6:10 a.m. followed by mess at 6:30. The daily routine included drilling from 7 to 4 each day, with a two-hour lunch break, lights out at 11.

The city held a big sendoff in September as the men moved out to Camp Bowie in Fort Worth (where real guns and actual uniforms awaited.) Ultimately, the Abilene boys became part of the 36th Division and saw action in France with the 4th French Army near St. Etienne in October 1918. Two years after falling into line, the troops were mustered out of service in 1919.

AUGUST 6, 1936

A Local Luminary: Alton Terry

Hardin-Simmons track and field athlete Alton Terry competed in the 11th Olympiad held in Berlin, Germany. Terry qualified for the finals of the javelin throw and managed a sixth place finish with a toss of 220 feet, 3 inches. It was the best throw by any American, however the contest was won by a German competitor, much to the pleasure of Hitler, who was in the stands this day. Prior to the Olympic competition, Alton Terry set an NCAA javelin record in Chicago, his meet record standing until 1952.

The sandy-haired boy from Brady enrolled at HSU in 1933 and quickly rose to prominence on the football field and basketball court but saved his biggest splash for the school's track team. Described as unassuming and well-liked, the right-handed tosser was the first Olympic athlete with an Abilene connection. This local luminary spent 31 years working for Dow Chemical before retiring to become a fishing guide. Hardin-Simmons inducted Alton Terry into the school's Athletic Hall of Fame in 1979. Alton Terry passed away in 2003 at the age of 90.

Olympian Alton Terry

AUGUST 7, 1891

The Abilene Country

In the city's early day, *The Abilene Reporter* regularly received letters from across the United States asking for information about the Abilene country. This hyperbolic 1891 response painted an Eden-esque Abilene.

A diversity of crops grow all over the Abilene country. Watermelons, muskmelons, potatoes and all other vines do remarkably well. Some of our farmers tell about melons that weighed over 100 pounds. Peaches and plums grow splendidly. There are a great number of beautiful streams all through the Abilene Country and they are full of fine fish too, such as trout, black bass, perch and various other kinds. Taxation is low, the average rate throughout the Abilene country being 60 to 80-cents on $100 worth of property. Property is assessed generally at about half its value, you can readily see how low taxes are. Roads could not be better and all the important streams have been bridged. A man is not ostracized on account of his politics, in fact a good Republican is just as welcome in the Abilene country as a good Democrat. (We hope that is true 130 years later.)

AUGUST 8, 1923

Good Losers

Three minutes after the news flashed reporting that the state locating committee chose Lubbock over Abilene as home for the proposed Texas Technological College, the Abilene Chamber of Commerce dispatched a telegram to its Lubbock counterpart. The telegram read: *"The people of Abilene extend heartfelt congratulations to the people of Lubbock on their victory and predict for Texas Tech a glorious future. One hundred and fifty*

Abilene business men will visit you on August 24 to shake your hands and help you celebrate." A similar sentiment was telegraphed from Abilene Mayor Charles Coombes to the Lubbock mayor. After all, Abilene already had two colleges, with a third set to open the next month. No point in being greedy.

AUGUST 9, 1962
Westgate Shopping Capital

Built on 42 acres in west Abilene at a cost of over $3 million, the buying public was welcomed to Westgate Shopping Capital as a 1,200-foot red ribbon, encircling the entire mall, was cut with gigantic 12-foot scissors. The grand opening for the newest in shopping trends was a four-day event with all 22 stores remaining open 9 to 9.

The mall project was the idea of local car dealer and airport owner Jack Hughes, who formed Globe Development Company with partner H.S. Higginbotham. Westgate Shopping took the place of Hughes Field, a one-runway airport in west Abilene. Construction on the 630-foot-long mall got underway in late 1961 with Rose Construction Company handling the oversized building project and enough paving to park

Westgate Shopping Capital

3,000 cars. Stores included J.C. Penney, Kresge's, Walgreens, two shoe stores, a barbershop, an optical shop and offices for KCAD radio and KPAR-TV. Lerner's and Casual Corner offered ladies fashions, while the fellas could shop at the National Men's Store, and kids could pick out their new styles at Kiddie Mart. 'M' System supermarket opened its sixth Abilene location at Westgate, this one featuring an exterior wall with a tile mosaic depicting scenes of the West Texas economy, including windmills, oil derricks, cattle and jet airplanes. Wyatt's Cafeteria offered seating for 350—with roving hostesses pouring free coffee and tea refills—and a central water fountain, with changing colored lights, serving as a favorite childhood wishing well.

Westgate began to slowly wither in 1977 when J.C. Penney announced that it would relocate to the new Mall of Abilene under construction in south Abilene.

AUGUST 10, 1955
Milano's Po' Boy Sandwich

Ten years after serving in the China-Burma-India theater during World War II, former Camp Barkeley soldier Sam Milano would return to Abilene and bring his culinary delights with him. While stationed at Camp Barkeley, Sam met and married a local girl, Francis White, before shipping overseas. After the war, the couple settled in California, but in June of 1955 the Milanos returned to Abilene with two sons in tow.

Having owned a delicatessen in Pasadena, Sam decided to open one in Abilene, renting space across from Fair Park on South Seventh Street. In the 600-square-foot restaurant, he introduced Abilene to authentic spaghetti and meat sauce, pastrami, and mouth-watering Po' Boy sandwiches—three delectable layers of cheese, salami, ham, mustard, pickles and coleslaw served on soft bread. A year after opening, Sam expanded, moving into the new River Oaks Shopping Center. In 1962, he relocated once more, this time to 4141 North First Street, where he operated his drive-in/dine-in restaurant. You may wonder why this bit of mainstream news made it into a book chronicling daily Abilene nostalgia. The answer lies in the fact that the author loved those Po' Boy sandwiches and misses them still.

AUGUST 11, 1966

Make 'Em Green

At its August 11, 1966, meeting, the Abilene City Council made two decisions. First, it voted to offer the old City Hall at North Second and Cedar for sale (although City Manager H. P. Clifton favored tearing it down to make a parking lot) and, secondly, to accept a proposal from the traffic department regarding street signs. The council approved a three to five year timeline for replacing the old black and white street signs, choosing green as the new background color. Council member Fred Lee Hughes, a dyed-in-the-wool Aggie, suggested the signs might look better if they were maroon and white. The reflectorized signs came in two sizes, six and nine inch widths. The smaller ones identified residential streets and the larger ones marked major thoroughfares. (Mr. Clifton won out and the old City Hall site became a parking lot.)

AUGUST 12, 1966

Sophomore Initiation

Abilene police busily responded to several early morning calls in the area near Abilene High School as the annual, unauthorized, initiation of sophomore girls unfolded. The ritual typically involved eggs, syrup, shoe polish, shaving cream, and the chance for the incoming 10th grade females to kiss the feet of the senior Eagle girls. A large crowd of teens, congregating just before 3 a.m. at the North 10th and Mockingbird Lane service station, first garnered police attention.

A second call at 3:07 dispatched officers down the street to the high school where they strongly advised the roving teens to "Go home!" Apparently, this unsolicited advice went unheeded by the youthful crowd because seven minutes later, a third call sent police back to the campus where officers recorded that the sophomore girls "were parading before boys in their shorty pajamas." Asked to comment about the late night shenanigans, Abilene High principal Escoe Webb said he knew nothing about it but noted that the annual sophomore girls' initiation had never been a school-sanctioned event.

AUGUST 13, 1964
Beatlemania

Tickets for the sole showing of "A Hard Day's Night" at the Paramount Theatre created such demand that the precious passes came from the airport to Westgate Shopping Capital in an armored car. The 1,193 tickets for the Beatles' movie touched down in Abilene aboard Trans-Texas Airway's 11:30 a.m. flight where flight attendant Kay Alderson handed the precious cargo off to Kittie Wood, daughter of M-System Grocery manager Bill Wood. Kittie and the tickets, safely placed in an armored car, were whisked to the Westgate mall where tickets would go on sale two days later at the Wyatt's Cafeteria location. Tickets, costing $1 a piece, were rationed at two per buyer, with some fans lining up the night before. In order to score his ticket, Richard Morgan camped out overnight and was first in line. By 6 a.m. he had 125 in line behind him.

Ticket sales opened at 9 a.m. and in 45 minutes over 800 tickets were snapped up. (The remainder were leisurely sold to those smart enough to hold off a few hours.)

The lucky ticket holders arrived at the Paramount early the following Saturday in order to get a good seat for the 10 a.m. show. Maintaining his habit of early arrival, Richard Morgan showed up at 10 p.m. the night before in order to be first in line. However, a late night call from Mother Nature forced Richard to temporarily vacate his spot, which he marked with an X. Theater manager Frank Sheffield ruled that marking your spot violated the unwritten laws of movie line waiting, thus promoting Jody Wayte, 17, and Rebecca Johnston, 14, into the top spots.

A week later, with teenage fervor fully subsided, "A Hard Day's Night" returned to the Paramount for a regular 10-day run.

AUGUST 14, 1923
Owen Green Calls His Shot

Grocery salesman and golf enthusiast Owen Green teed up his golf ball on the number three hole at the Abilene Country Club and prepared his swing. Before sending his tee shot away, he joked with his fellow golfers, suggesting they credit him with managing the par three hole in only two strokes in order to save time. They declined, replying, "Nothing doing." Green stepped up to his ball and remarked, "All right then I'll just make it in one." Taking his swing, he sent the dimpled darling greensward. His astonished golf mates stood slack-jawed as the ball rolled right at the cup and then dropped in. It was the second time that Green had aced that particular hole, pulling off the same feat the year before, albeit without calling his shot.

Taco Bueno Numero Uno

Abilene brothers Tom and Bill Waugh formally opened their very first Taco Bueno at 2549 South First Street, at 10:30 a.m. in hopes that the gathered crowd might choose to order up an early lunch after Mayor Ralph Hooks snipped the red ribbon. The brothers informally opened three weeks prior to the grand opening and sold an average of 10,000 tacos each week. In addition to tacos, the menu listed burritos, chalupas, the chili burger and frijoles with onions, cheese and chili. Every item on the menu was offered at 19 cents. The restaurant provided indoor and outdoor seating accommodating up to 38 diners.

The original Taco Bueno on South First Street

Hoping to expand and even offer franchises, the brothers trademarked the name in 1967 and Taco Bueno locations soon opened in a number of southern states. In 1981, Tom and Bill Waugh cashed out, selling their chain of taco restaurants to a British company for $32.5 million.

AUGUST 16, 1953

PONY Leaguers Reach the World Series

Fifteen young Abilene All-Stars arrived early at the municipal airport for a 5 a.m. chartered flight to Pittsburgh, Pennsylvania. For several of the PONY League baseball players, walking up the steps of the DC-3 marked their first time ever on an airplane. After landing in Memphis for breakfast, the Pony Express (as players dubbed the flight) reached Pittsburgh after lunchtime. Adorned in blue jeans and cowboy hats with hat bands reading, "Greetings From Abilene, Texas," the boys received a warm welcome at the airport before taking a bus to the suburb town of Washington, site of the tournament. Outfielder, and budding entrepreneur, Clint Murphy took along a shoebox full of horned toads and did a brisk business selling baby toads at 50 cents and the full grown ones for a dollar.

The All-Star team—one of 290 teams nationwide—secured its spot for the trip eight days earlier in San Antonio when the squad of 13 and 14-year-olds won the Region 7 PONY League tournament, besting the defending national champs, San Antonio Southside, 6–2. As the five-state champions (Texas, Louisiana, Arkansas, Oklahoma and New Mexico) the Abilene boys hit, ran and fielded their way to a spot in the eight-team PONY (Protect Our Nation's Youth) League World Series. Abilene businesses and fans donated to help cover the expense and several friends and family members made the 1,400 mile drive to watch the All-Stars. The roster included many future Abilene High baseball, football and track standouts—Kenny Schmidt, Jimmy Carpenter, Stuart Peake, Pat Jones, Rob Carothers, Bruce Boyd, Butch Adams, Glynn Gregory, Gerald Lewis, Henry Pinkston, Harold Stephens, Hubert Jordan, Billy Edwards, Clint Murphy and David Hughes. Twenty-six-year-old Fred

Stirman, a teacher and coach at South Junior High School [Jefferson], managed the team with help from J.T. Boyd.

The '53 World Series tournament was only the second year for the contest and pitted the eight regional winners from across the country against one another in a double-elimination format. The Abilene boys drew Brockton, Massachusetts, runners-up in the 1952 tournament, for their first game. Back home, Abilene tuned in to KWKC to listen to the afternoon game but were disappointed as youthful nerves resulted in five errors and Abilene losing 6-1. The loss moved them into the losers bracket to face the Chicago All-Stars the following afternoon for a scheduled seven-inning contest that went 14.

The Abilene PONY League All-Stars, 1953

Pitcher Kenny Schmidt went the entire game for Abilene, giving up only seven hits and striking out 15 Chicago batters. Chicago scored a run in the first and second inning before a solo home run in the third by Abilene centerfielder Butch Adams started things off for the Abilene boys. A run in the fifth by Henry Pinkston tied the score. All remained even until the 14th when a fly ball to left field brought in a Chicago run and a heartbreaking end to the World Series run for the Abilene All-Stars. Before the boys left Pennsylvania, the Pittsburgh Pirates hosted them as their guests for a night game against the Brooklyn Dodgers. They watched as Jackie Robinson came to the plate five times, getting four hits and leading the Dodgers to a win. One week after leaving Abilene, the PONY All-Stars arrived home at 6 a.m., ten hours late due to bad weather but greeted by a crowd of proud Abilene fans.

AUGUST 17, 1977
Broadening Barrow

A standing-room-only crowd flooded the Crockett Elementary cafeteria. Most attendees were there to register their displeasure with the Texas Department of Highway and the City of Abilene's joint plan to widen S. Mockingbird Lane and Barrow Street. Increasing the street width from 50 feet to 64 feet meant several residents would lose large chunks of their front yards and 18 families would lose their homes altogether. The plan also called for rerouting Barrow through Rose Park, cutting the football field off from the rest of the park. Affected homeowners and nearby neighbors along the 2½-mile route followed up with 120 letters of protest as the controversy made a regular appearance in the pages of the *Abilene Reporter-News* and became a common topic at coffee klatches.

The weight of the decision fell on District Highway Engineer Roger Welsch who had to make a recommendation to the state office. Welsch forwarded his proposal to Austin just before Christmas of 1977. It did not please the Mockingbird/Barrow crowd. Today, the street is 64 feet wide.

Will and Wiley Remembered

The Victory Men's Bible Class (named following WWI) held its regular Sunday morning Bible study class at the Paramount Theatre. However, the group set aside the usual scripture lesson, opting instead to use class time to honor Will Rogers and Wiley Post after the pair lost their lives in an Alaskan plane crash three days before. The shock presented by their deaths was acutely felt in Abilene. Many in Abilene had recently gone to see Rogers' latest movie, "The County Chairman," at the Palace Theater. Just five months before the crash, Rogers flew into Abilene early on July 3 aboard American Airlines and took a taxi from the Abilene airport to the Hotel Wooten where he breakfasted alone on ham, eggs, California prunes, toast and coffee before strolling about the lobby. Rogers then took a taxi to Stamford in order to take in the Cowboy Rodeo and renew acquaintances with friends connected to the Simmons University Cowboy Band. The humorist had been an honorary member of the band since 1926.

Additionally, many locals knew the family of Wiley Post because he and his parents lived in Abilene from 1902 to 1907. Nena Kate Ramsey led off the service by reading the poem "Laughter Is Stilled" followed by Ed Shumway singing "He's Rounded Up in Glory." Class teacher and local attorney James Stinson presented the eulogy before class members bowed their heads in a prayer of remembrance.

The Community Bulletin

Headlined with "Another Voice Is Heard," the Community Bulletin published its first issue. The aim of the new publication was to "give minorities a chance to be heard and understood by all." The paper was available every Saturday and Sunday afternoon for ten cents at the Chicken Hut on North Treadaway or at the office on Ash Street. Issue number one carried a note of thanks to Susie Johnson for her community work, noting her commitment to the Woodson High School PTA, along with a notice that Reverend Paul Young of Antioch C.M.E. Church was leaving Abilene after seven years and moving to Dallas. An inside article reported that Mayor Ralph Hooks and Reverend Young had recently formed the Abilene Human Relations Committee to provide an official body for minorities to bring their grievances, discuss problems and seek solutions to race-related issues. The Community Bulletin ceased publication in September 1968.

No Thongs Allowed

With the start of school only a week away, a group of 65 students from Cooper and Abilene High schools gathered at Rose Park to rally for changes in the school dress code. Topics included: boy's hair length, facial hair, skirt lengths and male footwear. A few days prior to the meeting, AHS senior Dave Knight was elected spokesman for the group, but—under pressure from an AISD teacher who happened to be his mother—he withdrew from the position prior to the rally.

In addition to the 65 students, 10 adults, a lone school board member and a black puppy arrived at the park to discuss the dress rules. Under the existing code, skirts could be above the knee but not "mini," defined as five inches above the knee and causing some teachers to regularly employ rulers. One proposed solution for skirting the skirt issue was for the school board to allow girls to wear the newest fashion fad, the pantsuit. During the fall semester, the school board gave a thumbs-up for girls to wear pantsuits and gaucho pants, but the boys must still keep their hair short and, as for male footwear, thongs were not allowed. (If you do not understand "thongs" in this sense, ask your grandparents.)

AUGUST 21, 1932
Loudell Lays Down

Seven-year-old Loudell Kelly was downtown with her parents this Friday evening. As the trio walked along the Pine Street sidewalk between Third and Fourth streets, Loudell ran ahead and set out to cross the busy street, halting to allow a southbound car to pass before darting out directly in front of a northbound auto. Before her parents could shout a warning, and before the driver could slam on his brakes, Loudell sized up the situation and dropped flat on the pavement allowing the car to pass clean over her. She jumped up after the close call, hollering to her ashen-faced and astonished parents, "I'm not hurt!" The driver of the car, a man from California, stopped and immediately jumped out fearing the worst, only to see a smiling Loudell finishing her run across Pine Street.

AUGUST 22, 1882
A Better Prairie Dog Trap

Austin Palmer of Abilene received a patent for his "Apparatus for Killing Rodents" on this day. His design was specific for the extermination of rodents who burrow in the ground and, although not named, his intended victims were prairie dogs. The two-part apparatus was to be placed over the outlet of the burrow while sulphur or

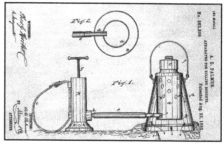

Palmer's rodent exterminator

other suitable toxic gases were then forced by pump action into the hole, suffocating the anonymous rodent.

ALSO ON THIS DAY IN 1932...
Local Luminary: Oscar Henry Cooper Dies

Famed educator Dr. Oscar Henry Cooper died in his Parramore Street home at the age of 79 and was laid to rest in the city cemetery. Cooper was born this day in Panola County, Texas. Known as "O.H.," Cooper came to Abilene from Waco in 1902, taking the reins as the fifth president of 10-year-old Simmons College. Prior to his position at Simmons, he served three years as the president of Baylor University. His abrupt departure from Baylor was prompted by his rash reaction to a student prank. Some Baylor lads snuck a dog into

Oscar Henry Cooper

chapel services being led by O.H. on the third floor of Old Main. Tucked away in a burlap bag, the dog began to yap. Infuriated by the lack of respect, Cooper grabbed the bag and tossed it out an open window. His resignation was accepted and he relocated to Abilene in the summer of 1902 to assume the presidency of Simmons. In 1909, Cooper left Simmons in order to open the Cooper Academy, a private prep school for Abilene boys but after four years he returned to campus, accepting a position as professor of philosophy and education, a job he held until his death. In 1960, 28 years following his death, Abilene school board members honored the contributions of Dr. Cooper by naming the new south side high school Oscar Henry Cooper High School.

AUGUST 23, 1930

Back Home and World Famous

The Hardin-Simmons Cowboy Band organized in 1923, but it was a trip through Europe in 1930 that turned the musicians from "The Famous Cowboy Band" to the "World Famous Cowboy Band," a descriptor that has stuck. Arriving back on campus August 23, the band boys had solidified their reputation as globally recognized showmen. The western-attired, high-struttin' band proved to be a smash hit with European crowds.

Leaving Abilene in June on a special train, the band members headed for New York where they played during a reception for Admiral Richard Byrd on his return from the South Pole. The band spent the night aboard the S.S. Leviathan before it left its berth on June 11. Their first concert at the London Palladium did not turn out to be much of a crowd-pleaser, prompting the boys to rethink their concert program.

The World Famous Cowboy Band with Simmons President Dr. Sandefer and Mrs. Sandefer, and Chief Justice Charles Evan Hughes.

They opted for a more upbeat approach comprised of feature numbers, lasso twirling, and whip cracking, which resulted in rousing, standing-room-only audiences for the remainder of the two-week tour. Concerts followed in Birmingham and Newcastle before crossing the Channel for Holland and a parade featuring "desperadoes from Texas." After playing Paris, the boys again boarded the Leviathan for the trip home, arriving this day and "World Famous."

AUGUST 24, 1942
The Love Goddess Visits

Six very willing and very lucky Camp Barkeley MPs anxiously awaited the 10:30 a.m. arrival of the Sunshine Special. The military policemen were assigned to meet 23-year-old Love Goddess Rita

Hayworth—the top pin-up girl for WWII GIs—and escort the red-headed bombshell during her two-night stay. Hayworth, on her first USO tour, was scheduled for six performances at the Army training camp just outside of Abilene and for one sold-out midnight benefit show at the Paramount Theatre. Appearing alongside Rita was Barkeley Army private and film actor Lew Ayres, known for his performances as Dr. Kildare (a role Ayres must have taken to heart as he was training at Barkeley to become a medic).

While at Camp Barkeley Miss Hayworth was drafted as an honorary member of the 357th Infantry commando platoon with the following order: "Because Rita Hayworth is truly a package of dynamite, packs the punch of T.N.T. and has the ability to slay any man with either eye, she is hereby drafted as a member of the 357th Infantry. This draft is the result of a vote by the commandos who have selected Miss Hayworth as the girl they would most like to have along when they raid Tokyo."

AUGUST 25, 1933
Stayin' Dry

Mounting the bandstand, McMurry College president James Hunt spoke to a crowd of 2,000 gathered on the Federal Lawn behind the post office where he urged voters to join with fellow Texans and oppose ratification of the Twenty-first Amendment. Also speaking out against making alcohol legal once again was President James Cox of Abilene Christian College along with a retinue of preachers. The statewide vote was scheduled for the next day.

Texans voted to implement the Twenty-first Amendment although Taylor Countians went against the grain, with 1,638 voting for legalization of alcohol and 2,479 opposed. Just as it had been since 1903, Taylor County remained dry as a bone.

AUGUST 26, 1926

The Joy in Living

An Abilene original, Roy Helen Ackers was born in nearby Pleasant Hill. Arriving in Abilene in 1938 at the age of 17, Roy Helen became part of the downtown business scene, working for attorneys and insurance men as an able assistant whose bubbly personality drew in business for her employers. Style-conscious from an early age, Roy Helen's vintage outfits, hats and brightly painted eyebrows became her signature look. Her weekly *Abilene Reporter-News* column "MizCheevus" became her alter ego. Taking on the assignment at age 79, she continued to report society news for the next 16 years. Spotting Roy Helen around Abilene was to be reminded of the joy of living. She died in 2017 at the spry age of 97.

Roy Helen Ackers

AUGUST 27, 1945

Unsung Hero: William Woodson Mitchell

At the age of 56, Bill Mitchell moved to Abilene in 1925 and began working as the caretaker of Abilene High School shortly thereafter. For 17 years, the jovial Mr. Mitchell looked after the hallways and classrooms of the school, endearing himself to the thousands of students he encountered and to whom he passed along life lessons. Mr. Mitchell planted a replacement

weeping willow on the west side of the
school in 1930 after the one near the front
walk was struck by lightning. He faithfully
tended the tree knowing that the students
enjoyed the shade and would for years to
come. Following his death in 1945 at the
age of 76, the school yearbook dedicated a
page to Mitchell captioned with, "You will
always live in the hearts of every student

William Mitchell

of Abilene High School. Your strong, firm, Christian character served as a
guide to those who knew you."

AUGUST 28, 1977

Reyes Flores Remembered

In 1977, Houston Park, located across from the city cemetery, was
renamed "Reyes Flores Park" in memory of this Abilene soldier. The park
was one in which Reyes often played as a boy and the cemetery is now his
final resting place.

The second Abilene boy to lose his life in Vietnam, Marine Private
Reyes Flores, was 21 when he was killed in 1965. (Lewis "Butch" Peterson,
18, was the first from Abilene to die in Vietnam, killed six weeks earlier by
sniper fire, 18 days after he arrived.)

Reyes Cisneros Flores, the son of Mr. and Mrs. Jesus Flores, and
a former Abilene High Eagle, lost his life in a firefight near DaNang on
October 30, 1965. Shrapnel from enemy fire ended his life as he fought to
protect a Marine outpost. Nine months earlier he had enlisted in the Marine
Corps, arriving in Vietnam in the summer as a member of Company A, 1st
Battalion, 1st Marine Regiment of the 3rd Marine Division.

Over 600 gathered for the funeral mass officiated by Father Thomas Leahy at St. Francis Catholic Church followed by the burial under rainy skies across the street in the City Cemetery. A six-man military detail fired three volleys of shots followed by a lone bugler sounding "Taps." Twelve years later, Houston Park was renamed Reyes Flores Park.

Lt. J.O. Robinson presents the family of Reyes Flores his Purple Heart, l to r, mother Josephina, brother Jesse, and father Jesus Flores, 1965

AUGUST 29, 1934

Hardin and Simmons...Nah, Too Hard to Say

Simmons University perfected the legal change of the school to become Hardin-Simmons University in August of 1934. Three months earlier the board of Abilene's oldest university unanimously agreed to change the school's name in recognition of the largest gift received to date. John and Mary Hardin of Burkburnett wrote checks totaling over $400,000, and their philanthropy was honored by changing the school name to "Hardin and Simmons University."

Because "Hardin and Simmons" was not a name combination that delightfully rolled off the tongue, the "and" was dropped and legal documents replaced it with a hyphen. It has been "Hardin-Simmons University" ever since.

Ready, Television Set, Go

TV finally arrived in Abilene in 1953 and we were ready. (People in Dallas had been watching since 1948.) If you had a set, it flickered to life at 1 p.m. on Sunday when KRBC (Reporter Broadcasting Company) began telecasting from its antenna placed atop Cedar Gap. Turning the dial to the only choice, VHF-9, you watched the dedication program broadcast live from the small station near the mountaintop transmitter.

If you did not own a set, they were available in a variety of Abilene stores, but you needed to write a sizable check to go get one. Bible Hardware was offering Motorolas for $179, the equivalent of $1,800 in 2021. At Lion Hardware they touted a "Giant 21-inch Screen!" for $200 ($2,000). Paschall's, in the Elmwood West Shopping Center, carried Packard Bell and Zenith sets, as did Busch Jewelers. Abilene Kitchen Center would let you pay out a Westinghouse set for under $9 a month or you could splurge and pick up a Philco offering "deep dimension picture" and setting you back $2,700 in today's dollars. Motorola, Admiral, RCA, Dumont, Magnavox, Raytheon and Sylvania beckoned with their soft black and white glows from a variety of retailers, including local tire dealers Connally-Stephens, Goodyear and Firestone. If you could not afford a set, you could always stand in the store to watch or loiter on the sidewalk after hours to see, but not hear.

The inaugural KRBC telecast opened with a prayer offered by Reverend Arthur Buhler of Second Christian Church followed by words from Abilene mayor Carl Gatlin and U.S. Congressman Omar Burleson, who accepted the station for the viewers of West Texas. Following the 30-minute dedication, the 1943 western titled "The Kansan" flickered on, granting that largely forgotten box-office flop the honor of being first on the Abilene small screen. Next up was a live program, "Fashions in Footwear," a half-hour show highlighting local shoe selections. A ten-minute vespers service ended the first day of programming at 10:50 p.m.

AUGUST 31, 1836
The Father of Abilene

Twin brothers Claiborne and John Merchant were born in the Republic of Texas on this day. Claiborne, better known as Clabe, came to West Texas in 1874, settling first in Callahan County where he established the "74 Ranch," before moving west in 1882 to Taylor County. With longtime partner James Parramore, the pair engaged in buying acreage and the cattle business for decades, going broke more than once. In 1880, Merchant purchased 1,700 acres in northern Taylor County, with some of that land becoming the site of Abilene in 1881.

Twin brothers John (l) and Clabe (r) Merchant

Merchant is credited with the naming of Abilene as well. Hoping the new town would become a cattle-shipping center, much like Abilene, Kansas, he suggested the name, earning for himself the nickname "Father of Abilene." Clabe and Mary Frances Merchant moved their family to Abilene in 1882 where they constructed an elaborate rock house in the 1200 block of Merchant Street. Clabe Merchant died in his home on March 9, 1926, at the age of 89.

SEPTEMBER

SEPTEMBER 1, 1887
High School Gets a Grade

In order to establish a high school operating in accordance with the University High Schools of Texas, a 10th year was added to the course of study in Abilene. Grades 7 through 10 constituted the revamped high school that met in the Riney Building along the railroad right-of-way near Sycamore Street. The building previously served as a warehouse for liquor, resulting in the school being christened as "The Beer and Ice Seminary." Professor G. W. Roach led the school, oversaw the curriculum, and taught several courses. For the 10th grade, Latin was optional. The general course of study included trigonometry, rhetoric, bookkeeping, English literature, philosophy, and a course in composition, elocution and writing.

Treasury Takes Block 20

In his role as Supervising Architect, James Knox Taylor dispatched a letter to James G. Lowdon of Abilene notifying him that the U.S. Department of the Treasury had selected Block 20 of the Original Town of Abilene as the site for the Federal Building and Post Office. Earlier in 1899, Congress authorized $75,000 for construction of a public building and 19 sites were offered to the government as a potential site—ten locations on the southside and nine north of the tracks, with prices ranging from free (N. Third and Cypress) to $10,800 for North Third and Pine. Most tracts were priced between $3,000 and $5,000. Block 20, at North Third and Pine, offered by Otto Steffens and occupied by a cotton yard, won the honor. It was the most expensive property of the 19; rather than pay the stated price, the Treasury Department instituted condemnation proceedings, ultimately paying an appraised value of $2,500.

ACC Reaches Higher Ground

After 23 years of operating their school along North First Street, the faculty and students of Abilene Christian College moved to a loftier location. The old five-acre campus moved to a 60-acre site in northeast Abilene dotted with eight buildings constructed over the previous twelve months—two dorms, an auditorium, dining hall, academy building, president's home, administration building and a gym. In 1927, the college purchased three tracts comprising a square mile of land, platting much of it as the Abilene Heights addition. The school then sold residential lots to

The new campus of Abilene Christian College, 1929

help offset the half million dollars spent on the new buildings. Lot sales opened in December of 1927, and by the end of the first week the cost of the entire property was recouped.

SEPTEMBER 4, 1922

The Nitros Take It in 17
and Give AHS a Mascot

Sixteen and a half innings of scoreless play came to a disappointing end when the Ranger Nitros brought three runs home in the top of the 17th. Unable to do the same or better in their final plate appearances, the Class D minor league Abilene Eagles handed the 1922 West Texas League championship to Ranger. The League failed to regenerate for the 1923 season but, rather than have the Abilene Eagles disappear for good, the high school adopted the eagle as its mascot. It has remained so ever since.

St. Joseph's Academy Opens

The Sisters of Divine Providence repainted and renovated the former Cooper School for Boys building (see September 6) after the Chamber of Commerce brokered a deal for the San Antonio based Catholic sisterhood to take over the two-story structure. The agreement stipulated that the new school be open to all Abilene students regardless of their religious beliefs. Doors to St. Joseph's opened September 5, 1916, with 35 students ranging from first grade through high school showing up for classes taught by Sister Philomena and five other nuns.

The high school curriculum for the Academy prescribed courses in Latin, French, German, sewing and needlework, with piano, violin and elocution offered as options. Graduates automatically gained admittance to the University of Texas. In 1920, an east wing was added to the school and in 1930, the west side received a three-story improvement which included an auditorium. The upper grades of St. Joseph's Academy moved in 1963 to a new school constructed in west Abilene and took on a new name, Central Catholic High School. The elementary remained in the original building with the last class dismissed in 1968 and the building razed months later.

St. Joseph's Academy along South Ninth Street

SEPTEMBER 6, 1909
Cooper School for Boys

Simmons College president Dr. Oscar Henry Cooper stepped down in 1909 in order to open Cooper Training School for Boys after receiving financial support from several Abilene families encouraging him to operate a prep school so Abilene boys might gain admittance to the nation's top colleges. The school first opened in the old Steffens home at North Fourth and Orange Street with 25 boys enrolled. In 1911, a two-story brick building went up along South Ninth Street between Meander and Amarillo streets. Cooper School closed in 1914 and Dr. Cooper returned to Simmons to teach. The building found new life in 1916 when the Sisters of Divine Providence in San Antonio took over the classrooms, opening St. Joseph's Academy.

SEPTEMBER 7, 1907
Local Luminary:
Rupert Norval Richardson Arrives in Abilene

The life of Dr. Rupert Richardson neatly weaves with Abilene's Hardin-Simmons University. Both were born in 1891, Rupert getting his start along Sandy Creek near Caddo in Stephens County. Rupert Richardson arrived in Abilene in September 1907 at the age of 16, enrolling at Simmons College. Upon graduating in 1912, he spent the next five years teaching at Caddo, Cisco and Sweetwater and serving in World War I. He returned to Simmons in 1917 to teach history, remaining there until his death in 1988.

Dr. Richardson held a lifetime fascination with bees, derived from an early encounter with a hive as a boy. At the age of 12, Rupert and his faithful dog, Ring, happened upon a humming hive on the family farm and the buzz of bees attracted him from then on. His annual Bee Speech—that beckoned from the start with, "Come; let us go out on a summer morning."—became an HSU tradition presented at chapel and included his admission, "Bees have been more than a hobby for me, they

Rupert Richardson
tending his beehives

have been an outlet for thought, for investigation, and really a spiritual inspiration." (When a hive of bees swarmed a car in downtown Abilene in 1953, settling on the car's steering wheel, Dr. Richardson was summoned and cleared the bees from the Chevrolet sedan.)

Richardson not only served as president of Hardin-Simmons from 1945 to 1953 but also wrote the school's history in a book of personal reflection titled "Famous Are Thy Halls." Other books include, "Adventuring with a Purpose: Life Story of Arthur Lee Wasson," "The Frontier of Northwest Texas," and "Colonel Edward M. House: The Texas Years." His seminal works were, "The Comanche Barrier to South Plains Settlement," and "Texas: The Lone Star State," a favored college textbook. In 1942, HSU bestowed an honorary Doctor of Literature degree on Richardson. Abilene's most venerated historian died on April 14, 1988, two weeks shy of his 97th birthday.

Wrong Way Comes Our Way

With news that the famously lost aviator, Douglas "Wrong Way" Corrigan—fresh off his July 18th wrong way flight from New York to Ireland (his flight plan called for a trip to California from New York)—was scheduled to visit Big Spring as part of a publicity tour, the Abilene Booster Club set out to land Corrigan for a visit. Club secretary E.G. Wood got on the phone to the Kansas City airport where Corrigan was soon due and was holding the line when Corrigan landed, but the flyer could not make it to the phone due to the welcoming crowd. Persistently, Wood phoned the hotel and was again on the line when Corrigan came into the lobby an hour after landing. However, once more, the famous aviator could not be bothered to take the call. Calculating that Corrigan would eat dinner and return to his hotel late, Wood rang up the hotel at 10:30 p.m., finally reaching his elusive quarry. Corrigan agreed, he would stop by Abilene.

Three days later, "Wrong Way" took off from Fort Worth at 7:45, landing at the Abilene airport at 9:32 a.m., piloting the same plane in which he had crossed the Atlantic. Climbing into George Harris' two-fronted car, Corrigan paraded down

Famed Flyer Douglas Corrigan parades along North Third

Chestnut, Pine and Cypress—led by a homemade plane flying in reverse—before arriving at the Hotel Wooten for a late breakfast with 250 guests, including some relatives who drove in from Rising Star. The good-humored Corrigan drank lemonade, telling the crowd he never ate breakfast, and he accepted the Abilene Booster Club gift of a watch geared to run in reverse. Escorted back to the airport, Corrigan oversaw his tank being topped off before lifting off at 11:06 headed west toward Big Spring.

SEPTEMBER 9, 1969

The Coliseum Opens

Grand opening duties for the Taylor County Coliseum were handled by three lovely young ladies: the Texas Hereford Queen, the West Texas Fair Sweetheart, and Miss Wool and Mohair. The ladies joined County Judge Roy Skaggs in snipping the red ribbon to formally open the new facility. Although work was still underway outside, the interior work was complete and ready to host the 1969 fair. County commissioners heaped praise on the dedication of contractor Oscar Rose in pushing the huge project to completion, noting that just minutes earlier the commissioners witnessed Mrs. Rose tending to last minute chores, sweeping out the coliseum.

SEPTEMBER 10, 1889

A Better Dish Dryer

Alice Wilson of Abilene received U.S. Patent No. 410,818 for her "new and improved dish-drier." The aim of the invention was "to save the work of wiping dishes." Her application explained that, once the dishes are washed, they are placed in the drier and hot water is poured over them prior to placing the lid in place and shaking with care. The

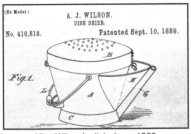

Alice Wilson's dish dryer, 1889

remaining heat "will dry the dish without further labor and with a better and glossier appearance than can be produced by wiping." The spout-like side piece was for insertion of cutlery. It is unknown if Alice Wilson retired to live a life of wealth and leisure.

SEPTEMBER 11, 1953

Moser Wins Opener, Again

Seventy-five hundred fans packed Fair Park Stadium to cheer the 8 p.m. opening kickoff of the high school season and to witness the Abilene coaching debut of Charles "Chuck" Moser. With only eight returning lettermen, the hope among the Eagle faithful was that the Abilene boys could hang close with the visiting Scotties of Highland Park. Coach Moser had nine years of coaching under his belt—two years in Missouri and seven in McAllen—before he was hired to replace Coach Pete Shotwell at a salary of $7,000. Moser had yet to lose a season-opener, but the September 11 matchup had all the makings of a streak-ender.

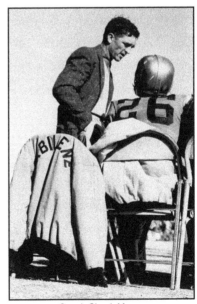

Coach Chuck Moser

The Eagles were outweighed on the line, had lost senior tackle Bobby Jack Oliver to a dislocated shoulder, and were facing Highland Park's highly capable quarterback, Syd Carter. Known for meticulous planning and practice, Coach Moser was also a master of surprise. A first quarter punt by Highland Park came to halfback Jimmy Millerman who faked a handoff to Don Rohden before racing 41 yards for a score. When the Scotties fumbled the ensuing kickoff, the Eagles needed just one play for Wendall Phillips to score on a 42 yard run. A touchdown pass in the second quarter and another score from Phillips in the fourth provided Coach Moser with his first Abilene win, 28-13 and extended his opening-game win streak.

Chuck Moser would spend the next seven seasons coaching the Abilene Eagles, leading them to become one of the winningest teams in Texas history and inspiring a long line of players who gave their heart to play for him. His last season opening game as a high school coach came on September 11, 1959, in the first game held at the new Abilene Public Schools Stadium [Shotwell Stadium]. A fumble recovery by AHS Eagle Dave Parks sealed the 14-12 win over state-ranked San Antonio Jefferson. Moser compiled a 141-28-2 in his career and retired as head coach in 1960 having never lost an opening game.

ACU Takes Baby Steps

Childer's Classical Institute opened with 25 students and more than 200 guests present. The school's aim was to "teach the Bible and build character." W.H. Free led the new school in singing, "All Hail the Power of Jesus's Name," a tradition observed at the opening of Abilene Christian University every year since.

SEPTEMBER 12, 1960
Cooper Welcomes Coogs

Students had to do some hunting for their proper classrooms as school at Cooper High took place for the first time on Monday, September 12, 1960, with more than 1,200 Cougars arriving at the new south side campus. For the inaugural year, the campus served as a junior-senior high school with the student body comprised of grades seven through eleven. All Abilene seniors remained at Abilene High. The Cooper junior high students departed the following year with the completion of Madison Junior High. Despite a non-functioning bell system, an intercom on the fritz, and no air-conditioning, opening day was considered a success. The cafeteria and gym needed final touches, forcing the Friday pep rally to be an outdoor affair. The unbeaten and untied Coogs (the team had only one game under its belt, a slim 15-14 victory over Baird) were preparing to take on Clyde.

The library opened a month after school started, and the auditorium was only in the early construction phase. The overall project ranked as the most expensive undertaking in Abilene school history, costing $2.7 million. The nine-building campus spread out over a 46-acre site, and architect Jack Luther designed the circular library with its distinctive umbrella roof as the campus hub. Student parking was placed near the buildings on the east and west sides of campus, attempting to avoid the mistake six years before of situating the Abilene High parking lot across a busy street.

SEPTEMBER 13, 1892

Opening of Simmons College

The start of Simmons College came a year later than the original plan; nevertheless, the school got off to a rousing start on a bright, cool Tuesday morning in September of 1892. It was a resolution by the Sweetwater Baptist Association (covering West Texas from Eastland to El Paso) that awarded the school to Abilene following the donation of land by hardware merchant George Phillips and two Fort Worth real estate investors, Emory Ambler and Theodore Vogel. To honor their donation, the southern and northern streets bordering the campus took on their names. Neither Ambler nor Vogel were Baptist; both were Episcopalian. The fulfillment of the Abilene dream opened with a song by school president William Friley accompanied by two of his daughters and two other female students. The overflow crowd then rose in the auditorium and sang "Jesus, Lover of My Soul" followed by a prayer offered by Dr. Blair of Merkel. Reverend R.T. Hanks, the school's residential pastor, then brought the opening address. The dedicatory service closed with the singing of "Nearer my God to Thee."

SEPTEMBER 14, 1958

Truth or Consequences

Bob Barker drew in over 10,000 who crowded around the outdoor stage at the West Texas Fair hoping to be called up to play Truth or Consequences. Although not televised, the game show crowd's enthusiasm was high as thousands raised their hands when Barker asked for volunteers from the "studio audience." Abilenians Jerry Cantrell and Herman Bridges were selected from the throng and faced Barker's question, "What did Eli Whitney say to his wife?" As expected, neither contestant offered the correct answer—"Keep your cotton-pickin' fingers out of my gin." The consequence? A "horse race" involving inner tubes. Cantrell won the race and the prize, a watch.

Ivan Bonham was called up next and again missed his question. The consequence was for a blindfolded Bonham to test who kissed the best—blonde Kay Graham, redhead Betty Richie, or brunette Martha Lightfoot? Puckering without peeking, Bonham judged that redheaded Richie offered the top smackeroo. Once he regained his vision, Ivan learned that all three kisses came from his none-too-pleased wife, Darlene.

Sally Shepherd and Patricia Hartman, both 13, could not guess why a locomotive cannot sit down. (It has a tender behind.) They then attempted to move helium-filled balloons across the stage using a paddle. After several minutes, Barker called the race a tie since the West Texas wind made finishing all but impossible.

SEPTEMBER 15, 1924
The West Texas Baptist Sanitarium

The West Texas Baptist Sanitarium opened its doors for the people of Abilene and the surrounding area, ready to treat any person regardless of race or religion. Just one day earlier, an open house drew over 1,200 who came to tour the much anticipated hospital. Visitors were told that the hospital had been built far enough from the railroad tracks so passing trains would be no bother to the patients. The five-story building provided 75 beds along with two rooms for the treatment of cancer and three operating rooms—two for major surgeries and one for eye, ear, nose and throat procedures.

The hospital opened with a staff of 10 nurses, and 18 Abilene doctors were afforded privileges. On opening day, 11 patients were admitted and six operations performed, with the first surgery

The West Texas Baptist Sanitarium in 1924

patient being Mr. Gabriel Paxton, the 80-year-old father of hospital board member George Paxton. The board agreed that, in the spirit of charity, there would be no charge for the surgery. In 1936, the West Texas Baptist Sanitarium was renamed Hendrick Memorial Hospital.

SEPTEMBER 16, 1946
Miracle in the Maize Field

Attempting to keep the Pacific National airliner aloft, Captain R. M. Krieg radioed the Abilene airport after11 p.m. alerting the tower that he lost both engines and was hoping to glide his crippled DC-3 in for an emergency landing. He did not make it.

In addition to the three-man crew, there were 21 passengers on board, nearly all of whom were heading home following military discharge or were sailors on leave for the first time in two years. The charter flight left San Diego at 4 o'clock en route to New York and had already stopped in El Paso before heading for a scheduled stop in Dallas. Krieg had been a pilot for seven years while co-pilot Judd Reed, a former test pilot, had been flying for 16. The third crew member, R.J. Rentschler flew B-24s in the war.

At 11:47, just east of Sweetwater, the left engine developed trouble with a runaway propeller. Krieg, Reed and Rentschler struggled to unravel the problem before finally deciding to shut off the engine, causing the right engine to have the same difficulty. Visible in the distance were the lights of Abilene, but with both engines now out, and the airport nearly 30 miles away, Krieg radioed the tower but was doubtful of making it that far. In fact, the only choice for Captain Krieg was to set the plane down in the inky darkness. Slowly descending, he hoped that whatever lay beneath, was smooth ground. Passengers were told to fasten their seat belts, but were not told that the landing was not at an airport.

A 100-acre maize field on the Lewis Kinsey farm, 11 miles east of Sweetwater—encircled by trees and heavy brush with a power line nearby—served as the landing spot. With the landing gear up, Captain Krieg skillfully set the tail down first, before belly landing to a rough stop, blindly managing to miss the deep gullies and nearby low rocky hills. One of the plane's propellers tore loose, gashing the right wing, missing the gas tank—still carrying over 600 gallons—by inches. After skidding to a stop, passengers quickly disembarked and were quite surprised to find themselves in a field of maize. Several of the war veterans mentioned they assumed the plane was just landing at a poorly lit airfield. No one sustained as much as a scratch. Rentschler and three passengers hiked a mile and a half to reach the highway, hailing a passing motorist who took them to Sweetwater. Taxis were dispatched to bring the passengers to town, which, much to their chagrin, was in a dry county.

Diez y Seis Boom

Scores of Abilene citizens were jolted awake at dawn by an unusually large explosion and quickly jammed the phone lines calling the police to report the bed-rattling burst. Forewarned, the police explained it was a 21-blast dynamite salute set off as part of the three day Diez y Seis celebration, or Mexican Independence Day. Nerves did not easily quell as, near simultaneously, fire trucks raced to a cotton gin fire on Locust Street. The blast marked a day of activities including a parade at 3 p.m. followed by speeches, singing the Mexican national anthem and the "Star Spangled Banner." At Carver Park, Mayor Roscoe Blankenship crowned Lucia Barrera as queen of the festivities, and ACU Professor J.W. Treat addressed the crowd, congratulating them on their "double national inheritance of freedom."

SEPTEMBER 17, 1966
Local Luminary: Clyde "Bulldog" Turner

Former center for the Hardin-Simmons Cowboys, Clyde Turner was inducted into the NFL Hall of Fame this day. Turner played for HSU from 1937 to 1939 and earned his "Bulldog" nickname after a picture of him hoisting a calf on his shoulders gained him national attention. Following graduation, Bulldog was drafted by the Chicago Bears. He played center for 13 seasons, was selected All-Pro eight times, and was part of four NFL championships. Turner was selected as a member of the 1940s NFL All-Decade Team and is ranked as one of the 100 greatest Bears of all time, with the team retiring his jersey—number 66.

In 1953, Turner left pro football and accepted a coaching position with Baylor before returning to help coach the Chicago Bears and finally the New York Titans. Clyde "Bulldog" Turner died in 1998 at the age of 79. He is buried in Gatesville, Texas.

Clyde "Bulldog" Turner

SEPTEMBER 18, 1961
Page One Begins Its Run

The morning edition of the *Abilene Reporter-News* began running a front-page column by Katharyn Duff titled "Page One." Duff's column would run for the next 18 years. The Rotan native and HSU alumna joined the staff of the *Abilene Reporter-News* in 1943, remaining there for 37 years and holding every reporter's beat before being named assistant editor in 1957. Along the way, Duff won numerous awards from the Texas Associated Press and received the Thomas L. Stokes Award for her contribution in bringing conservation of natural resources to the nation's attention. She enjoyed local history and produced a wide-ranging book titled "On Catclaw Creek" followed

New Tomorrow: 'Page One'

The Abilene Reporter-News Monday morning will begin a new front page column, called Page One.

It will be written by Assistant Editor Katharyn Duff, and will appear each morning Monday through Friday.

It will be a column of diversified interests and topics dealing with people, events and situations over the West Central Texas region served by The Reporter-News.

Watch for it beginning tomorrow morning!

Katharyn Duff

Front page notice announcing Page One

by "Catclaw Country: An Informal History of Abilene in West Texas."

Duff's sense of humor, eye for detail, and ability to turn the mundane into a captivating tale became a morning staple for many Abilenians, making "Page One" the first place thousands turned to at the start of their day. Her column first ran this day in 1961 and continued right up to her retirement in 1979. The initial column took a look at local stock investment clubs and their popularity among Abilene housewives. Katharyn Duff passed away in 1995 at the age of 80.

SEPTEMBER 19, 1944
Near Miss

A wave of bombers took off from Ardmore, Oklahoma, headed for Abilene in a simulated attack on the Abilene Army Air Base. Just before 10 a.m., P-47 Thunderbolt fighters from the base west of Abilene scrambled to intercept the faux enemy aircraft. Leading the P-47 squadron formation was 24-year-old Lieutenant Thomas Toedt who made a pass at one of the bombers that caused his fighter to fall into a violent spin at 20,000 feet. With no hope of regaining control, Toedt rode the spiraling plane several thousand feet before bailing out. His parachute guided him to a landing near Catclaw Creek just north of Sunset Motor Lodge on South First Street. As he floated earthward, his pilotless plane roared down, hitting the pavement at South 11th and Sayles with a tremendous explosion.

Barely missing the home of Mr. and Mrs. Harold Austin at 1041 Sayles, the impact created a hole several feet wide and two feet deep. The plane miraculously missed houses, cars and people as well as nearby Alta Vista Elementary School. Flaming wreckage hurtled into yards, causing one parked car to catch on fire. The largest piece of the plane came to rest near the Sayles home of Dr. and Mrs. Guy Patillo with engine parts launched onto their roof. The plane's control panel landed in the backyard of the Ross Jennings home at 941 Sayles. (Mrs. Jennings noted to a reporter that 13 years earlier her car was narrowly missed by Amelia Earhart's crashing auto-gyro at the Abilene airport.) More wreckage was strewn across a vacant lot near the corner of South 11th and Sayles.

Against the pleas of their teachers, scores of Alta Vista students ran the half-block to survey the scene. Many Alta Vista Roosters went home that afternoon with pieces of the P-47 stuffed in their pockets.

SEPTEMBER 20, 1923
McMurry Starts

The McMurry auditorium filled to capacity and then some as extra chairs were brought in to handle the crowd assembled to witness

Old Main at McMurry College, 1923

McMurry College set sail. In a chivalrous show of support for all Abilene college students, prior to the start of the program, the inaugural McMurry student body gave a yell

for McMurry, Simmons College and Abilene Christian. The audience stood to sing "America" before Methodist elder W. M. Lane offered the invocation followed by a reading of Proverbs 3:13-26 beginning, "Happy is the man that findeth wisdom, and the man that getteth understanding." Abilene mayor Charles Coombes welcomed the college, followed by the president of Simmons College. The *McMurry Bulletin*, a student newspaper, was available and carried an anonymous poem titled, "I'm Goin' To McMurry," the opening verses being;

> I have washed my overalls and patched my old brogans,
>
> And trimmed my fingernails and soaped and scrubbed my hands.
>
> I'm freckle-faced and Roman-nosed and I'll admit I'm green,
>
> But I'm goin' to that college they have built in Abilene.

SEPTEMBER 21, 1885
Denominational Duel

In September of 1885, the Abilene faithful publically squared off against one another. Well-known Baptist evangelist William Evander Penn came to Abilene to preach a revival; however, during his Abilene sermons, the pulpit-pounding Penn intimated that local Church of Christ preachers were guilty of requiring baptism for salvation. In an open letter addressed to Abilene Baptists and published in the *Abilene Daily Reporter*, the elders of the Church of Christ tossed down the gauntlet and challenged Reverend Penn to a debate. The evangelist was given 20 days to respond to the challenge. Penn wasted no time, replying the following day with a scriptural spear taken from Nehemiah, chapter 6, in which Nehemiah replies to his enemies: "I am doing a great work so that I cannot come; why should I leave it and come down to you?" Touchè.

SEPTEMBER 22, 1909
Hotel Grace Sets Out the Welcome Mat

At noon, the doors were unlocked and the curtains drawn back, welcoming all into the Hotel Grace. Across the street, a khaki-clad crier stood alongside the train tracks beckoning visitors to walk across North 1st and register at Mr. Beckham's new hotel. Employees lined the lobby ready to attend to the guests, and within an hour of opening, 13 travelers signed the hotel register, with L.B. Ellis of Ft. Worth coming in as guest number one. Other guests hailed from Chicago, New Orleans and Omaha. Three Grace first-nighters were from Merkel and two from Ballinger.

SEPTEMBER 23, 1997
My, My Myrtle!

Myrtle's sultry curves and coy come-hither posture were the talk of the town as 10 hot pink billboards showing her sensuous likeness went up across town. Alongside Myrtle's sexy shape was the tagline, "Myrtle's Coming! Get Your Bed Ready!" While some saw the ad campaign as cleverly innocent, others saw it as an overt reference to s-e-x. The intent was to arouse interest in planting crape myrtle trees

The billboard that stirred Abilene passions

and bushes in order to beautify the city. Abilene Clean and Proud, led by Donna Albus, hoped to inspire Abilenians to plant over 5,000 crape myrtles in their (flower)beds. But, once Myrtle went up, orders flooded in, and the effort sold more than 8,300 of the bright-blossomed plants...with their smooth limbs, inviting fragrance, and bosomy boughs.

It Takes Two to Race

On a day when Fair officials from the Pickles and Jelly Department bestowed honors in 39 categories, the real Fair excitement was centered on the first ever Abilene automobile race. The contest had only two entrants: W.A. Coggins of Colorado City, driving his two-cylinder Buick, lined up against a three-cylinder Ford out of Rotan piloted by W. O. Hubbard.

The race consisted of four laps around the half-mile Lytle Lake track adjacent to the fairgrounds. Coggins managed to keep his Buick out front for most of the dusty race, but in a dramatic finish Hubbard's Ford nosed ahead only yards from the line. Hubbard also established an original track record, covering the two miles in 4 minutes and 18 seconds.

In the other big show, Mrs. Jesse Scott edged past Lady Vandenbark for Best Sweet Pickle honors while Lavinia McDaniel made a remarkable showing, sweeping the field in Canned Pears, Pepper Mangoes and Tomato Catsup and bringing home silver in Canned Peaches, Apricots and Best Chili Sauce.

Plotkin Paintings

The West Texas Fair showcased paintings by Peter Plotkin, a Russian-born artist who taught at Simmons University from 1929 until 1931 before moving to Los Angeles. Seven large canvasses were shown, including two portraits of Robert E. Lee with his horse, Traveler, and scenes such as "The Raising of Jarius' Daughter" and "A Texas Stampede," which later hung behind the front desk of the Hotel Grace. A full-length portrait of Stonewall Jackson and smaller ones of Dr. J.D. Sandefer, Simmons president, and McMurry's Dr. J.W. Hunt were exhibited next to one of Sam Houston on his horse. For over 25 years, the full-length portrait of Sam Houston and one of the Robert E. Lee canvases framed the stage at Abilene High School.

SEPTEMBER 26, 1927

The Lone Eagle Lands, Twice

Just four months after his epic Atlantic crossing, Charles Lindbergh flew into town piloting his famous Spirit of St. Louis under partly cloudy skies and a brisk wind onto the grass landing strip at Kinsolving Field just before 9:30 a.m. Fooling the crowd looking westward, he unexpectedly arrived from the east, having flown to Abilene from Santa Fe, New Mexico.

The Abilene crowd cheered as the Spirit of St. Louis taxied to a stop and the trans-Atlantic flyer climbed out. The first thing Lindy did was sign the field book, leaning the register against the side of his airship. Escorted to a waiting car, Lindbergh declined to take a seat on a throne-like chair attached to the rear of the car. The chair was quickly dispatched and Lindbergh climbed into the backseat of the open car, inviting his escort for the day, native Abilenian and First Lady of Texas Mildred Paxton Moody, to sit next to him for the parade into town.

A 74-car procession brought the Lone Eagle along a three-mile parade route to the downtown Federal Building. An estimated 30,000 Abilenians (essentially the entire population), along with 40,000 out-of-towners, gathered at the airport, along the parade route, and massed

downtown to greet
and gawk at the
lanky young flyer,
the most acclaimed
and   eminent
person alive at the
time. Schools and
college classes were
cancelled as every
business shuttered

Charles Lindbergh in the backseat next to Mildred Moody. Abilene mayor Hayden in front passenger seat with Louis Derryberry driving

in order to glimpse the most esteemed Abilene visitor.

Downtown, the star-struck throng pressed in to hear his speech from the bandstand following an introduction by the First Lady, who invited the "Columbus of the air" to speak. With his famous half-shy smile, Lindbergh blushed, waiting for the applause to subside, before giving a five-minute speech about the future of aviation. Having requested that he not have to shake hands, Lindy was surprised when Mayor Hayden then invited the crowd up to shake the hand of a startled Lindy. After several minutes, he politely begged off, saying, "Thanks, I've got to quit." Mrs. Moody hustled Lindbergh into her father's car, driving him back to the airfield. Following a 90-minute Abilene visit, Lindy lifted off for Fort Worth.

A year and a half after Lucky Lindy dropped in on Abilene, he made a second visit, this one unexpected. It was on a slow Saturday in February of 1929 when Charles Lindbergh landed once more at Kinsolving Field, this time in a black and orange Travelair. On this occasion, it was only the airport manager and a lone field attendant greeting the famous flyer. Mr. Johnson, the attendant, upon seeing the pilot emerge, thought, "This guy looks like Lindbergh. But it can't be." As Johnson began servicing the plane, it dawned on him that indeed the heralded hero was standing before him. After fueling the plane with 30 gallons of gas, Lindy climbed back in and flew south, destination unknown. Signing the field register on this trip, Lindy filled in all information—arrival time, plane type, owner, tail number, name of pilot and license number, origin of flight— but left "destination" blank. It later became apparent, love-struck Lindy was heading for Mexico City to be with his fiancee, Anne Morrow.

SEPTEMBER 27, 1946
Parallel Parking Creates Parallel Arguments

The Abilene City Commission ordered that parking along Cypress Street from North First to North Fifth would immediately convert from "head in" to "parallel." Downtown merchants quickly cried foul, requesting the commission study the situation further and consider the effect such a parking change would have on businesses. Store owners complained that parking parallel cut available space in half, robbing them of potential customers. Commissioners agreed to postpone any further action on parking for two weeks.

The anti-parallel crowd made strong headway with the public, or at least with that portion of the public who took time to write the newspaper editor. A straw poll taken by merchants showed over 500 opposed to parallel parking and only 20 in favor. At a heated meeting three days before the final vote, one store owner warned the commissioners, "If you put in parallel parking, you won't be re-elected!" To which one commissioner replied, "If it's up to you to re-elect me, I don't want to be elected." Three days later, commissioners voted to go ahead with parallel parking.

In 1959, Abilene abandoned parallel parking downtown. Head-in seems to work just fine.

SEPTEMBER 28, 1960
In the Driver's Hot Seat

Abilene police issued 27 traffic tickets (a ticket book only held 25 forms) to one local driver who managed to rack up $1,350 in fines. Appearing before Judge Don Wilson, the 27-year-old asked if he might wait to enter a plea as he needed to think about things. Wilson promptly sent him to jail so that he might think. The night before, five patrol cars pursued the driver in his 1941 Ford for 15 minutes. The chase began when he burned rubber leaving Casey's Drive-In on North Treadaway and, after reaching speeds up to 100 miles an hour, ended when the souped-up sedan hit the curb at Vogel and Pine. Officers issued five speeding tickets, eight citations for running stop signs and red lights, three more for failure to yield the right of way, six for driving on the wrong side of the street, four for driving without headlights and one for burning rubber.

The driver pled guilty to 13 of the offenses and the court agreed to drop the others. In order to pay the fine, he sold his car.

SEPTEMBER 29, 1962
Diablo Jr. Goes to Hamby

Three weeks earlier, Duncan Renaldo—much better known as the early-1960s television star Cisco Kid—helped launch the opening of the Westgate Shopping Capital. Cisco and his horse Diablo were on hand to pass out autographed photos (Cisco did most of the passing out) while the Westgate merchants offered unlimited chances to sign up and win a brown and white pony that Cisco dubbed Diablo Jr. The Westgate pony drawing took place on September 29 and Marcia Esman, 9, of Hamby was the winner of Diablo Jr., who came with a saddle and bridle to boot.

SEPTEMBER 30, 1971
Freedom of Speech

Seniors in Cecil Springer's honors English class at Abilene High penned letters to the newspaper editor with 13 printed in today's edition and a promise to print more throughout the school year. The student letter writers covered the waterfront when it came to topics worth addressing or in passing out a good ol' fashioned finger wagging. Future AHS baseball coach Jim Reese expressed his displeasure at those who voted down a recent school bond, calling such naysayers selfish. Carol Snell and Margaret Sanders were both hot about the school's poor-performing air-conditioning system. Snell pointed out that it was difficult to concentrate in the stifling heat, rhetorically adding, "Doesn't anyone care?"

Diane Jividen pointed out that some convicted murderers received very light sentences while Cindi Herndon urged citizens to turn to prayer as a means of aiding the fight against a range of world problems. Bobbie Hatfield filed her complaint about the lack of newsprint devoted to the band as compared to ink detailing the football squad. Sherry Hansen branched out even further, claiming the newspaper showed a clear favoritism for Cooper over AHS. Most constructive of all was Jeannie Lewis who asked the city to consider installing more count-down stop lights, like the one on North Mockingbird, that showed the time remaining before the light changed.

OCTOBER

An Increasingly Expensive Evening in Abilene

The Abilene Restaurant Association sponsored its third food fest at the Civic Center. Dubbed as "An Evening in Abilene," some 1,200 shelled out $3.50 to sample the offerings. Tickets for the first "Evening," held in January of 1973, had sold for $1. The price for the second "Evening" buffet, held in September of that same year, cost $2.50 a head. Tickets for the 1975 Evening in Abilene rose to $4.

The 1974 edition featured Eddie Barton's Cafeteria handing out salads to complement steaks grilled by Towne Crier, Golden Stage Coach, and Saddle & Sirloin. The Westico truck stop was serving up chili, while Poco Peso handed out sopapillas. The Buffalo Gap Steak House enticed with its onion rings and you could wash it all down with milk provided by Gandy's and Foremost. Except for Gandy's, none of those old Abilene favorites remains in business.

In 1976, the event took on a name change, becoming "A Taste of Abilene." Tickets rose to $5. By 2019, they were $40 for general admission and $125 for the VIP package.

OCTOBER 2, 1938
Dam Ready

The 85-foot-high Fort Phantom Hill dam, blocking the free flow of Elm Creek, was finished and awaiting rainfall to drop down and back up behind the 3,800-foot-long barrier. Two months earlier, with the work not yet complete, heavy rains nearly spelled disaster as a rapidly rising lake filled with five million gallons of water to a depth of 45 feet and threatening to pour through an unfinished gap. The rising waters subsided and the reservoir project was completed.

Work on the Phantom Hill dam

The idea for the lake first arose in 1929 with the city purchasing hundreds of acres. The Great Depression squeezed financial resources, setting the project on the back burner. In 1936, Abilenians felt that the project had to move forward and, by a slim 150 votes, a $600,000 bond to pay for the dam passed. By 1939, the lake was nearly full.

OCTOBER 3, 1918
No News is Bad News

The daily offering of the *Abilene Daily Reporter* was scant indeed on this day, only four pages, making it almost impossible for delivery boys to gain any real throwing distance. Page one carried an explanation for the lack of news, advising that the entire newspaper workforce was out sick except for the editor and two women working in the front office. The lone editor wrote that the sickness and symptoms were consistent among the absentee staff and noted that many doctors were referring to the illness as the Spanish flu.

The only local news, if you can call it that, was a front-page story recounting that the Lions Club was treated to a program by H.P. Maddry who yodeled "Sleep Baby Sleep" followed by an encore of "Wilson's Lullaby." Things had not improved by the next day as another four-page edition went out with management promising the best service possible under the trying conditions. With fevers breaking and some staff up and about by the 6th, the press managed to churn out a paltry 14-page Sunday edition.

OCTOBER 4, 1930
Class Privileges

McMurry College advised that female students living in a college hall were subject to certain rules and regulations determined by one's classification. Freshmen ladies were allowed two weekend dates a month; however, if the date was off campus the couple had to be accompanied by a chaperone unless the outing involved two or more couples. Sophomore girls were also allowed two weekend dates a month with the added bonus of one weeknight date. Juniors earned weekend date privileges plus two extra nights Monday through Friday. In a stroke of retention genius, senior ladies, and any co-ed over age twenty, were allowed "discretionary privileges," i.e. date to your heart's content. Regardless of classification, failure to report to the dorm hostess within 15 minutes after an evening ball game was put down as a date. Should a young lady wish to see a non-McMurry lad, her parents would need to write to the dorm hostess advising all was on the up and up. All girls were expected to refrain from dating during exam week.

A Red-Letter Bible Day

On this Sunday afternoon, the campus of McMurry College was a beehive of excitement as a citywide bash took place to celebrate the first new translation of the Bible since King James set one in motion back in 1611. In the new Revised Standard translation, second-person pronouns such as "thou", "thee" and "thy" no longer applied to mortal man, only in reference to Deity. And, mankind no longer "didst" anything, only "did." Copies of the newest Bible were given to the local college libraries, along with one for Abilene High. Also leaving the party with complimentary copies were the retired pastors of the largest local Baptist, Presbyterian, Christian and Methodist congregations. (In 1989, the New Revised Standard edition superseded the 1952 Revised Standard. Abilene sat that book release out.)

Penny the Pachyderm

Penny the elephant was a gift from the Abilene Woman's Republican Club to the Abilene Zoo. It was Penny Hunt, age 5, of State Street who suggested the name, writing "My name is Penny and I go to first grade. I would like to name the new elephant Penny because all the boys and girls will bring a penny to help pay for the baby elephant's food." (Some speculated that was not *Penny* Hunt's true motivation.)

Penny arrived in 1965, taking up residence in the former cage of Charlie the Chimp who had been shipped off to Brownwood after years of causing a long list of trouble. The baby elephant's long trip originated in Kenya, first sailing up the Red Sea on a freighter, then passing through the Suez Canal, across the Mediterranean and the Atlantic before arriving in New York. Penny then flew to Dallas on a Braniff cargo plane landing at Love Field. In order

Penny in Charlie the chimp's old cage

to complete her long journey from Africa to Abilene, a modified trash truck was dispatched to Dallas to transport Penny to the zoo at Fair Park. One of the zoo employees rode in the back of the truck with the crated pachyderm to keep her calm.

Six years later, Penny was sold to the Kansas City zoo.

OCTOBER 7, 1909
First Cadillac

At a time when the average annual income in the United states was $574, George Paxton, president of Citizens National Bank, plunked down $1,850 ($51,550 in 2020 dollars) to take home Abilene's first Cadillac. The luxury car was a 1910 Model-Thirty, so named because it boasted a 35-horsepower engine. It also came equipped with acetylene-gas headlamps, a windshield, horn, tools, and a tire repair kit and touted under the slogan, "You can kill a horse, but not a Cadillac." Upon

George Paxton's Cadillac with daughters in the front seat and son George Jr. standing alongside

its arrival by freight train, local auto dealers Will and John Spaulding accepted delivery and took the Model-Thirty to their South First Street garage where it was temporarily put on display before Mr. Paxton drove it away. Eight months later, Paxton sold the car to a man from Colorado City. Unable to bear life without such a machine, Paxton bought his second Cadillac in July of 1910.

OCTOBER 8, 1917
Elevator Thrill

Citizens National Bank threw open the doors to its new four-story bank building at the corner of Pine and North First Street. The bank building introduced Abilenians to the elevator and drew folks in from near and far just to experience that minor thrill. Tenants on the upper floors began luring visitors with newspaper ads inviting clients to "come ride the elevator" to our offices.

OCTOBER 9, 1974
King-sized Crowd

A sellout crowd of 8,606 skipped Wednesday night prayer meeting, shelled out up to $10 a ticket, and headed to the Taylor County Coliseum to swoon, sway, shriek and soak up the swinging energy of Sir Swivel Hips. Elvis was in town. The King of Rock-n-Roll drew 273 more ticket-buyers than the previous coliseum record-holder, Lawrence Welk. (Presumably, audience crossover was minimal.) One of Presley's band members reported that the Taylor County venue was the second smallest he could remember. The night before, Elvis performed before 10,000 in San Antonio.

Following three warm-up acts, the Memphis Flash finally took the stage at 9:30, putting Abilene police on their toes as they tried to maintain decorum amongst the Abilene's fairer sex who were elbowing in close. For the occasion, Elvis opted to wear a white suit, trimmed with metal studs and sporting a belt buckle on par with a West Texas rodeoer. Around his neck glinted a rhinestone cross (perhaps a nod to his recently recorded—soon to be Grammy-winning—version of "How Great Thou Art.") Throughout, he accessorized with a series of silk scarves, successively used to mop his famous brow, then tossing each in the general direction of a female jumble, much akin to pitching meat near a pride of lions.

At one point Elvis knelt down and bestowed the thrill of a lifetime to one young Abilene admirer, a peck on the cheek. He cranked things up with "See See Rider" then knocked off "All Shook Up," "Don't Be Cruel" and "Heartbreak Hotel." The lead backup singer for the

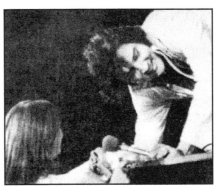

Elvis greeting an Abilene fan at his 1974 concert

entourage was former Abilenian and AHS graduate Kathy Westmoreland (her sister sang backup for Bobby Vinton) who had earlier gained some screen time, appearing in the movie "Elvis on Tour." Thirty-nine year-old Elvis ended his 60-minute Abilene songfest with "I Can't Help Falling In Love With You," offering those pouty eyes throughout.

Postscript: Elvis returned to the Taylor County Coliseum in March of 1977. On that trip, he interfered with Sunday night church, likely resulting in a reduced crowd of 7,500 who forked over as much as $15 for a ticket. Feeling his age at 42, he took the stage an hour earlier than before but still managed to belt out 22 songs in 75 minutes. Wearing his gold-trimmed, cream-colored suit, the King opened and closed with the same two songs from his 1974 appearance. After walking off-stage at 9:45, the house lights went up and the announcer made it clear an encore was not forthcoming, informing all with "Ladies and gentlemen, Elvis has left the coliseum."

OCTOBER 10, 1937
Didn't See That Coming

Officials managing the West Texas Fair requested the Abilene police usher the fair's fortune tellers out of town before the end of the annual event. It seems the fortune tellers not only predicted one's future, but they also were quite adept at picking pockets. Before seeing them to the city limits, police forced the ball-gazers to refund several "suckers" who had fallen prey to the sticky-fingered palm readers.

ALSO ON THIS DAY IN 1953...
Frozen Fish

Following a chase by Abilene police, a Kansas truck driver was hauled to jail for driving on the wrong side of the road and running a Greyhound bus off the road. The truck's refrigerated trailer contained 24,000 pounds of fish that had to be parked near the jail so the driver could be let out of his cell every few hours to ensure the fish did not thaw.

OCTOBER 11, 1974

Flying Fortress Flies Again

An unusual site flew over Abilene. After sitting idly by at the Abilene Municipal Airport for 13 years, a former World War II B-17 bomber—a four-engined aircraft known as a Flying Fortress—flew to a new home at Dyess AFB. However, the old bird did not lift off under its own power; rather, the retired aircraft was lifted aloft by a CH54 helicopter crane and slowly flew over Abilene to its new home at Dyess. Abilenians across town stood outside to look up at the

Relocating the Flying Fortress to Dyess AFB

unusual site of the 25,000-pound bomber dangling beneath the oddly shaped helicopter. After a soft landing near the entrance to the airbase, the Flying Fortress received a full makeover and was renamed "Reluctant Dragon." The warbird remains on display there today, one of only 46 surviving.

OCTOBER 12, 1981

Too Much of a Good Thing

Floodwaters inundated several Abilene neighborhoods as Catclaw, Cedar, Lytle, Buttonwillow and Little Elm creeks overflowed their banks when a slow moving storm dumped 15 inches of rain. Lytle Lake sent a rush of water over the spillway and into low-lying neighborhoods downstream.

Water rose waist-high in the Lytle and Fairway Oaks areas and across north Abilene. As the city made a plea for boats, Mayor Elbert Hall also requested the National Guard stand by as police were busy

Lytle Lake runs over the spillway, 1974

assisting families trapped inside their homes while Dyess personnel manned helicopters to pluck others from rooftops. One Abilene man clung to a mesquite tree in the middle of Cedar Creek for 90 minutes before rescuers could bring him ashore. In all, more than 300 abandoned their homes and 135 homes were destroyed. Miraculously, no lives were lost.

OCTOBER 13, 1918
A Churchless Sunday

For the first time in anyone's memory, Abilene churches did not open for Sunday services. Four days earlier, the ministerial alliance decided to forego worship in order to keep people apart at the height of the deadly Spanish flu pandemic. (However, all were invited to come to the Red Cross offices at the courthouse from 9 until 6 to help fill an order for 500 face masks.) Pews were empty again the following Sunday as social-distancing (a term not yet invented) was the order of the day. Simmons College reported that the flu was under control on campus and the City-County Health officer stated that the influenza epidemic was "decidedly on the wane with only three or four cases reported daily." He estimated that 16 to 18 Abilene citizens had succumbed to the flu.

Following a two-week hiatus, church doors swung open again,

offering services on October 27 with First Baptist drawing a larger-than-average turnout. Pastor Millard Jenkens, earlier in the week, announced he would present his decision about remaining in Abilene or moving to Waco to accept the pastorate at Columbus Avenue Baptist Church. (He stayed put.)

The next time Abilene experienced a churchless Sunday came 102 years later in the midst of the COVID-19 pandemic.

OCTOBER 14, 1932

Plennie Walks Plenty

Eighteen months and 13 pairs of shoes after leaving Abilene, Plennie Wingo back-pedaled into his home on Butternut Street, wrapping up his semi-successful attempt to circle the globe while walking in reverse.

Wingo managed the coffee shop in a local hotel when he decided that the thing to do was walk around the world backwards. Plennie attached two small rearview mirrors to his glasses, got a walking stick and a good pair of shoes, kissed his wife and daughter good-bye and headed east – but facing west. He decided to leave from Fort Worth, hoping to garner more publicity and to enlist sponsors whose ads he would carry on his back in order to finance the backwards stroll. Twenty-two days after leaving Fort Worth, he backed into Muskogee. Then, it was on to St. Louis in reverse gear and full speed astern to Chicago.

Plennie Wingo sporting
his mirrored glasses

Averaging 24 to 30 miles per day, Plennie reached New York, backed on up to Boston and onto the gangplank of a ship sailing for Europe. From Germany, Plennie reversed on to Turkey, yet when he reached Istanbul, his passage was barred. So he leapfrogged over Asia altogether, landing in Los Angeles where he again took up his rear-facing walk. After 13 pairs of shoes and 18 months, he back pedaled into Abilene on this day.

OCTOBER 15, 1920

The Things You Do In College

While in town for a football game against Simmons College, some members of the North Texas College team filched a banner. Tied to the side of a bus, the banner announced the game, reading, "Foot-Ball Today. Simmons vs Denton. Simmons Park 4 P.M." Although not valuable, once stolen, the banner became priceless. The amount of pride suddenly placed upon the advertisement by the Simmons squad zoomed to a lofty level, and a plan to restore the banner, and local honor to Abilene, quickly hatched.

The Simmons squad dispatched Lynn McAllister and "Spinks" Pearson to Denton with instructions to bring the banner back to Abilene at any cost. Arriving in Denton, the pair began their sleuthing. Hitting on the idea that McAllister

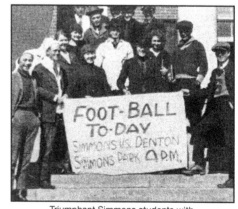

Triumphant Simmons students with their reclaimed treasure

could approach the North Texas coach, offering to play, he infiltrated the enemy camp. At practice, McAllister chatted up the players about the banner snatching as well as a good place to stay and was directed to a boarding house where some players bunked. It just so happened to be the very house in which the banner was located. McAllister asked to borrow the banner to show to a friend but was turned down flat, so, like any good spy, he bided his time and waited for the right moment before nabbing the treasure and dashing away. Triumphantly returning to Abilene with the highly-precious banner, Pearson and McAllister insisted it be locked away in the trophy case.

Young Mr. Wooten Arrives

In the fall of 1879, John and Sarah Wooten gathered their five young children—three daughters and two sons—and headed west for Taylor County. They brought their possessions, along with a six-month supply of food and enough lumber to build a small home. Their trip along the Center Line trail took 32 days. On day 31—October 16, 1879—the Wooten family reached a grassy plain 15 miles northeast of Buffalo Gap, a plain that would become the site for the city of Abilene. Fourteen-year-old Horace Wooten recalled in later years that his family camped next to Elm Creek close to where the future North and South First street bridges would span the muddy creek.

Years later, the successful Abilene businessman recollected, "We came in a wagon and camped on Elm Creek. There was no timber, no mesquite, nothing but prairie dogs and rattlesnakes. The snakes were of tremendous size and we killed one of the biggest I ever saw. The grass was knee deep and we wore boots for self-protection." What the young Horace Wooten could not know as he lay beneath the wide October night in 1879 was that the ground on which he slept would become a city, and that he would be among that band of forward-leaning men and women who would push up and grow a town from the waving grasses along Elm Creek.

ALSO ON THIS DAY IN 1976...

Ove Johansson Hits From Afar

In its homecoming football game, ACU led East Texas State [Texas A&M-Commerce] 7-0 late in the first quarter. From their own 48-yard line, the Wildcats faced fourth down when coach Wally Bullington sent in his Swedish placekicker Ove Johannson. Before the game, Bullington had seen Ove make a pair of field goals from 70 yards away. Just a year earlier, Johannson had never played American football, now the Swede was sent in to try something as yet unaccomplished in high school, college or professional football. With a north wind at his back, Ove set up soccer-style and waited for the snap of what would be only his fourth field goal attempt. Kicking from his own 41 (which also happened to be his jersey number), Ove booted the ball toward the south end zone. His 69-yard field goal try cleared the bar easily, setting a world record and clearing the bench as he was swarmed by

Ove Johansson prepares to make history out of the hold of backup quarterback Dean Low

his fellow Wildcats.

Just hours earlier, Texas A&M kicker Tony Franklin was penciled into the NCAA record book with a 65-yarder in a game against Baylor. That record was erased only hours later Johannson's world-record became the new standard. A record that still holds.

OCTOBER 17, 1946
A Suburban Theater

Adelman Theaters opened Abilene's first suburban theater at 1726 Butternut Street. At 6:30 p.m. the projector first flickered on at the Metro, showing a romantic comedy, "Ding Dong Williams." The first-run movie house provided an auditorium with leather-cushioned seating for 526 and a 17-foot high screen. The Quonset hut construction gave the theater a look unlike any other local venue while the adjacent parking lot for 125 cars was a convenience no downtown theater could offer.

The Metro Theater under construction on Butternut Street, 1946

A year after opening, the Metro was sold to the owner of Abilene's Linda and Texas theaters who managed to operate it for six months before closing the doors in April of 1948. The theater reopened in September operated by its third owner in three years.

Stars and Stripes Forever

Seventy-four-year-old conductor John Philip Sousa brought his band to Simmons University as part of his 36th annual nationwide tour. Abilenians had long hoped for Sousa to include Abilene on his tour list but failed to secure his appearance until 1929. An afternoon concert was put on for Abilene local schoolchildren, and the Eagle band from Abilene High played under Sousa's direction. The evening concert at Simmons drew a standing-room-only crowd of 2,000 to hear his 75-member band. Just five weeks earlier, the band had been in a train wreck in Colorado, injuring seven members. Sousa stopped touring in 1931 and passed away the next year.

Up a Pole and In a Pickle

Tradition held that should McMurry freshmen successfully fly their class flag over campus for 24 hours, restrictions on the first-year students had to be lifted. So, when upperclassmen saw the frosh flag fluttering from a 220-volt electrical wire connected to a stadium light pole, action was taken. With six hours remaining in the necessary 24, Sweetwater junior Bob Brookshire volunteered to bring the flag down and deny the freshmen their campus freedom. After turning the electricity off, Brookshire donned pole-climbing spikes and a safety belt and managed to reach the top of the 100-foot pole. With the flag about 10 feet away from the pole, he used his safety belt to slide along the wire out to the pennant, unceremoniously detached it and flung it victoriously to the waiting upperclassmen below.

The triumphant Brookshire now began inching back toward the pole but found it impossible to close the gap. His own weight caused the wire to sag, making his exit strategy futile. With the strap around his waist, Brookshire hung from the wire for nearly 30 minutes before the firemen arrived with their ladder truck and rescued the dangling daredevil.

Freshman had paid an electrician $7.50 to put the flag up there.

A Stain on Abilene Youth

Judge Milburn Long of the 42nd District Court granted a temporary injunction allowing County Attorney Frank Smith to close two recreation clubs. The Abilene Recreation Club located in the basement of the Radford Building at North Third and Pine (longtime home of Condley and Company) and the Broadway Rec Club in the basement of the Hotel Grace were locked up tight by the city. The operation of such clubs violated local ordinances and both establishments had become hangouts for Abilene youth who loitered about playing pool and picking up bad habits in general.

Cherry Picked Up

Piloting a B-17 from Honolulu to the South Pacific, Captain William Cherry of Abilene radioed that he was running out of fuel and would need to ditch in the vast ocean. An intensive search for the eight men on board began immediately, making front-page news for three weeks since one of the downed men was famed flyer Eddie Rickenbacker. Drifting in life rafts, the crew's food ran out after three days. On the eighth day, a seagull landed on Rickenbacker's head and he was able to catch it; the men ate the bird and used some parts as fishing bait. One crew member died after drinking sea water. Two weeks of searching by Navy patrol planes failed to spot any survivors and the search was set to end, but Rickenbacker's wife persuaded the military to continue looking for seven more days. Most newspapers now reported that all were presumed dead. On day 23, Captain Cherry was spotted 600 miles north of Samoa and rescued with Rickenbacker. The rest of the crew were plucked from the ocean the next day.

OCTOBER 22, 1920

Abilene Wins McMurray (But We Can't Seem to Spell It)

A two-sentence telegram sent from Clarendon by Rev. James Hunt to the *Abilene Daily Reporter* confirmed that West Texas Methodist College would be located in Abilene. Hunt, pastor of Abilene's St. Paul Church, cabled, "The Conference overwhelmingly voted to accept Abilene's offer for the college. The Board of Education was empowered to consummate the deal." The Board of Education for the Northwest Texas Conference of the Methodist Episcopal Church South had earlier endorsed Abilene's offer after Bishop William McMurry indicated his Abilene leanings—which spoke well of the Bishop's magnanimity since the Abilene newspaper consistently misspelled his name with an unnecessary "a," printing it as "McMurray."

The lure placed before the Methodist Conference by Abilene

included $200,000 in contributions from local Methodists and an additional $100,000 pledged by the Chamber of Commerce. On top of that, there would be a donation of a 32-acre building site along the southern fringes of the city and the site would be connected by an extension of the Abilene trolley line from South Seventh along Grand Avenue to the campus. The cherry on the cake? The city tossed in free water in perpetuity. (Today McMurry pays for its share of city water.)

The details were set down in writing and a contract between the Methodists of the Northwest Texas Conference and the Abilene Chamber of Commerce was formally signed in April of 1921. The *Abilene Daily Reporter* noted that the meeting further produced an agreement to name the college in honor of Bishop William Fletcher McMurry, spelling his name correctly.

OCTOBER 23, 1883
The County Gets a New Seat

With more than 100 Taylor County landowners signing a petition requesting an election to move the county seat from Buffalo Gap to Abilene, Taylor County Judge John Murray called for such a vote to take place on October 23, 1883. For a month prior, heavy campaigning by both sides took place. In order for Abilene to become the county seat, a two-thirds majority was required, and Buffalo Gap worked hard to overcome the large base of Abilene voters. All for naught. Abilene won 905 to 269. Only one county box went for Buffalo Gap—its own. (Getting the county records transferred to Abilene was a separate fight altogether.)

OCTOBER 24, 1889
Banner County!

In the fall of 1889, when Abilene was just a wee child of eight years, a big dream came true as the county brought home the first place prize from the State Fair in Dallas, and Taylor County was named the "Banner County of Texas!" It was happy, front-page news. The newspaper proudly touted, "The Glorious News Received in Abilene With Great Joy! A Jollification Meeting, Firing of Anvils, Music By The Band, Parade By The Military Company. A General Love Feast And Everybody Happy!"

OCTOBER 25, 1947
The Lakes! They are Arisin'!

A two-day rain, subsiding around dinnertime on October 25, 1947, gained Abilene a six-month water supply, adding an estimated one billion gallons to Lake Abilene, Lake Kirby and the Phantom Hill reservoir. Drought had caused the city to cease taking water from Kirby and Lake Abilene starting two weeks earlier. The 48-hour deluge brought a 49-inch rise in the level of Kirby while Lake Abilene rose two feet and Lake Fort Phantom Hill came up 20 inches. By nightfall, Lytle Lake was within two inches of the spillway, having risen nearly nine feet, and was overflowing by sunrise.

Local Luminary: Fred Lee Hughes

Born in Merkel on this day, Fred Lee Hughes made a name for himself in the big city of Abilene. In 1960, the Abilene Jaycees selected 33-year-old Hughes as the city's Outstanding Young Man, and in 1972 the Abilene Chamber of Commerce bestowed on him the honor of Outstanding Citizen. The red-headed Buick dealer committed his life to public service, joining the Rotary Club, Chamber of Commerce, Jaycees and United Way, serving as president of each. In 1966, he was elected to the Abilene City Council and in 1975 became the city's 28th mayor, serving one term.

Former Abilene mayor
Fred Lee Hughes

The always-smiling, effusively optimistic civic leader, and passioate Texas Aggie was credited with nearly single-handedly landing the B-1 bomber squadron for Dyess Air Force Base. As the century closed in 1999, an 11-person committee of civic leaders, tasked with identifying "Abilenians of the Millenium," selected the retired car dealer as the top civic leader from the 20th Century. When told of the honor, Fred Lee Hughes' jaw dropped and he exclaimed, "Oh my horrors! My gracious! Out of all these people? Really?" This local luminary passed away in 2018 at the age of 90.

OCTOBER 27, 1952
Nixon Drops In

Among the early arrivals to the old Tye Army Air Base hangar were Edward and Louise Eisenhower of North Second Street who hoped to find a good spot to spy the running mate of Edward's second cousin, General Dwight Eisenhower. California Senator Dick Nixon and his wife Pat were due to land at 6:03 p.m., and although the *Dick Nixon Special* DC-6 touched down a bit tardy at 6:30, the crowd gave the 38-year-old Senator and his slim, 40-year-old wife a raucous welcome.

Abilene was the final stop in a grueling day that saw the Nixons in Texarkana, Longview, Beaumont and Corpus Christi campaigning for the '52 presidential election. Abilene mayor Ernest Grissom introduced the vice presidential nominee to the estimated 7,500 who crowded the hangar at the Army Air Base. Before Nixon arrived, three teenagers induced a loud chorus of boos as they paraded through the crowd carrying placards for the Stevenson-Sparkman ticket. Abilene doctor Cyrus Ray snatched the signs and, to the delight of the Republican horde, tore them up.

The Hardin-Simmons Cowboy Band struck up "The Eyes of Texas" as Nixon mounted the speaker platform. During his 30-minute speech he was interrupted with applause 20 times as the crowd expressed its common approval at ending the war in Korea, the poor job performance of Secretary of State Acheson, and the promise of honest government should the Eisenhower-Nixon ticket prevail. The Abilene crowd paid little heed to a brouhaha that rose up barely a month before—addressed in Nixon's famous Checkers speech—in which he defended himself over accusations related to political expense improprieties and made it clear that he and Pat intended to keep one gift they had received, a black-and-white Cocker Spaniel.

In the November election, over 56 percent of Taylor County voters cast their votes for the Republican ticket of Eisenhower and Nixon.

Frances McMichael Drops In, Too

Sixteen-year-old Frances McMichael, who dropped out of South Junior High to take a job as an elevator operator at the Windsor Hotel, was reported in good condition after miraculously surviving a 51-foot fall down the hotel elevator shaft. Although suffering with bruises and from shock, she broke no bones and suffered no internal injuries. From her hospital bed, she told the startled doctors that she only remembered grabbing at cables on her way to the basement floor. Turning to her mother, she ruefully noted, "If I had stayed in school, I wouldn't be here."

A Montgomery Wards Rush

While the Hardin-Simmons Cowboy band provided the background music, a pair of six-foot long scissors sliced the red ribbon at 9:45 a.m. followed by 2,000 shoppers surging in to check out the new two-story, 100,000-square-foot Montgomery Ward. Before opening the doors to the $1.2 million store—the west anchor store for the planned Westgate Shopping Capitol—Chamber of Commerce president Oliver Howard spoke, followed by Taylor County Judge Reed Ingalsbe, Mayor George Minter, and the general manager of Ward's south-central division. Anxiously awaiting a chance to shop,

Opening day for Montgomery Ward, 1959

patient Abilenians listened to a slew of introductions, including Westgate developer Jack Hughes, who told of the mall planned for the property east of Wards.

With the outdoor ceremonies finally concluded, the crowd moved inside. The store had been opened 20 minutes when the first lost child was reported over the loudspeaker. All were asked to be on the lookout for a 3-year-old girl with pigtails and new ribbons, last seen in the camera department.

Product demonstrations for sewing machines and wood turning lathes were staged along with others throughout the store. Gas ranges were on sale for $179, mattresses for $34 and electric typewriters were going for $90. Wards boasted an auto service department on the west side of the store, providing car care while you shopped, and the store also offered tax specialists ready to help you file your return. Montgomery Ward closed on Sundays, but was open Monday through Saturday at 9:30, doing so until going out of business nationwide in 2001. The Westgate Shopping Capitol came and went, but the Wards building still stands as just a bit of history in plain sight.

OCTOBER 30, 1925

Plying the Avocation of a Flirt is a No-No

Mayor Charles Coombes and the City Commissioners approved an ordinance "forbidding public flirting on the streets, thoroughfares, sidewalks, alleys, or in any store, theater, automobile within the incorporated limits of the City of Abilene." Per the ordinance, flirts and flirting was defined: "This includes any person who by word, sign, gesture, wink, facial expression or look shall seek to attract the attention of or form the acquaintance of any person of the opposite sex for the purpose of making a mash or a flirt." Specifically stating "men were forbidden from coughing, whistling at or making goo-goo eyes at any woman traveling the public sidewalks and streets of the city." And if you did happen to wink at someone, the fine was $200.

The news of this local law was picked up nationally, solidifying Abilene's reputation as the "Buckle of the Bible Belt." In 1934, a local male was convicted of plying the avocation of a flirt and incurred a fine. A second enforcement occurred in 1952 when a young masher was picked up after throwing a rock at the Thompson house on North Sixth and following up by hurling flirtatious language towards the Mrs. He paid up $100, as did a 21-year-old fella from Merkel who came over to the big city, got busted and was ordered to move out of Taylor County.

OCTOBER 31, 1947
The Eagle Has Landed

The large metal eagle that customarily adorned the AHS side of Friday night football stadiums turned up missing on October 26 but returned to roost on October 31. Seems the mascot had flown west but the guilt-ridden culprits came to the Abilene police station at 1 a.m. hauling the oversized eagle in with them. Officers decided that the safest place for the metal mascot was at the headquarters, at least until after the Abilene-Sweetwater football game scheduled for that evening under a Halloween moon in Sweetwater.

A late fourth-quarter touchdown by Pete Shotwell's Eagles gave Abilene a 14 – 7 win. That'll teach them to steal our mascot.

NOVEMBER

NOVEMBER 1, 1952
Late Night Shenanigans See the Light of Day

Abilene police were on their toes as late night Halloween pranks continued well past midnight. Anticipating extra calls, Abilene Police Chief C.Z. Hallmark called out extra shifts to keep up with the widespread activity. Residents awoke to find that garbage cans, lawn chairs and potted plants were missing while others found that their car windows were soaped. In a pre-emptive move, many downtown store owners applied protective coatings to plate glass windows, hoping to blunt soap attacks. The school superintendent placed watchmen at school campuses, an historic Halloween mark. Eggs were lobbed at front doors and car tires deflated all across town. Streets were barricaded with garbage cans, tires and tree limbs. A Coke bottle shattered a window on Ash Street and a small blaze burned through the awning at W.T. Grant Department Store on Pine but was extinguished by boys armed with water pistols before the fire department could arrive.

NOVEMBER 2, 1949
Got Tuberculosis?

A mobile X-ray unit set up along North First in front of the Elks Lodge by the Texas Tuberculosis Association offered its services free to anyone over age 15. With the line stretching east down the sidewalk past the Drake [Grace] Hotel and around the corner on Cypress, 709 people lined up this day to see if they had tuberculosis. The next day, 656 stood in line for the free screening. The operation was a countywide effort to survey for the disease. Averaging two X-rays per minute, the mobile unit operated six hours daily for 18 days.

High school students were bused to the site for testing, and businesses with large numbers of employees—such as Mrs. Baird's Bakery, Wooten Grocery Company, Dr. Pepper Bottling, Lone Star Gas, Abilene Christian College and the City of Abilene—arranged for all their employees to partake in the TB survey. (Just a reminder of how far we have come in the realm of healthcare, tuberculosis killed 43,800 Americans in 1948, and on this day three patients were admitted to the polio ward at Hendrick Hospital.) Before the mobile unit moved on, 9,420 Taylor Countians had their chests X-rayed, with 194 showing positive for harboring the highly communicable disease.

NOVEMBER 3, 1928
Raining Ruths

Savory delights rained down on Abilene as a thousand tiny parachutes floated earthward, each bearing a Baby Ruth candy bar. The Curtis Candy and Gum Company of Chicago contracted with Captain Dallas Spear to pilot his open cockpit plane over town while his sole passenger, public relations man George McCarty, chunked the chocolaty peanut-caramel treats to the children below. More than one Abilene youngster was unceremoniously elbowed aside as adults too joined in the scramble to nab the cascading candy. Captain Speer noted that he flew in and out of airfields across the country but it was rare to drop in at a port as nice as Abilene's little airport.

ALSO ON THIS DAY IN 1899...
Give a Man His Due

Attorney Henry Tillett lodged a complaint with the *Abilene Daily Reporter* requesting that the newspaper correct its error. Mr. Tillett had carried off blue ribbons at the Fair for "Best Beaten Biscuit" and "Best Soda Biscuit." The newspaper inaccurately reported that Mrs. Tillett had earned the honors.

NOVEMBER 4, 1909
The Great Race Winner Drives Into Town

Over 300 Abilenians waited in the dark outside the Hotel Grace for the arrival of the most famous car in America—the intrepid globe-circling Thomas Flyer, winner of the New York to Paris race (going west) staged in 1908. The car was a 1907 Thomas model powered by a four-cylinder, 60-horsepower engine that propelled the open-topped four-seater 13,000 miles overland in 169 days, arriving in Paris 26 days ahead of the second place finisher. (In the race, the car was shipped from San Francisco to Asia.) After besting seven other entrants, including one German, one Italian, three French and one other American car, the Flyer swept into Paris along crowded boulevards filled with cheering French.

The famed Thomas Flyer on its West Texas tour

The durable Thomas left Albany after 3 p.m. heading to Abilene, arriving six hours later. The much-celebrated machine was on a West Texas tour promoted by the *Fort Worth Star-Telegram* when it rolled into Abilene.

NOVEMBER 5, 1963

Hollywood Arrives

With a price hike of just 25 cents, you could buy a ticket to the world premiere of "Take Her, She's Mine" debuting simultaneously at the Paramount and the Queen theaters. For $1.25 you not only got a first peek at the movie, you got an in-the-flesh look at the film's stars—lanky Jimmy Stewart and lovely Sandra Dee. The pair arrived in Abilene one day earlier, touching down in a chartered plane, greeted by 300 locals lining the airport fence and serenaded by the sounds of the Lincoln Junior High band. Donning Abilene gifts of cowboy hats (a pink one for Sandra) they were

whisked away in two new Thunderbirds to the Public School Stadium [Shotwell Stadium] where some 2,000 students, let out of school early, waited to see the stars.

In his famous drawl, Stewart stood before the microphone and thanked

Jimmy Stewart and Sandra Dee
receive cowboy hats at the Abilene airport

Abilene truant officers for letting the students skip class. Lunch at Dyess and dinner at the Westwood Club was followed the next morning with a press conference, a United Fund luncheon and an appearance by Miss Dee at the Dyess Youth Club. While searchlights swept the skies, a parade featuring local bands drew a crowd of 35,000 downtown to see the Hollywood pair. Before the film began to roll, Stewart took to the Paramount stage and played "The Eyes of Texas" on the accordion as the Abilene crowd stood, sang and clapped in appreciation.

NOVEMBER 6, 1943
Smooching for Uncle Sam

Patriotism appeared to play a secondary incentive for bond-buying soldiers stationed at Camp Barkeley. The true driving force in soldiers investing to help fund Uncle Sam's prosecution of the war was that soldiers who purchased war bonds received a series of no-strings-attached kisses from the civilian girls employed at the camp. The pecks on the cheek inspired sign-up among soldiers of the 333rd Quartermaster Depot Company to nearly 100 percent, making it one of the bond-buyingest outfits around. The girls felt it was the least they could do for the war effort.

NOVEMBER 7, 1953
Miraculous Exit From a '51 Mercury

While traveling at 60 mph, 5-year-old Roger Van Horn fell out of the family's four-door Mercury sedan and lived to tell the tale. With mom and dad in the front seat, Roger and his 7-year-old sister in the back, the family was about 25 miles from Abilene traveling along Highway 277, near View, when Roger, believing he was rolling down the window, actually turned the handle on the right-hand door. Hinges on the rear doors of a '51 Mercury were located at the back of the door, so opening the door at 60 mph caused the door to catch the headwind and fly open. With Roger holding onto the handle, he was flung out onto the road shoulder.

First on the scene was Cleo Havins, a firefighter stationed at Goodfellow AFB in San Angelo, who administered CPR before placing the unconscious Roger into his own car with Mrs. Van Horn, speeding off towards Abilene. Coming on the scene in the opposite direction were Raymond Thomason Sr. and Bill Brookover of Abilene, who stopped, got into the Van Horns' car and drove Mr. Van Horn and his daughter to Hendrick Hospital. Roger regained consciousness as Havins drove into town. At the hospital, Dr. Leland Jackson stitched up a severe cut and checked for broken bones but found only bruises. Miraculously, having exited a moving car, Roger was no worse for the wear and was discharged three days later.

NOVEMBER 8, 1933

The Parker Home Comes Down

Purportedly the first two-story frame home in Abilene, the home of Robert and Sallie Parker at the southeast corner of South Second and Butternut came down this day. The home went up in 1885 and became a frequent spot for gatherings of Abilene society. Mr. Parker was in the lumber business and built his home using longleaf yellow pine. The final owner,

the Radford estate, razed the landmark, using much of its lumber to repair other Radford properties. The Parkers raised 11 children—two sons and nine daughters—in the home, and a fair number

The Robert Parker home that once stood at South Second and Butternut Street

of Parker descendants still call Abilene home. The entire Parker brood posed on the front porch for the photo taken in the 1880s.

NOVEMBER 9, 1919

A Local Luminary: Carl Ulysses Carrington

Carl Carrington was born on November 9, 1919, in Tyler where he would later graduate from high school before joining the US Navy. The son of Clara Bonner and stepson of Abilene's New Light Baptist pastor Rufus Bonner, Carl was the first African-American from Abilene to lose his life in World War II. The Bonners lived at the corner of Ash Street and North 6th where Clara took in seamstress work and looked forward to weekly letters from her son.

Carl Carrington

Carl served as a Mess Attendant 2nd Class aboard the USS Pollux, a general stores issue ship assigned to the Navy's Atlantic Fleet. On February 15, 1942, the Pollux departed Maine for Newfoundland, carrying a cargo of war materiel and under the escort of two destroyers. As the convoy approached Newfoundland, a strong winter storm developed, causing the Pollux to run aground on the rocks off Newfoundland's south coast and sink.

Of the 233 men aboard the Pollux, 93 did not survive the night, including Carl Carrington. He is buried in Abilene's city cemetery.

A B-1 Crash Near Dyess

Captain Michael Waters managed to steer his crippled B-1 bomber away from Dyess AFB and populated areas before he followed his three crew members in ejecting from the doomed aircraft. A fire centered in the left wing disabled two of the jet's four engines and caused critical controls to be lost. The plane crashed in a ball of fire two miles north of Interstate 20 at 3:30 p.m. with the crew parachuting safely to the ground.

NOVEMBER 10, 2008
Pushing the Boundaries of Grammar

The much-anticipated new tagline for Abilene to use in promoting business development and convention and visitor tourism was debuted before a large crowd via a splashy video presentation on the big Paramount Theatre screen. The Abilene Branding Partnership—a joint venture between the city, the Cultural Affairs Council, Chamber of Commerce and several Abilene businesses—hired a Nashville company to come up with a marketing slogan that captured the spirit of Abilene. For the price tag of $107,000, surveys were conducted, locals interviewed, and research into Abilene's past produced a spot-on phrase encapsulating the city's can-do attitude and wide-open spaces – ta da…

ABILENE FRONTIERING!

Even before the theatre lights were brought back up, derisively whispered comments floated forth and telling glances passed amongst the crowd. In the following days, a wagonload of criticism was dumped on the visionary tagline. More than one piqued letter-writer pooh-

poohed the slogan, pointing out that "frontier" has no verbal form, thus "frontiering" was not a word. Others balked at the idea of Abilenians becoming Frontieringers. It was a case of language risk-takers vs grammatically-minded purists. A year later, the registered trademark for "Abilene Frontiering" quietly lapsed into oblivion.

NOVEMBER 11, 1918
World War I Ends

As Abilene went to bed on November 10 of 1918, World War I was in full swing. When the city awoke on the 11th, it was all over. The armistice, signed at 5 a.m. Paris time silenced the guns six hours later at 11 a.m. Taking into account the time difference, the early morning banner headline read, "FIGHTING ENDED AT 5 A.M."

With peace at hand, expressions of gratitude and relief popped up all over town. Abilene children arrived at school to find that lesson plans changed. They would now parade through the downtown streets waving flags and kicking off a daylong celebration. Stores closed at noon as assembled students from Simmons College led a second parade—including the Boy Scout band, the Red Cross Canteen, and Simmons faculty—to the depot park where a crowd estimated at 10,000 waited excitedly on

the lawn. Speaker stands were set up on the east and west ends of the park in order for citizens to address their fellow citizens and express their impromptu joy over the news. Abilene dignitaries addressing the throng included Judge Wagstaff, Mayor Kirby, Simmons President Sandefer, and Mrs. Dallas Scarborough.

That evening another crowd gathered at First Baptist Church to hear from the Ministerial Union and offer prayers of thanksgiving. The male quartet from Abilene Christian College sang, followed by church pastor Dr. Millard Jenkens reading a telegram received from Congressman Tom Blanton: "Terms of armistice are unconditional surrender. No American need be ashamed of armistice terms. All draft calls are cancelled. Our brave soldiers will be streaming safely home shortly." The crowd sang, "Nearer My God to Thee" and ended with a rousing rendition of the "Star Spangled Banner." The Abilene boys began arriving home six months later.

NOVEMBER 12, 1897
Football Kicks Off

Local football became a reality in November of 1897 when, as an added attraction to the Abilene Fair, the newfangled gridiron game debuted. A crack squad of 15 lads from Simmons College took on a collection of local players known (rather liberally) as the Abilene All-Stars. The All-Stars had been recruited by the Simmons coach, Professor Karl Krause, who had come to Simmons from Yale and had played football at the University of Chicago for Amos Alonzo Stagg. Kickoff took place in a field at North Second and Mesquite Street and, after the dust cleared, it was the Simmons boys claiming the first Abilene football victory 12-0. A rematch on the Simmons campus in January of 1898, saw the All-Stars get their revenge, 14-13.

NOVEMBER 13, 1933

Making Airwaves

The Texas Radio Act of 1927 made it illegal for unlicensed radio stations to broadcast beyond state borders. A case being tried in the Abilene district court alleged that Curry Jackson, operating a six-watt station known as "The Voice of Abilene," had been picked up by a portable receiver located in a field seven miles south of Hobbs, New Mexico.

At the trial, the only witness for Jackson's defense was Jackson himself, who was practically deaf. Attorneys stood right next to his most-receptive ear shouting their questions. Conviction carried a penalty of five years and a $5,000 fine. Following a day and half of testimony, jurors deadlocked 8 to 4 and a mistrial was declared. Jackson's new trial got underway beginning the next day. A second jury spent 50 minutes in deliberations before returning a guilty verdict, and Judge Atwell set punishment at 10 days in jail. The exhausted Mr. Curry noted that two trials in one week had been so strenuous on him that he was looking forward to the 10-day rest.

NOVEMBER 14, 1851

Everybody is Disgusted

Lieutenant Colonel John Abercrombie along with five companies of soldiers arrived at the Post on the Clear Fork of the Brazos north of the future site of Abilene. Construction immediately got underway on the fort, unofficially known as Fort Phantom Hill. Stones from a quarry about two miles east of the site were hauled in to construct camp buildings. Among the group was Lt. Clinton Lear who paused his construction efforts to write a letter to his wife in which he reported:

> When I say to you that we have a beautiful valley to look upon,
> I have said everything favorable that could be said of this place.
> We are camped in a grove of blackjack two or three hundred
> yards from the creek, which is salt. Everybody is disgusted.

Two and a half years after its establishment, Fort Phantom Hill was abandoned. By all accounts, no one was disappointed to leave.

NOVEMBER 15, 1967
A Child's Mite

Abilene Christian College announced two gifts had come to the school. First, Mr. and Mrs. Dean Walling of Glendale, California, donated $100,000 for construction of a lecture hall. ACC president Don Morris announced that the Executive Board of Trustees voted to name the 280-seat hall Walling Lecture Hall. Dean Walling graduated from ACC in 1930.

The second gift, donated by Lisa Grey of Austin, totaled $2.44. The 5-year-old philanthropist decided to donate her piggy bank to the Abilene college and informed her parents of her intent. Mr. and Mrs. James Grey got in touch with President Morris advising him of their daughter's wish. Young Lisa was invited to campus where she met with Morris in the president's conference room and where she handed over her penny-filled bank. (Lisa's father was a graduate of Texas A&M and Southern Methodist while Mrs. Grey attended Lamar State College.)

Community Christmas Tree

Jewell Bourland of 882 Ross phoned Mr. Orange Farnsworth, chairman of the Chamber of Commerce Christmas Planning Committee, informing him she wished to donate a 35-foot tall Arizona Cypress tree growing in her front yard to the city so it might serve as a community Christmas tree. A June thunderstorm first gave Mrs. Bourland the idea, as she feared the swaying tree might one day fall on top of her small frame house. Farnsworth hustled over to size up the tree, bringing his axe along should it measure up to the task. It did. The felled tree was removed from the Bourland yard and relocated to Everman Park where it was decorated and the lights turned on November 29 to coincide with a visit from St. Nick.

Football Fall

Fourteen-year-old Harris Wooten, star running back on the Central Ward football squad, went to bed with his football, falling fast asleep and dreaming of gridiron glory. While vividly dreaming of a flying tackle, Harris flew right out of the second story of the family home on Sayles Boulevard, awakening in a bush below. Harris was put on the disabled list with a dislocated arm for the next matchup.

NOVEMBER 17, 1945
Getting Horsey

Neighbors in the Abilene Heights Addition surrounding Abilene Christian College came to City Hall weighing in on the neighing (and braying and whinnying) occurring in their neighborhood. It seems that one area resident had turned a vacant lot next to his house into a horse pasture. For an hour and a half, City Commissioners listened to pro- and anti-equine arguments. The ensuing debate among commissioners raised the ante, with at least one pro-horse commissioner suggesting that perhaps poultry and cattle ought to be banned as well. City Attorney Overshiner, in a clear overstep of his role, suggested that cows should remain legal as they supplied much-needed milk. The final decision this day was to postpone the final decision to another day.

That "other day" arrived two weeks later. With one of the four commissioners out sick, the mayor and two commissioners voted to ban horses in the Abilene Heights area. However, Commissioner Ben Richey refused to vote, citing two reasons. First, he felt that the horse-owning subject at the center of the dispute should be reimbursed for expenses incurred in putting up a stable. Second, he took great offense to one anti-horse neighbor who publicly suggested that Mr. Richey was "selfish." In the end, horses, mules, jacks and jennies were banned. Apparently, asses were still allowed.

NOVEMBER 18, 1948

First State Bank Comes and Goes

Business began for Abilene's First State Bank at 9 a.m. as customers began arriving at the offices located on the corner of South Fourth and Chestnut. Organized by a group of Abilene businessmen—including Elbert Hall, Jack Hughes, O.B. Stephens and E.L. Thornton—the bank was led by 32-year-old Raymond Tanner and it touted an Abilene first – a drive-up window. In 1960, a new four-story bank building went up just south of the original home of the bank. Thornton Motor Company and Orange Crush Bottling buildings were razed to provide parking. (In 2021, that building is owned and occupied by county offices.)

First State Bank would alter the Abilene skyline in 1984 with the completion of its new 20-story bank building catty-corner from its original location. The bank took up residence on the first seven floors while the top floor became home to the Abilene Petroleum Club. The building was known as the First State Bank Building. However, business ended for Abilene's First State Bank at 6 p.m. on February 17, 1989, when the FDIC declared it to be insolvent and locked the doors of the 41-year-old bank. The bank's assets were transferred to NCNB Texas National Bank. In 2021, the building is known as The Enterprise.

Abilene's first drive-in banking facility

Abilene's Honor Roll

In a plan to build up the Abilene economy, over 65 families and businesses pledged for the years of 1913, 1914 and 1915 to contribute into a Chamber of Commerce fund that would be used for such purpose. Known as "Abilene's Honor Roll"—those who pledged to pay four percent on their real estate and two percent on their personal property based on the valuations for 1912—the names were printed in the newspaper. The honor roll contained familiar Abilene names—Legett, Parramore, Merchant, Kirby, Sayles, Sandefer, Fulwiler, Tittle, Sewell, Minter, Wooten, Radford, Paxton and Scarborough among others. The goal was to create a fund of $100,000 for attracting new businesses.

A chamber pep rally dinner held weeks later saluted the Honor Roll members. The rah-rah dinner was held at the Hotel Grace. In his toast, Mayor Kirby took civic naysayers to task—referring to such curmudgeons as "knockers." He recommended that after such wet blankets knocked to their heart's content, they then be hauled to the City Commissioners so that the city fathers might knock some sense into them. The mayor pointed out that more gets done when we stand shoulder to shoulder in unity of purpose than when we fray apart.

Amen.

NOVEMBER 20, 1891

Mr. Frizzell Meets His Maker

William Frizzell, 27, was a Kansan who was a temporary Abilene resident in 1891. His local address was the Taylor County jail. Mr. Frizzell had the unique distinction of being the only person to ever hang for his crimes in Taylor County, and although he walked the scaffold here, his crime actually occurred in Comanche County. Seems he trotted out his six-shooter as an attention-getter in trying to coax his wife to take him back. She was not convinced. The original murder trial was held

in Comanche County but one juror said he would like to wring Frizzell's neck, so he was given a new trial and a change of venue to Taylor County.

Newspaper drawing of William Frizzell

Mr. Frizzell went to the scaffold on Friday, November 20, 1891, and some 1,500 Abilenians—pretty much the whole town as well as some arriving from the country— showed up for the solemn send-off. Frizzell rose early that morning, bathed, shaved and dressed. Kemp's restaurant prepared him a breakfast of broiled chicken and fish along with oysters and potatoes. At 2:20 in the afternoon he was led out of his cell, across the street, and up to the scaffold set up on the courthouse lawn.

Sporting a black suit, white shirt and black tie, Frizzell said he felt as though he was headed to Sunday School. Rev. Wingo, the Baptist preacher, along with Rev. Stuart, who led the Episcopalians, conducted a short service while the young Frizzell sat and smoked a cigar. Following the congregational singing of "What A Friend We Have In Jesus," the condemned was given a chance for any last words. He said, "I have very little to say." He then went on to speak for 45 minutes.

At 3:18 the noose was put around his neck and he made his final request—asking the Abilene crowd to fill the air with one more song, requesting, "There's Never a Day so Sunny." Following Abilene's a capella choral send-off, the county's only condemned man went to meet his maker.

NOVEMBER 21, 1918
Lt. Chester A. Adams

Twenty-four year-old Lieutenant Chester Ashley Adams was laid to rest in the city cemetery this day, following a funeral service at First Baptist Church. Adams, the fifth child of eight born to Edward and Mary Adams of Abilene, was a member of the Simmons class of '17 whose classmates described him as someone who "sees the humorous side of every occurrence and never fails to enjoy a good laugh." Soon after graduation, Adams enlisted in the Aviation Service and won his wings at Love Field in Dallas. His proficiency in teaching others to fly thwarted his desire to go and fight in France as he proved himself invaluable as an instructor and was assigned to Ellington

Headstone of Chester Adams
at the Abilene cemetery

Field Gunnery School near Houston. Adams lost his life on November 18. While instructing a student in an open canopy bomber and flying upside down, his safety belt failed, causing him to fall 1,500 feet to his death. Although his death occurred one week after the end of World War I, his death is counted among the casualties of that war.

NOVEMBER 22, 1963
The Day President Kennedy Was Killed

President Kennedy was on his way to the Dallas Trade Mart for a noontime speech when he was killed by Lee Oswald in Dallas. In Abilene, flags were immediately lowered at Dyess, the post office, City Hall, and at all schools. The 850 employees at Abilene's Timex plant were sent home at 2:30 and the Paramount closed at 5:30 after showing Walt Disney's "The Incredible Journey." In downtown Abilene, people gathered in small groups, their faces registering disbelief and shock. McMurry, Abilene Christian and Hardin-Simmons dismissed classes and a memorial service was held on the McMurry campus at 6 p.m. with school president Dr. Gordon Bennett arriving just as it began. He had been in Dallas and was part of the crowd waiting for the president to speak. Also in the crowd was HSU president Dr. James Landes. They were already seated and had started to eat when word reached the Trade Mart.

Rosary was said at Sacred Heart Catholic Church while congregations across the city gathered to pray and encourage one another. Discussions were held by the school district, but Superintendent A.E. Wells and board president Morgan Jones decided to press ahead with the 7 p.m. kickoff for the Abilene High – Cooper football game. The 10,000 fans listened as the combined bands played "Crusader's Hymn" at halftime.

NOVEMBER 23, 1913

The Dam Has Busted!

The Lytle Lake watershed took in more rain than the 16-year-old earthen dam could contain and at 10 a.m., the damn thing gave way, sending 800 million gallons roaring along the eastern edge of downtown. Following heavy storms near Cedar Gap, Lytle Creek brought in more water than the already-full lake could contain. As its limit was reached, a 150-foot-wide breach near the western end of the dam gave way with a crumbling swoosh and a torrent estimated at 12 feet high began racing downstream.

The fire department rushed to the scene with its caliope alerting those within earshot that something terrible had occurred. Word also quickly spread as an alert telephone operator began indiscriminately ringing up homes yelling, "Dam's busted! Dam's busted!"

The rushing water washed away the T&P pumping station and the city water pipeline and damaged a bridge along North Second Street. Miraculously, no one was killed or injured, although several cattle found themselves standing idly by on temporary islands.

Roads to the lake quickly congested as all of Abilene felt a need to see the damage. Many residents took the opportunity to do some hand fishing in the small pools and depressions that held thousands of white perch, catfish and buffalo fish. The struggling seafood were gathered up by the sackfuls from the muddy

BIG LYTLE LAKE DAM HERE IS SWEPT AWAY SUNDAY MORNING

800,000,000 Gallons of Storage Water Escapes Into Stream Below and Loss Estimated at Twenty Thousand Dollars.

WILL BE REPLACED WITHOUT DELAY BY BETTER DAM

depression that once held the lake. People stood about discussing possible causes for the calamity, one of the most popular being that a crawfish likely bore a hole allowing water to pass through and erode the dam.

Three days later an improvised dam was constructed to span the breach and plans were made to rebuild and strengthen the dam holding Abilene's water supply.

NOVEMBER 24, 1911
The First Take-Off

Aviator Robert Fowler was arguably the first pilot to land and later take off in Abilene. Attempting to make a trans-continental trek, Fowler took to the air in Pasadena, California, on October 21, 1911. Fowler briefly touched down in Colorado City on November 21. Despite a side wind pushing his Wright biplane into the bushes as he tried to take off, he was able to struggle aloft and head for Sweetwater, arriving just after ten in the morning. Fowler took off for Abilene just before noon, covering the 41 miles in 47 minutes and setting down on the grounds of the gun club at 12:45.

As he approached, steam whistles shrieked to announce his impending arrival and some 5,000 Abilenians gathered to watch the mechanical bird alight. High winds disrupted Fowler's plan to continue east and he announced that he would take off the following morning. However, an even windier morning grounded him for a second night. On the morning of November 24, Fowler decided conditions were favorable and he lined up his machine at 11:20 for Abilene's first take-off.

Mother Gooseland Stirs Things Up

On Thanksgiving night of 1965, the Abilene Chamber of Commerce officially kicked off the Christmas season by staging the grand opening of Mother Gooseland at Rose Park. Admission was free, resulting in 5,000 people showing up. The idea for "Christmas in Mother Gooseland," was the brainchild of Norman Crohn, manager of Levine's store, who suggested the new chamber project after the group decided to axe the annual Christmas parade.

Open from Thanksgiving until Christmas Day, the $5,000 circular exhibit showcased a variety of painted nursery rhyme cutouts, including Jack Horner, Three Blind Mice, Humpty-Dumpty, the Old Lady in the Shoe, and the Three Little Pigs, all painted by Leo Smith and lit by 45,000 watts of bulbs installed by Key City Electric. A 30-foot tall Mother Goose watched over the scene with her blinking lights for eyes. A stage just inside the arched entrance served as a platform for Santa (played by Wally Akin) who arrived atop a fire truck with a sackful of candy to pass out. Throughout the month-long run, nightly live entertainment was presented by school choirs and there was even a visit from Santa's reindeer (borrowed from the zoo).

Mother Gooseland was deemed a rousing success after 40,000 came to the park for the 1965 debut. However, not everyone was on board with the community project. As preparations for an expanded festival in 1966 got underway, a flurry of letters appeared in the newspaper protesting the commercialization of Christmas. Counterpunch letters soon followed, forcing the editor to referee the fray with an opinion piece noting that Mother Gooseland was not created to replace the true meaning of Christmas.

The last year for Mother Gooseland in Abilene was 1969. The

chamber sold the displays to a shopping center in Brownwood who staged its own Gooseland in 1970 before returning the time-worn characters back to Abilene. In the end, the chamber donated the characters to the Abilene State School. Rather than stage a Christmas celebration in 1970, the Abilene Chamber of Commerce provided free tickets to the "Messiah" concert.

NOVEMBER 26, 1946
Bird Blight

The flock moved in on November 26, settling in the big cottonwood trees next to the depot and creating a nightly racket, spoiling fresh-washed cars and fouling the sidewalks. Identified as starlings, blackbirds, cowbirds or grackles, the birds were unwelcome by any name. Abilene commissioners announced that cutting down the cottonwoods (first set out in 1882) would not be the answer to the problem. Removing the trees was just one suggestion for outsmarting the birds roosting by the thousands each evening. Commissioners pointed out that cutting down the trees would do little as the nearby telephone lines were ready and waiting roosting spots. Other citizen suggestions included using Roman candles or taking the Junior Optimist Club up on its offer to gather each evening and pick off the noisy visitors with air guns.

The annual bird infestation was first observed in Abilene in 1937 (although, for some reason, the winged pests sat out 1940). Records kept by Mrs. Otto Watts show that the birds typically arrived in Abilene in late November, hanging around until the early weeks of March. The depot cottonwood trees are long gone, however, the grackles still come to Abilene to hang around and annually create a noisy mess.

Just Twenty Minutes, Please

A petition quite successfully made the rounds of the boys' dormitories at Abilene Christian College. The plea was addressed to the school's powers-that-be, asking them to grant relief in the area of dating difficulties. Five pages long, signed front and back by all male boarders— except one lonely holdout—the petition asked for a chaperone-free 20-minute period following all campus meetings during which the boys might linger and look lovingly into the eyes of the female Wildcats. The actual wording was more along the lines of "getting refreshments together" but the intent lay more along the game plan of loving looks.

Behind closed doors, faculty members considered the proposed change affecting the complicated world of wooing and agreed that a 20-minute period of social engagement was in the best interest of all concerned. Rejoicing reigned campus-wide, save for one boy's lonely dorm room.

Remembering the Mad Bomber

When Redskins linebacker Dave Robinson clobbered Roger Staubach, knocking him silly, the door opened for former ACC Wildcat Clint Longley to get off the bench (after locating his helmet) and without any warm-up, run onto the field at Texas Stadium and into the history books. Donning the number 19 Cowboy jersey, the backup quarterback— known to his teammates as the Mad Bomber" (after nearly hitting Coach

Tom Landry in the head with a wild throw during training camp) or as "Snake Hunter" (since he liked to hunt rattlers in the off-season)—managed to bring elation to turkey-stuffed Cowboy fans on Thanksgiving Day.

Having played in only two pre-season games, Longley came into the game during the third quarter with Dallas trailing 16-3. After hitting Billy Joe Dupree for a 35 yard touchdown, he followed it up with a 70 yard scoring drive, giving the Cowboys a 17-16 lead. However, Washington countered with a 19 yard touchdown run by Duane Thomas, putting the scoreboard back in their favor, 23-17. On the Cowboys' next possession, they fumbled, giving the Redskins a shot at a 24 yard field goal but Ed "Too Tall" Jones managed to live up to his nickname, blocking the attempt.

With 1:45 on the clock and no time outs, Longley set out on his 15 minutes of fame. On fourth and six from the Dallas 44, he connected with Bob Hayes who eked out a first down. The next play was a dropped pass by Drew Pearson (mind you, this was before the sticky gloves when dropped passes were a regular occurrence.) With 35 seconds remaining, Longley faced a Redskin nickel defense. Dropping back he launched a bomb from the Dallas 40, hitting Pearson in stride with a perfect pass over his right shoulder, splitting two Redskin defenders and scoring the tying touchdown. Efren Herrera kicked the extra point—Cowboys 24, Redskins 23, and Clint Longley had a very happy Thanksgiving.

NOVEMBER 29, 1908
Trolley Trouble

For a city to have electric trolley service in the early 1900s was to have arrived as a true metropolis. Only the most progressive communities had such a modern convenience, and Abilene was not going to be left behind. The local dream became a reality in 1908 when the Abilene Street Railway Company, a private concern led by Mr. W.G. Swenson, prepared to begin trolley runs. The Abilene tracks ran from Simmons College, through downtown, then continued down Chestnut to South Seventh where rails veered to the west and out to the edge of town – to West End Park, or Rose Park today. (The trolley tracks would later be extended south on Grand Avenue to McMurry.) Running at 15-minute intervals, it was a 30-minute trip to travel the six miles from Simmons to West End Park.

Following a hard rain, the trial run of the Abilene trolley took place on a Sunday afternoon in November of 1908. The little car was

packed with a crowd of 36 local movers and shakers, including Mr. Swenson who handled the throttle and brake for the inaugural run. All climbed aboard out at the Simmons campus

The Abilene trolley along Pine Street

and headed south waving to the Abilene crowds gathered along the route to see the Abilene dream pass by.

A half hour later, as the car approached the end of the line near the Sayles home out on South Seventh Street, Mr. Swenson pushed the lever to apply the brakes but found there was a noticeable lack of grip. He was still pushing the brake handle as the little Abilene trolley slid pleasantly off the tracks, through a barbed wire fence, across a muddy ditch, and straight into a pole, propelling the clump of city leaders into a muddy heap.

Mr. Radford turned his ankle, Morgan Weaver suffered a cut jumping over a mesquite bush, and the newspaper editor sprained his writing wrist. Mud was caked on just about everyone except Mr. Swenson who, having detected the trouble early on, braced himself and held fast. The front-page story the following day noted that it was the "funniest thing that had happened in Abilene."

NOVEMBER 30, 1935

The Hendrick Gift

A gift of $110,000 not only saved the West Texas Baptist Sanitarium from possible collapse, but also prompted the board to change the name to Hendrick Memorial Hospital. Former Odessans Tom and Ida Hendrick, who had lived in Abilene since 1932, made the life-saving gift with one stipulation — that the funds first be used to retire any

Hendrick Memorial Hospital with the Hendrick Wing added to the east

outstanding indebtedness. The remainder of the gift was to be used to add a four-story wing on the east side of the 11-year-old hospital.

DECEMBER

Mother Hubbard Stuffs Stockings

A small notice tucked into page 6 of today's newspaper read, "If you have nothing for your children for Christmas, write 'Mother Hubbard,' care of the *Abilene Reporter*. Your letter will be confidential. Tell me where you are and how many children in the family." The Mother Hubbard Anti-Empty Stocking campaign supplied 185 Abilene children with goodies on Christmas morning, including toys, candles, fruits and nuts, most of it contributed through Abilene churches. Fifty-eight families received groceries and clothing. Beginning in 1914, the Mother Hubbard campaign was aided by a group of "good fellows" and, over time, the good fellows became the Goodfellows, who carried on the tradition of supplying Christmas cheer.

DECEMBER 2, 1950
A One, A Two...

Donning tuxedos and formal evening dresses, over 1,000 Abilenians packed into the Abilene High School auditorium (the South First Street version of AHS) to hear the opening sounds of the Abilene Symphony Orchestra. Conductor Jay Dietzer took up his baton at 8 p.m. and brought the 65-piece orchestra to life. Four faculty members and seven students from Hardin-Simmons joined eight McMurry players and a dozen Abilene Christian musicians to form nearly half of the orchestra.

Beethoven's "Egmont Overture" and Schubert's "Unfinished Symphony" were among a repertoire also featuring Wagner and Grieg selections for the debut concert. The Abilene Symphony Orchestra presented three more concerts before wrapping up its first season in May of 1951. A decade after forming, the Abilene Symphony Orchestra merged with the Abilene Civic Music Association to form the Abilene Philharmonic Association, making beautiful music together ever since.

DECEMBER 3, 1938
A Final Fling

Well after midnight, Abilene police arrested a youth at North Fifth and Hickory. He was prone in the street, gazing mournfully upward at an empty whiskey bottle perched on the street curb. In his pocket was a marriage license.

Tone It Down and Straighten Up

Abilene High principal Byron England said that, although membership in the school pep squad could substitute for gym class participation, it was a fact he regretted, believing that more physical harm than good is done through incorrect posture encouraged at the games and the extreme emotional excitement.

DECEMBER 4, 1961

The Crescent Moons

Following the showing of a "near-nudie" late movie at the Crescent Drive-In on South Treadaway, Abilene police swept in. The movie "Not Tonight, Henry!" was deemed to be in violation of a local obscenity law. It seems that Henry's intentions well exceeded allowable standards by some distance, resulting in owner, manager, projectionist and ticket-seller (who did not even have a clear view of Henry) all being hustled off to the pokey.

Attorney for the Crescent crew defended the movie and Henry's actions, deeming all to be within the normal range. The trial resulted in a hung jury as two of the six jurors were not all that offended by Henry and his gal pal. For the retrial, the court rented the Palace Theater in order to show the evidence to the six-man jury, who were joined by over 100 spectators. The second trial produced a conviction and a $100 fine for the Crescent owner, while charges against the manager, projectionist and ticket-taker were dropped.

Abilene on Catclaw Creek

Abilene Printing and Stationery completed the printing of Katharyn Duff's book, "Abilene on Catclaw Creek," and prepared to pass it off to Chapman bookbinders for the final step in creating a local classic. Duff, assistant editor and Page One columnist, suggested to Andrew "Stormy" Shelton, publisher of the *Reporter-News*, an idea for a book detailing the past days of Abilene. She hinted the newspaper could serve as the book's publisher. Shelton agreed but envisioned a mimeographed pamphlet of a few pages stapled together, a publication a couple of notches below a store catalog.

The 300-page hardback book—secured with glue, not staples—sold for $6.50, or you could pony up $25 for the fancier Phantom Hill edition. Subtitled as "A Profile of a West Texas Town," the book still serves as the standard reference book for the history of Abilene.

Opening Swing

A new golf course broke ground in south Abilene on a cold, blustery Tuesday. Sculpted out of a mesquite-filled pasture, the Fairway Oaks golf course would be the centerpiece of the 450-acre development owned by Abilene investors. The par-72 course, designed by Florida golf architect Ron Garl, with help from PGA pro Charles Coody, offered a 7,200-yard challenge and included four par-five and four par-three holes. The back nine of the course ran along Buttonwillow Creek and a small lake was created by damming up the stream. Subdivision plans called for a clubhouse (designed by Tittle, Luther and Loving) situated along a boulevard with an adjacent swimming pool and tennis courts. At the groundbreaking, Coody took the first swing of a club at the soon-to-be course, showing off his form using a long-handled shovel to send a tennis ball on the inaugural tee shot, estimated to be around fifty yards.

DECEMBER 7, 1914

Frank Grimes Arrives

The former editor of the *Brenham Banner* and the *Temple Telegram* arrived for his first day as the city editor of the *Abilene Daily Reporter*. His last day on the job would come 47 years later, upon his death in 1961. Described as "a long, lean man who cast a long, bright shadow over his beloved city on the Catclaw," Grimes' writings were "wry, whimsical and could clear out the underbrush of complex problems." In 1951, he was a finalist for a Pulitzer Prize and during the 10-year period from 1949 to 1959 was a four-time winner of the Texas Associated Press editorial award. Grimes was a poet as well, with his "The Old Mesquites Ain't Out" becoming a West Texas staple. On many days, Frank Grimes would write six editorials. In 1944, his editorial-page readership bested the national average by 57 percent.

Grimes was father to four, including son Rudyard Kipling Grimes, who died in a Japanese prison camp during World War II. Frank Grimes died from pneumonia on July 28, 1961, and was laid to rest next to his son.

Longtime *Abilene Reporter-News* editor Frank Grimes

DECEMBER 8, 1941

Dog(s)gone

An ongoing series of collegiate pranks carried out prior to the 1940 football grudge match between McMurry and Abilene Christian resulted in the sudden appearance of 12 stray dogs wandering the ACC campus. The McMurry boys delivered the pooches under the cover of darkness, hoping to produce a mongrel mess. But after a year of daytime sunning and hanging around the cafeteria hoping for handouts, the doggy dozen had become campus favorites. Despite students heaping a fair amount of loving attention on the mangy, flea-bitten horde, campus admins had had enough, calling in the dog catcher to take care of the leftover prank.

ALSO ON THIS DAY IN 1973...

ACC Brings Home a National Championship

Abilene Christian Wildcats handed a big loss to the Fightin' Christians of Elon College, earning the ACC football team an NAIA National Championship. The ACC offense put up over 600 yards and 42 points behind the running of tailback Wilbert Montgomery and the passing of quarterback Clint Longley, both of whom would go on to play in the NFL.

DECEMBER 9, 1977
Catch Me If You Can in Abilene

A 29-year-old former con man and fraudster, Frank Abagnale, was in Abilene at the invitation of the Better Business Bureau. Several hundred local business owners attended one of the two seminars held at McMurry's Radford Auditorium, anxious to hear an erstwhile crook explain how to spot a practicing crook.

Abagnale schooled the crowd on spotting counterfeit currency and forgeries and identifying illegitimate checks. Paroled from federal prison only four years earlier, Abagnale explained how he successfully posed as an airline pilot, attorney, doctor and college instructor. Twenty-five years after his Abilene visit, Abagnale's story hit the big screen with Leonardo di Caprio portraying the swindling con artist who dared law enforcement to "catch me if you can."

DECEMBER 10, 1937
Quit Cuttin' Down the Trees!

The manager of the Abilene State Park, Jimmie Bates, issued a stern warning to locals—"Go get your Christmas trees somewhere else! Quit cutting down the cedars at the park!" Bates added, not only was it a serious offense to cut down trees, but it was equally illegal to cut shrubs and branches for decorations. For that matter, wildflowers were off limits too. Cash-strapped Abilenians suffering during the Great Depression would just have to swipe their Yuletide greenery elsewhere.

Hero Homecoming

Following his triple gold medal performance in the 1956 Summer Olympics held in Melbourne, Australia, ACC track star Bobby Morrow took center stage upon his return to Abilene. The 21-year-old sprinter and Abilene Christian sophomore received the full complement of hometown honors—red carpet, a key to the city, a parade through the streets led by the Air Force drum and bugle corps, a room for him and his wife at the Thunderbird Lodge, and a testimonial dinner. As he alighted from his plane at the Municipal Airport, he was met by his parents, the presidents of all three local colleges, Mayor Gatlin, and as many other city dignitaries who could squeeze in.

Bobby Morrow signing autographs
on his return to Abilene

At that evening's dinner, Morrow was serenaded in song and received praise from a litany of speakers: his high school coach, the ACC student body president, school president, board president, deputy commander of Dyess, the mayor, school board president, and three celebrity Texas athletes—golfer Byron Nelson, football All-American John Kimbrough, and baseball great Tris Speaker. Telegrams received from President Eisenhower, Governor Shivers, and Senators Lyndon Johnson and Price Daniel were read to the admiring crowd. However, it was an emotional Coach Oliver Jackson—who had accompanied Morrow to Australia—whose words touched Morrow the deepest. With tears in his eyes, Coach Jackson spoke of his pride in seeing such a deserving and dedicated young man bring home gold medals in the 100-meter, 200-meter, and 400-meter relay races.

The Pecan Bowl

Abilene school district administrator Jack Stuard took home the grand prize—a Dumont color television set—for suggesting the winning name of the Chamber of Commerce's Name-the-Bowl Committee contest. The NCAA was looking to stage the Midwest College Football Championship in Abilene at the Public School Stadium and it needed a name for the game. Stuard's entry was one of over 1,000 received, and his was the first to suggest a name later proposed by 27 others. Mr. Stuard recommended that the contest be dubbed the Pecan Bowl.

The Athletic Committee of the Abilene Chamber of Commerce handled all arrangements and promotion for the first of seven Pecan Bowls. The initial game took place on a sun-filled December 12, 1964, with a 2 p.m. kickoff before 7,500 fans. The contest pitted the Lamar Tech Cardinals against the Panthers from State College of Iowa. (The Panthers won 19–17.)

The Pecan Bowl was hosted as an annual affair in Abilene through the 1967 season before relocating to Arlington. The Pecan Bowl faded into history after 1970, becoming the Pioneer Bowl and relocating to Wichita Falls.

DECEMBER 13, 1930
Santa Brings Out a Crowd

Abilenians and out-of-towners thronged downtown streets early, and by noon stores and sidewalks were jammed as a crowd estimated at 30,000 awaited the 2:30 parade featuring Santa Claus. Spectators lined the 20-block route along Oak, Pine, Cypress and Chestnut to catch a glimpse of St. Nick, accompanied by his wife, Mary Christmas, along with the toyshop crew and 10 reindeer pulling the sleigh, retrofitted with wheels.

Led by two motorcycle officers, the parade extended for half a mile, requiring over 30 minutes to pass as bands, veterans, horseback riders and wheeled-contraptions slowly passed by. Riding in open-topped Chryslers, Buicks, Studebakers and Essex automobiles were the mayors of Abilene and Aspermont, the superintendent of Rule, and dignitaries from Colorado City and Snyder. College and high school bands vied for the top $50 prize (collected by the Buckaroo Band of Breckenridge). Crowd control was managed by 38 Abilene policemen, state patrolmen, National Guardsmen and local Boy Scouts.

Santa and his entourage returned one year later, parading through Abilene on the exact same day.

DECEMBER 14, 1957
All Good Things...

All along the way, everyone knew that sooner or later it had to end. Your team cannot win forever. But, boy oh boy, it was a heck of a ride while it lasted. When the Abilene High Eagle football squad bested Borger Bulldogs in the fourth game of the 1954 season, no one imagined that Coach Moser's Black and Gold would dominate 4A football in Texas for the next four years.

In the first game of 1954, the Eagles blanked the Highland Park Scotties 40-0. The next week the Sweetwater Mustangs were scoreless as well. However, when the Buckaroos of Breckenridge came to town, 10,000 faithful sat in disbelief as Buckies fullback—and future Oklahoma Sooner standout—Dick Carpenter powered Breckenridge past the Abilene boys, 35-13. Coach Moser spent the next week prepping his boys for the first district game, slated for October 8 at home against the Borger Bulldogs.

Behind the passing and kicking of H.P. Hawkins and the running of Henry Colwell, the Eagles routed the Bulldogs 34-7. They would go on to win the next 48 games.

The October 8, 1954, win at Eagle Field marked the start of an exceptionally remarkable and singularly storied gridiron performance, extending to a heartbreaking end that arrived

Standout AHS running back Glynn Gregory

at the Dallas Cotton Bowl on December 14, 1957. Along the way, the
Eagles of Abilene High were State Champs in 1954 (14-0 over Houston
Austin), 1955 (33-13 over Tyler John Tyler) and 1956 (14-0 over Corpus
Christi Ray).

Moser and his Eagles continued racking up wins throughout
1957, appearing as unstoppable and constant as ever. Favored by two
touchdowns, the Eagles confidently entered the Cotton Bowl for the
state semifinal playoff game against Highland Park. Things were heading
the Eagles' way, leading 20-14 with 2:49 on the clock, and it seemed
preordained that Abilene would make it to the state championship game
for the fourth year in a row. But, on third and nine, Scottie QB Bob
Reed set up in short punt formation and, with blocking providing him
a chance, heaved a desperation pass that was hauled in by halfback Jack
Collins, who managed to cover the 25 yards to the goal line, tying the
game at 20. Collins kicked the extra point, giving the Scotties a one point
advantage, but a penalty forced a second kick and Collins knocked it
wide.

Tied at 20, AHS moved to the Scots' 24 but four passes by Freddy
Martinez went incomplete. Texas high school football did not have an
overtime option in 1957; tie games were decided by the number of times
a team had penetrated its opponent's 20-yard line. Highland Park had
done so five times, Abilene High just three. The unprecedented 49-game
win streak came to an end…as do all good things.

Local Luminary:
Mary "Willie" Houston Morrow

Thirty-five year-old Mary "Willie" Morrow arrived in Abilene in 1885 along with her husband John and their three young children. Not long after settling in Abilene, John Morrow died, but Mary Morrow remained an Abilene resident for 46 years. Mary was the fourth child of two-time president of the Republic of Texas, Sam Houston. In 1850, Houston and wife Margaret (who had eight children in all) named their newest daughter

"Mary William," resulting in her being nicknamed "Willie." During Willie's youth, her father (who had already served as the first and third Republic of Texas president) represented Texas in the United States Senate and served as the seventh governor of Texas. (He had previously served as governor of Tennessee,

Abilene grave of Mary Houston Morrow

making him the only person to govern two different states.)

In 1889, President Benjamin Harrison appointed Willie Morrow as Abilene postmistress, a post she held for 23 years. Willie lived at 440 Cypress and walked to her job at the post office, before retiring in 1911 at age 61. Willie Morrow died at the age of 81 and was laid to rest, next to her husband and son, in the Masonic section of the City Cemetery on December 15, 1931. At the time of her death, Willie was the oldest living child of Sam and Margaret Houston.

DECEMBER 16, 1950
Incapable Squirrels

Half a dozen squirrels were pressed into civic service. Their task: scare the starlings out of trees in Everman Park (See November 26). In an ongoing battle with the avian agitators, city officials decided to hire mercenaries, rounding up six youthful squirrels to scamper among the boughs and scare the birds away. To acclimate the hit squad, the squirrels were brought to the park in a cage where they remained cooped up for a few days so they might scope out the surroundings while enjoying city-supplied pecans, carrots, peanuts and bread. Fat, happy and primed to the task, the cage door was left open and the furry terrors were set free to handle the matter. Alas, the lion lies down with the lamb. The squirrels and starlings paid little heed to the other species, with the park trees providing ample room for both.

DECEMBER 17, 1940
Ain't Happenin'

The Dallas Morning News corrected the false impression conveyed in a story it ran two weeks prior—one that Abilene Christian College president Don Morris took great exception to. It seems the Dallas newspaper reported that well-known Dallas dancer Lydia Tarnower was headed to the ACC campus to teach a master class in modern dance and provide demonstrations at Hardin-Simmons and McMurry. In fact, Miss Tarnower had been invited to Abilene by the Texas Intercollegiate Theater Festival, and her visit was in no way sponsored by the Church of Christ school. Morris advised the newspaper that such a class would be contrary to the principles and policies of the shimmy-free school. The embarrassed Tarnower asked the paper to correct the story and added that Dr. Morris had been very courteous about the misunderstanding.

DECEMBER 18, 1950
May I Have This Dance?

The vote was 5 to 2. The resulting uproar was impressive. Five Abilene School Board members opted to sanction social dancing as an approved activity for students, even authorizing the use of school facilities for the swayin' and steppin'. Prior to the sock-hoppin' decision, the board sat through a lengthy discussion during which three Abilene pastors—two Baptist, one Methodist—protested any prancin' and dancin' on public property. Anti-dance arguments included: dancing will exacerbate, not solve, moral laxity; students who conscientiously object to dancing will be embarrassed as they witness their cavorting classmates; dancing on taxpayer-funded property was wrong; felicitous relations between Abilene churches and the school board will be strained; and faculty members opposed to dancing will, nevertheless, be forced to supervise and witness their own students tripping the light fantastic. Threats to vote out the five pro-dance board members came early and often.

Congregations covering the religious spectrum took up the cause, with several passing resolutions demanding the school board step out of the conga line and into the straight and narrow. At First Baptist, over 500 voted to approve such a resolution while only eight voted against (it was noted that several of the eight were students.) In all, 10 Baptist churches, one Methodist, and all of the city's Church of Christ congregations presented anti-dancing petitions to the board.

Students at Abilene High School were evenly split on the issue, with some feeling that a moral standard was indeed being lowered. Others felt a bit of a boogie was quite harmless. One 17-year-old noted, "All this talk about sex stimulation from dancing would never have occurred to us if the grownups hadn't brought it up." A city election in April 1951 saw one pro-dance board member retain his school board seat while two anti-dancers were sworn in. However, the music slowly faded on the topic and the board never took up the subject again.

DECEMBER 19, 1967
"It Was So Close"

If your team is still playing football in December, well, that is tough to beat. Unless you get beat. A huge civic sigh fell across Abilene as the top-ranked Cooper Cougars fell to Austin Reagan by one point, the game ending with an inches-short goal line push by quarterback Jack Mildren.

Cooper quarterback Jack Mildren

Coach Merrill Green's undefeated Coogs were a three-touchdown favorite over Austin Reagan, which had reached the championship game in only its second season. Fought at TCU's Amon Carter Stadium on a cold, gray and rainy day before a shivering crowd of 12,000, the game was heading Cooper's way, leading 19-7 at halftime However, Cooper lost its advantage going into the fourth quarter, trailing by one. With seconds left, the Coogs managed to move the ball two feet from the winning score. Having no time outs and with time ticking, Mildren waved off field goal kicker John Villareal and called for a quarterback sneak. Jack came within inches of capping a remarkable season with a Hollywood ending. Alas, it turned into a character-building play and not one for winning a state championship.

On the season, Mildren ran for 24 scores and tossed 20 more. The soon-to-be-named Outstanding Texas High School Player—and the top schoolboy recruit for 1967— would go on to puff up Abilene pride over the years, starring as an All-American quarterback at the University of Oklahoma, winning the Sugar Bowl in 1971, playing professionally for the Baltimore Colts and New England Patriots, and later elected Lieutenant Governor of Oklahoma.

Following the disappointing 1967 loss to Austin Reagan, as Coach Green addressed his dejected team in the locker room, Abilene athletic director Chuck Moser stood in the back muttering, "It was so close."

DECEMBER 20, 1969
The Big Mac Arrives

At 11 a.m. city dignitaries cut the ribbon and formally opened the first McDonald's restaurant in Abilene. The ribbon, consisting of fifty $1 bills taped end to end, was snipped and then donated to the West Texas Rehabilitation Center. To further hype opening day excitement, Ronald McDonald arrived by helicopter. Ben Stitzberg relocated to Abilene from Chicago to manage the restaurant at North First and Westwood.

In addition to the Big Mac, the menu board offered double hamburgers, cheeseburgers, filet-o-fish, hot apple pie and, of course, French fries. Stitzberg noted that the Abilene McDonald's was the eighteenth in Texas and introduced the "no waitress" concept, relying instead on customers to claim their own meals, sometimes in less than a minute. He further pointed out that the national uniformity of

food preparation helped deliver quality food, and he also noted that
McDonald's offered a "family friendly" dining experience. Juke boxes
and cigarette machines were not allowed.

DECEMBER 21, 1953
The Zoo Feud is Finished

Seventy-five year-old Abilene zookeeper J.D. Burns shed no tears
as his long-running feline feud concluded this day—Bingo the lion
succumbed at the Abilene Zoo. Burns and Bingo had known one another
for nearly 30 years, and their relationship, rocky from the start, was sealed
in bad blood after a brief escape on the part of Bingo.

Back in 1948 (see February 26) Bingo managed a short escape.
Burns, fighting in the lightweight class, was no match for the heavyweight
who pushed past his cage door. The King of Beasts expressed his inner
feelings by reaching out and clawing Burns on his arm just as he fled,
easily clearing a nearby fence in a bounding leap. Burns claimed, "Bingo
was looking at me like a dog looks at a rabbit." The liberated lion paced
nearby while Burns weighed his options, ultimately deciding to climb on
top of the cage and holler insults at the loosed lion. In order to get a good
look at his prospective lunch, Bingo re-entered the cage as Burns quickly
leaned over and closed the door. Discord only deepened between Keeper
and Kept as the remaining years passed.

Upon learning of Bingo's death, Burns ran a finger over his scarred
arm, declaring, "If I'd had my way, I'd have done away with him five years
ago."

Peter the Great

The Abilene High Eagles met the Waco Tigers at a muddy Fair Park Stadium on a cold, rainy day in Dallas to determine which football team would walk off as state champs. For the better part of four quarters the two battled it out, neither squad able to reach the other's end zone. With the clock ticking towards a zero-zero tie, Abilene High had the ball on Waco's 18-yard line. On first down, Roy Stevens gained three yards behind the blocking of the right tackle. On second down Lloyd Browne was stopped at the line. The following play, Browne tried to go around the left end but, once more, was unable to generate any progress. On fourth down, with the ball on Waco's 15-yard line, team captain Pete

Hanna—known as Little Pete—was handed the full weight of the drama. In the dimming light, Hanna dropped back to the 25 and managed to drop kick the mud-caked ball through the goalposts, giving the Eagles a 3-0 advantage.

Pete Hanna's kick headed for the game winning field goal

With time ticking down, Waco started from its own 48. A 26-yard pass play moved the ball to Abilene's 37 and a second pass netted 12 more yards, putting Waco on the AHS 25-yard line. A third pass was blocked at the line of scrimmage and a second-down run failed to gain any yardage. Waco opted to try for a game-tying field goal, trusting the highly accurate foot of "Boody" Johnson. Kicking from the 32, Johnson's kick sailed wide and short, with Herring Bounds recovering the ball at the 5. Two plays later, the clock reached zero and Coach Pete Shotwell's Eagles brought home the state title on Little Pete Hanna's field goal. From that day forward he was known as Peter the Great.

DECEMBER 23, 1964
An Early Christmas Gift for HSU

A late December check from the Sid W. Richardson Foundation for $750,000 became the second largest gift received by Hardin-Simmons up until that point. (Largest was a nearly $1 million gift from Mr. and Mrs. John Hardin in 1934.) Sid Richardson attended Simmons College in 1911 and 1912 but had to withdraw when his funds ran out. Richardson, who made his fortune in the oil business, died in 1959. However the foundation he established in 1947 made the grant to his alma mater for construction of a science building. Perry Bass, Richardson's nephew and director of the foundation, presented the gift which was enthusiastically accepted by the school's board who voted to name the future building in Mr. Richardson's memory. The Sid Richardson Science Center opened in March of 1968.

ALSO ON THIS DAY IN 1960...
Ulterior Motive?

One Abilene man saved his wife the trouble of ratting him out. The middle-aged hubby phoned police himself, telling them that he needed to drive downtown to buy some light bulbs, adding, "My wife is claiming I am drunk and she is planning to call y'all. So I'm saving her the trouble." Over the phone, he described the make, model and color of his car as well as the route he would take along Butternut Street. Within ten minutes, officers stopped his car and booked him into jail for driving while intoxicated. Perhaps preferable to returning home?

DECEMBER 24, 1927
A Stocking Run

The first—and hoped for annual—city Christmas tree lighting took place on the Federal Lawn (just north of the old North Third Street post office) with more than 6,000 children heading home with stockings filled with fruits, nuts and candy. Santa passed out the goodies with the help of his elves—local Boy Scouts—who were cautioned to give the goodies to the under-12 crowd. Ladies from various churches had sewed the stockings, filling them with treats.

The specially constructed Christmas tree, strung with multi-colored lights and topped with a bright white bulb, was ceremonially lit to a solo performance of "There's a Star in the Sky," by Scout leader Ed Shumway. The entire group then joined in singing "Silent Night" and "O, Little Town of Bethlehem." Father Harry Knufer led a group of children from Sacred Heart Catholic Church presenting two more songs in Spanish. With the speeches and songs complete, the throng of Abilene children rushed forward for the stuffed stockings, all 6,000 quickly passed to outstretched arms. Near the close of the program, the festival turned into a mild panic as parents tried to locate sons and daughters lost in the surging crowd.

DECEMBER 25, 1960
Abilene's Greatest Christmas Gift

Lifelong Abilenian Ruth Legett Jones, joined by her two daughters, Judy Matthews and Edith O'Donnell, met on Christmas morning 1954 at the Fort Worth Club in downtown Fort Worth. The occasion was not for exchanging gifts, rather to bestow a gift, an unbelievable gift to the people of Abilene, a gift whose impact is still felt. At the Christmas meeting, the widow and daughters of Percy Jones established a charitable foundation, opting to name it in memory of Dodge Jones, son and brother who had died in 1946 at the age of 22. Mrs. Jones acted as chairwoman at the Christmas meeting, calling it to order at 10 a.m. Ruth Jones was pleased that the foundation was established on the anniversary of her

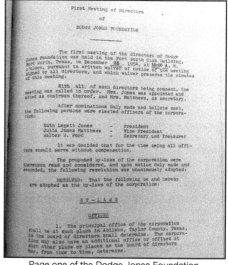

Page one of the Dodge Jones Foundation minutes book

Christmas day marriage to Percy Jones back in 1915.

Under the direction of Ruth Jones and later Judy Matthews, the Dodge Jones Foundation would give away millions of dollars over the next 64 years, transforming Abilene and improving the lives of Abilenians.

Ruth Jones died in 1978. Judy Matthews passed away in 2016 and Edith in 2020. The Dodge Jones Foundation closed on December 31, 2018.

DECEMBER 26, 1931

Safe Crackers Hit Grissom's Store

Descending from a rope beneath a second-floor skylight, holiday burglars robbed the Christmas cash from the Grissom's Department Store safe. After entering the Cypress Street store, dropping down into upstairs warehouse space, the thieves strung electric wiring down to the balcony-floor office where they rigged up a battery used to set off their nitro-glycerine. The blast ripped open the six-foot high safe, tossing it on its side, and flung an iron stove across the room. The burglars scooped up cash and diamonds valued at $4,700 before going on a shopping spree, picking up some fur neckpieces, two men's suits, a variety of neckties and matching shirts. In exchange, they left behind some hammers, pliers and extra wire. Using a store ladder, the squad made its way out through the same rooftop skylight. Police had little to go on, but were on the lookout for two well-dressed men, smelling of smoke.

DECEMBER 27, 1946

Charity Indeed

Late in the evening, a local charity organization phoned the Abilene police requesting two squad cars be sent around to arrest a family of eight. The father's complaints about the food and the facility had created a disturbance at the local shelter. Police arrived to find mom, dad and six children, ranging in age from ten to three years old. Further investigation determined that the California family was bound for Fort Worth but had only one dollar. Rather than arrest the group, police put the eight travelers into the squad cars and delivered them to the train station where the officers chipped in, buying train tickets and providing extra money for food. Charity indeed.

DECEMBER 28, 1943

Ed Dyess is Laid to Rest

Ed Dyess was laid to rest in Albany's city cemetery following a funeral held in the Matthews Presbyterian Church. In the six days since their son's death, Dyess' parents received stacks of letters, cards and telegrams offering sympathy. From the hundreds of condolences received from across the country, just one telegram was read at the service. It read, "Please accept expressed profound sympathy of the man spared from disaster by the final brave deed of your son. Greater love hath no man than to give his life to save another." Signed, J. M. Fladwed.

Six days earlier, just before noon, 27-year-old Lt. Colonel Ed Dyess stopped by the Glendale Air Station in Glendale, California, to take a new fighter plane, the twin-engine, fork-tailed P-38 Lockheed Lightning, up for a quick check ride. He climbed in and a mechanic knelt on the wing to bring him up to speed about some idiosyncrasies of the plane. For one, there was a tendency for the Allison engines

Ed Dyess

to backfire while accelerating because, stateside, the Air Corps used a lower octane fuel. The mechanic said, "If you hear it backfire, hit the brakes." Dyess closed the cockpit, lined up on runway 3-0, and pushed the throttle forward. It was ten minutes past noon on a bright California day.

Just as he reached liftoff speed and pulled the plane up, the mechanic's warning came true—the left engine began to pop. His speed was such that the only option was to struggle aloft but with the gear still down, one engine out and smoking. A few hundred feet was all the altitude he could manage. The P-38's twin engines counter-rotated, so losing one meant the plane immediately began to roll.

It was not the first mid-air problem encountered by the young man from Albany, Texas. All he needed was a wide spot to set the plane down. There to his left, laid out right in front of him, was a broad, straight four-lane thoroughfare—West Olive Avenue in Burbank. Although it was noon, war time gas rationing played in his favor—there were very few cars out, the street was virtually empty. Losing altitude and fighting the roll, Ed Dyess lined up his faltering plane. But, then, just up ahead, a dark blue Buick sedan turned off of North Lincoln Street and onto West Olive. The driver was Joseph M. Fladwed, a father of two young children, who had been home for lunch and was heading back to the Warner Brothers Studio lot where he worked as a foreman.

According to several eyewitnesses, in an instant Dyess pulled the nose of the fighter up to avoid the car. With a vacant field off to his left, he banked hard that direction, coming within a foot or two of clearing the peak of St. Finbar's Catholic Church. However, just clipping the top of the roof sent the plane plummeting into the front yard of a duplex, barely stopping near the front porch in a ball of fire.

Rather than have their son buried in Arlington National Cemetery, Richard and Hallie Dyess decided to lay him to rest in his hometown of Albany on this day.

DECEMBER 29, 1928

The Fabled Prince

Once upon a time, a handsome young Prince left home just before Christmas yuletide, bringing a deep sense of alarm and anxiety to Shaheen Manor. Prince, the 2-year-old Belgian police dog belonging to oilman Ferris Shaheen, was prone to wandering away from the South Seventh Street castle but never for long. Lovingly devoted to the two Shaheen children, the highly valuable black-coated pet seldom left their side for a long time. The distressed oilman placed an ad requesting that throughout the land all seek the whereabouts of Prince, resulting in fruitless leads as far away as the hamlet of Coleman. Alas, Prince was not in that distant land.

Seven sunrises after leaving the pleasurable comfort of the Shaheen estate, a peasant farmer spotted the regal Prince in a fielded forest near the village of Hamby, north of Abilene. The handsome young Prince was in the company of a lesser, non-pedigreed mongrel. As the wizened farmer approached, he noticed that both monarch and mutt had a tin can affixed to their tail. Unable to shake their metallic pursuers, Prince and pal had thus distanced themselves farther and farther from home, their tormentors never far behind.

Seven days of running left them quite lost and far from South Seventh Street. Accompanied by his own dog, the farmer approached the hapless pair. Prince, acting upon his inbred police dog instincts, set upon the farmer's dog and…well, things turned out ugly. Having seen the missing dog ad, the farmer coaxed Prince and companion into his Model-T carriage, returning to the castle. Oilman Shaheen and his children were overjoyed seeing Prince bound onto the lawn. The farmer's good deed was warmly received and, further, he was paid $15 in damages for the loss of his own dog.

Charlie Blank's Nite Club Burns

Sixty years after Italian immigrant Charlie Blanks built his eclectic nightclub in southern Abilene, an arsonist brought the landmark rock structure to its end. Eight units of the Abilene Fire Department fought the fire for 90 minutes, unable to save the well-known spot. Opened in 1937 as Charlie Blank's Nite Club, the establishment along the Potosi Road acquired a bawdy reputation early on, but with dance bands brought in during the 1940s, it became a lively hangout with soldiers stationed at Camp Barkeley. The concrete tables and multi-colored inlaid tiles were the handiwork of Blanks himself, whose family occupied an upstairs living area. The club closed in 1961 but was later occupied by the "It'll Do Club" followed by the "Clover Club."

Shootin' In the New Year

A saloon on the corner of Chestnut and South First Street provided the original venue for an Abilene tradition that spanned 67 years. On New Year's Eve 1884, a rowdy cowboy stuck his arm out of Walker's Saloon and fired off a few rounds at the stroke of midnight. Police Chief John Clinton dashed inside, only to find a smoking gun on a table. One year later—as 1885 turned to 1886—Chief Clinton happened to be at South First and Chestnut again. Figuring "what the heck," two years in a row on the same corner offered reason enough to begin a tradition. At the New Year, he pulled out his Colt .45 and fired three rounds into the midnight air, ushering in 1886 and signaling to the nearly two dozen local saloons that it was time to close.

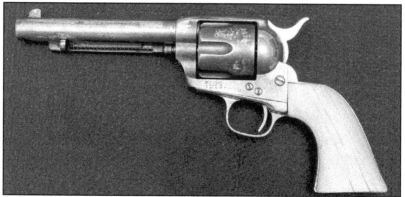

Chief Clinton's New Year's Eve pistol on display at the Abilene Police Department

Clinton returned on the final day of each year to shoot in the New Year, continuing the tradition until 1921. After the death of Chief Clinton in 1922, his annual ritual passed to Jinks McGee who inherited the ivory-handled revolver, firing it off annually for the next 29 years. The tradition ended at midnight on December 31, 1951, when Jinks McGee fired the old pistol for the final time. He died in his sleep eight days later. Clinton's pistol is on display at the Abilene Police department.

PHOTO CREDITS

January 1	HSU Collection
January 4	Taylor County Historical Commission
January 8	City of Abilene
January 15	Episcopal Church of the Heavenly Rest
January 19	Don Hutcheson Collection
January 20	The Grace Museum
January 31	Portal to Texas History
February 1	HSU Collection
February 6	West Texas Rehab Center
February 9	author
February 10	author
February 13	author
February 19	City of Abilene
February 23	author
February 24	author
February 25	author
February 27	author
February 29	Abilene Reporter-News
March 3	author
March 10	HSU Collection
March 14	The Grace Museum
March 15	author
March 23	ACU Collection
March 25	City of Abilene
March 26	author
March 29	Lloyd Jones Collection
March 31	HSU Collection
April 1	Don Hutcheson Collection
April 5	author
April 3	author
April 6	author

April 5	McMurry University
April 6	author
April 8	HSU Collection
April 9	author
April 11	Texas A&M University
April 14	HSU Collection
April 18	author
April 20	author
April 24	Abilene High School
April 26	author
April 27	author
April 29	author
May 5	Abilene Cultural Affairs Council
May 14	author
May 17	The Grace Museum
May 18	author
May 19	McMurry University
May 23	HSU Collection
May 27	McMurry University
May 30	National Institutes of Health
May 31	HSU Collection
June 5	author
June 6	Abilene Reporter-News
June 12	City of Abilene
June 16	Joe Specht Collection
June 20	author
June 25	author
June 28	Garrett Family
June 29	U.S. Air Force Dyess AFB
July 2	author
July 4	Parramore Family Collection

July 7	author	October 2	HSU Collection
July 10	Estes Family	October 6	City of Abilene
July 12	author	October 7	Paxton Family
July 13	Jack Holden Collection	October 10	Abilene Reporter-News
July 21	Gerhart Family	October 11	City of Abilene
July 22	City of Abilene	October 12	Abilene Reporter-News
July 24	HSU Collection	October 14	Pat Lefors Dawson
July 26	HSU Collection	October 15	HSU Collection
July 31	author	October 16	ACU Collection
August 5	author	October 17	HSU Collection
August 6	HSU Collection	October 26	City of Abilene
August 9	HSU Collection	October 29	Abilene Reporter-News
August 15	Abilene Reporter-News	November 4	Fort Worth Star-Telegram
August 16	Bob Carothers	November 5	Abilene Reporter-News
August 22	HSU Collection	November 8	author
August 23	HSU Collection	November 9	Curtis House Museum
August 26	Abilene Reporter-News	November 11	Taylor County Historical Commission
August 27	Woodson Family		
August 31	author	November 18	HSU Collection
September 3	ACU Collection	November 21	author
September 5	author	November 30	Hendrick Medical Center
September 7	HSU Collection	December 7	ACU Collection
September 8	Taylor County Historical Commission	December 11	ACU Collection
		December 14	Jack Holden Collection
September 10	UNT Libraries	December 15	author
September 11	Abilene High School	December 19	Mildren Family
September 15	Hendrick Medical Center	December 22	author
		December 25	author
September 17	HSU Collection	December 28	Dyess Family
September 18	Abilene Reporter-News	Decembre 31	author
September 20	McMurry University		
September 23	Donna Albus		
September 26	HSU Collection		

ACKNOWLEDGEMENTS

Online access to newspapers from around the country and, of course, historic Abilene newspapers, helped make this book possible. Additionally, research by earlier local historians helped uncover events, dates and a variety of stories. Those historians and authors are familiar names to anyone interested in the story of Abilene: Dr. Rupert Richardson, Katharyn Duff, Ed Wishcamper, Dr. Robert Sledge, Hugh Cosby, A.C. Greene, Dr. Vernon Spence, Tommie Clack and Juanita Zachry among others.

Printed in the USA
CPSIA information can be obtained
at www.ICGtesting.com
LVHW051954020124
767178LV00010B/10